Lecture-Free Teaching

**A Learning Partnership
Between Science Educators
and Their Students**

Lecture-Free Teaching

A Learning Partnership Between Science Educators and Their Students

Bonnie S. Wood

NSTApress

National Science Teachers Association

Arlington, Virginia

National Science Teachers Association

Claire Reinburg, Director
Jennifer Horak, Managing Editor
Andrew Cocke, Senior Editor
Judy Cusick, Senior Editor
Wendy Rubin, Associate Editor

ART AND DESIGN
Will Thomas Jr., Director
Tim French, Senior Graphic Designer, cover and interior design

PRINTING AND PRODUCTION
Catherine Lorrain, Director

NATIONAL SCIENCE TEACHERS ASSOCIATION
Francis Q. Eberle, PhD, Executive Director
David Beacom, Publisher

LIBRARY OF CONGRESS CATALOGING-IN-PUBLICATION DATA
Wood, Bonnie S., 1946-
  Lecture-free teaching : a learning partnership of science educators and their students /
Bonnie S. Wood.
     p. cm.
 Includes bibliographical references and index.
 ISBN 978-1-933531-32-8
 1. Science--Study and teaching (Higher) 2. College science teachers--Attitudes. 3. Lecture
method in teaching. 4. Active learning. 5. Teacher-student relationships. I. National Science
Teachers Association. II. Title.
 Q181.3.W66 2009
 507.1'1--dc22
                    2009023654

 eISBN 978-1-936137-96-1

Table of Contents

Dedication

To my husband, Stephen, and my two sons, Justin and Tyler, for their help and encouragement and, most of all, for being proud of me.

To my sister, Suzie, whose meticulous grammar and spelling kept me in good writing form during our daily e-mail exchanges.

To my sister-in-law, Debbie, who is writing her first novel and with whom I shared the challenge and exhilaration of a first book.

To my friend Deb, with whom I have shared animated conversations about science pedagogy during more than a decade of early morning bicycle rides, hikes, and cross-country skiing.

To my friend Anja, a trusted colleague, whose perspective from a different discipline provided insightful critiques of chapter drafts.

To colleagues and administrators at the University of Maine at Presque Isle, who encouraged me to take risks by exploring new teaching methods.

To each of my students—past, present, and future—whose feedback makes possible a true partnership of learning.

About the Author

Bonnie Wood grew up in Northern Virginia and first made her way to New England to attend Wellesley College in Massachusetts. After graduate school at Cornell University Medical College in New York City, two years in rural Montana teaching at a college outreach program on an Indian reservation, and a postdoctoral fellowship at the University of California at Davis, she settled in Northern Maine with her husband and two then-young sons. She has lived and worked in Presque Isle since 1979 and joined the full-time faculty at the University of Maine at Presque Isle in 1989.

Chapter 1

Introduction

My passion for teaching reform took root in 1998, more than two decades after earning my PhD in medical sciences. Before that, I did what most postsecondary educators do—I taught as I had been taught.

During my first decade of teaching at the University of Maine at Presque Isle, I accumulated a large collection of transparencies and annotated my lecture notes so that I would project the transparencies at the appropriate moments. I punctuated my lectures with humorous statements I had conceived over the years and updated my notes to reflect current research. At each class meeting I moved smoothly and energetically through the scheduled topics while my students furiously scribbled notes. I knew they were attentive because they asked probing questions such as "Could you repeat that, please?" or "Will this be on the test?" My goal at that time was to perfect my lectures.

Although they wrote flattering evaluations at the end of each semester, I began to realize that neither the weaker nor the stronger students could reliably apply what they had learned—an important skill for both science majors and nonmajors. After more than a year of considering possible solutions to this problem, I submitted a proposal titled "Incorporation of Active Learning Methods Into General Biology and Sciences Courses" and was awarded sabbatical leave for the spring 2000 semester. That semester awoke more creative energy than I had ever experienced while performing the traditional laboratory research for which I had trained.

My stated intention was to improve two of my general education curriculum courses by engaging in some kind of active learning exercise during every class meeting. I initially adapted ideas gleaned from books and journals. As I became more comfortable with my new teaching style, I designed my own activities. Within a couple of years I had abandoned lectures and replaced them with what I called *Lecture-Free Teaching*. Improving introductory science courses is still my focus, but my new methods have spilled over into all of my upper-level courses.

My next phase of reform was to increase the time allotted for each class meeting. After I incorporated activities into my classes, students began to complain that 50-minute class periods were too short. Both my students and I felt rushed, and the topics lacked coherence when activities ended abruptly or had to be completed at home or during the next class. I changed class meetings from 50 minutes, three times a week, to 75 minutes, twice a week.

Ultimately, I erased the arbitrary boundary between lecture and laboratory. In contrast with the traditional weekly schedule of three 50-minute lectures plus a three-hour laboratory at a different time of the week, sometimes with an instructor other than me, my classes now meet with me alone in the laboratory twice a week for approximately three-hour sessions. I gradually replaced instructor demonstrations and cookbook-style laboratory exercises with inquiry-based activities. In cooperative learning groups, students apply the scientific process to develop hypotheses and then design and perform experiments. To complete the circle of reform, I investigated methods of formative and summative assessment and created classroom assessments to complement and reinforce my active-learning and inquiry-based approaches.

The steps to Lecture-Free Teaching discussed in Part I represent the entire process of course design and delineate a never-ending feedback loop that provides information to both the students and the instructor. For one semester the students and their instructor are members of a partnership that contributes to their mutual goal of significant learning that remains meaningful beyond the final exam.

The first step in this process is to consider unchangeable factors so that subsequent course design will complement these elements. Next, the instructor determines specific learning goals for the course, followed by a third step of creating assessments, a crucial part of the feedback loop. Assessments should provide significant information to both the students and the teacher about their mutual progress toward accomplishing the learning goals. Formative assessments are most effective when the opportunity remains for students and educator to make changes that will contribute to success. The fourth step is to choose a teaching strategy that both achieves learning goals and responds flexibly to feedback from the assessments. The teaching strategy must be much more than a collection of active learning methods selected by the educator. Instead, it must provide coherence within each class meeting and from one week to the next. Next comes the fun of developing in-class activities and homework assignments that satisfy the original learning goals and support the teaching strategy while providing cohesiveness to the course.

The remaining steps described in Part I fall into place easily: choosing a grading system based on both formative and summative assessments, assembling a topic schedule, and preparing outlines of important terms and concepts for each content area ordinarily covered during a lecture. One of the final steps is to compose a detailed syllabus that explains each of these features while emphasizing the shared responsibility of the student and the teacher for achieving learning goals. The topic schedule, syllabus, content outlines, activity worksheets, and assessments are organized into a three-ring binder called *The Coursepack*. Having these items in one place helps students understand the overall course design and make connections among its different components. The outlines, which compose the meat of the coursepacks, are interspersed with relevant in-class activities, laboratory exercises, and formative assessments. On my campus, coursepacks are sold for the cost of copying in the bookstore as one of the required texts. Excerpts from my coursepacks are included as examples throughout this book.

During the first 15 minutes of the first day of class, students are organized into heterogeneous learning teams within which they work for the entire semester. Teamwork underscores the partnership of learning. Although I design the entire course well before opening day of the semester, the process of teaching and learning is never completely predictable. The elements of surprise and discovery keep class meetings lively, participative, and intellectually stimulating for both the educator and the students.

When I tell other people that I use Lecture-Free Teaching, their curiosity is aroused because they cannot envision teaching a class without lecturing. In Part II of this book, I describe the rhythm of the semester to provide a sense of what actually happens during a course from day to day and week to week. This section of the book provides details of what I briefly mention in Step 12 of the process described in Chapter 3 (p. 39): a description of the preparation by both the students and the instructor, a depiction of how I erased lecture-laboratory boundaries, methods of regular communication with students, and the importance of writing activities.

The fourth step in the Lecture-Free Teaching process, as listed in Chapter 3, is to select a teaching strategy that will ensure coherence; Part III describes a variety of instructional strategies. Each chapter is designed to be freestanding and can be used to gradually incorporate any new methods the educator chooses.

Administrators may want to begin their reading with the final three chapters of the book. In Part IV I discuss the process and progress of change in science education that I have observed, experienced, and contributed to over the past four decades. I also describe what we as individual educators and administrators can do to improve science education significantly.

As I made the transition from learner to teacher in the field of science pedagogy and began to share my knowledge through papers and workshops, I received numerous requests for more comprehensive information. I wrote this book as a practical, rather than a theoretical, guide to offer step-by-step assistance to veteran science educators who are disenchanted with the lecture and wish to gradually refashion their teaching; to professors in teacher education programs who wish to introduce their students to innovative teaching methods; and to educators beginning their careers who are not yet constrained by old habits and ineffective teaching methods. Because Lecture-

Free Teaching can be a powerful retention tool, administrators within the entire K–16 spectrum can read Chapters 2, 17, 18, and 19 for research-based support of simple, cost-free methods that engage a more diverse population of students than those who have traditionally thrived in science. I also hope to lure skeptical science educators away from reliance on the traditional lecture and cookbook laboratories with my examples of successful and satisfying approaches to teaching.

In this book I describe a fresh approach to teaching that releases both educators and their students from the confines of lecturing. Teachers can choose from a variety of methods without completely abandoning the lecture, or they can use the book to move gradually toward lecture-free teaching. Although lectures may remain prevalent in the near future, especially in higher education, my intention is to contribute to recent efforts to alter this situation. I believe that most educators lecture because they are modeling the methods by which they were taught and achieved success. The content-heavy lecture is no longer appropriate for a society in which factual information is so readily available. Lecturing is not the best method for teaching today's students, and it weeds out many who would otherwise flourish in science courses.

Although I am now confident in my ability to teach lecture-free, I want readers to understand that I have not perfected this method; the process is never static. The feedback loop I describe in Part I nourishes my enthusiasm. In the past I felt overwhelmed watching the journals to which I subscribe accumulate, unread, during the academic year. Now I look forward to diving into them, anxious to discover an idea I can use immediately. I seek students' feedback while figuring out how to improve a new activity or wondering if I should repeat it in future semesters.

My expectation is that *Lecture-Free Teaching: A Learning Partnership Between Science Educators and Their Students* will enable teachers at all levels to achieve the degree of change they desire. I am eager to communicate my experiences—both good and bad—to a broad audience and to share the energy of the learning partnership. Most important, I hope this book will result in new and exciting dialogues by fueling creativity and inspiring readers to devise their own innovative methods to share with the rest of us.

National Science Teachers Association

Chapter 2

Why Not Lecture?

Lecturing is the predominant teaching method in postsecondary education, which suggests that most academics consider it satisfactory, or at least believe that its strengths outweigh its weaknesses. Over the past two decades evidence against the lecture format has mounted, and many researchers consider it ineffective for teaching students of any age. Disadvantages of lecturing can be summarized in five broad categories:

- Most lectures are too long for effective learning. Attention remains high for the first 10 minutes of the lecture and then progressively decreases.
- Lectures do not promote long-term retention of information and understanding of concepts. Students retain minimal understanding of content after completing a lecture-based course, and lectures do not effectively rid students of previous misconceptions.
- Lectures cannot teach learning, thinking, and other behavioral skills. Lectures are not well suited to developing higher-order cognitive skills such as analysis, synthesis, and evaluation, all of which are more important than content for success after college.
- The lecture gives the teacher too much control with little flexibility to respond to student feedback. A lecture presumes that all students enter the classroom with the same level of understanding and learn at the same pace.
- The lecture came into being to impart knowledge. Today's technology places knowledge at one's fingertips and thus has rendered the lecture obsolete.

A common thread running through all research comparing lecturing to other teaching methods is that when instructors lecture, students are passive.

The researchers' consensus is that the lecture has a place but when used alone is rarely adequate to achieve learning goals. Lectures should be used only if blended with other instructional methods. I contend that if the instructor so desires, the formal lecture can be abandoned altogether and replaced with the thoughtful use of active learning strategies in a collaborative, cooperative, supportive classroom environment in which the students and the instructor build a partnership of learning to explore ways of applying knowledge.

THE DEFINITION OF ACTIVE LEARNING

A book by Bonwell and Eison (1991), one of the first I read concerning active learning, is often credited with popularizing the term and the pedagogy. But active learning strategies evolved from the work of much earlier theorists, including John Dewey, a well-known educational reformer from the beginning of the twentieth century. Bonwell and Eison defined active learning as "anything that involves students in doing things and thinking about the things they are doing" (1991, p. 2).

This broad description leads some educators to ask: What's not active about attentively listening, taking notes, and acquiring information during a lecture? The research literature, discussed in the next section of this chapter, suggests that for students to be actively involved in learning, they must use higher-order cognitive skills such as analysis, synthesis, and evaluation (Bloom 1956; Crowe, Dirks, and Wenderoth 2008). The traditional lecture, during which teachers talk and students listen, does not provide students with an opportunity to make use of these skills (Mazur 2009). In a science classroom, a student-centered active learning approach minimizes one-way lectures and maximizes teamwork and feedback among the teacher and students, who work together to apply scientific principles and reasoning to real-world problems.

A recent personal experience illustrates the conclusions of the research literature. I rarely have the opportunity to experience the classroom as a student, but I decided to observe a small, informal cardiopulmonary resuscitation (CPR) recertification class taught by a friend. Years ago I had been a CPR instructor myself, so psychomotor skills from the 1980s were forever etched into my brain. I knew there had been changes in the recommendations for performing CPR and the Heimlich maneuver, so I asked to watch the class without being officially certified; I simply wanted to learn about the new procedures and practice a bit on the dummy. Feeling confident that I had absorbed the new information, I took the written exam, which I passed easily. The instructor then offered to assess my practical skills so I could be recertified in CPR. To test me she scored my performance in response to her descriptions of several medical scenarios; I struggled to apply my newly acquired factual information to these novel situations. Even with a previous background as a CPR instructor, my participation by passively, albeit attentively, listening to a lecture and watching demonstrations of correct procedures did not translate to the ability to apply the knowledge—and this competency is what one needs most during a cardiopulmonary emergency.

ENDORSEMENT OF ACTIVE LEARNING IN SCIENCE CLASSROOMS

In 2004, the journal *Science* published one of the most compelling arguments for science education reform. By writing in this prestigious journal, the authors hoped to grab the attention of scientists who do not ordinarily read about pedagogy. The authors question why outstanding research scientists continue to use and defend—on the basis of intuition alone—teaching methods shown to be ineffective. They provide evidence that active participation by students during class meetings, along with discovery-based laboratories, not only improves learning and knowledge retention but also helps students develop the habits of mind that drive science. Students taught by active learning demonstrate better problem-solving ability, conceptual understanding, and success in subsequent science courses than those who learned in more traditional ways. The authors strongly recommend that research universities lead the reform of science education (Handelsman et al. 2004).

Even more recently *Science* published two articles that endorse the substitution of more interactive teaching methods for the lecture. The first, an autobiographical article, is by Harvard physics professor Eric Mazur (2009). The second article reports his extensively researched methods of Peer Instruction in physics to be equally effective in other science disciplines (Smith et al. 2009).

Evidence of Better Learning Outcomes for Students

Widespread use of the Force Concept Inventory (FCI) provided a standard measure for comparing the relative success of different teaching strategies in physics. This test requires students to make choices between Newtonian concepts and commonsense alternatives or misconceptions (Hestenes, Wells, and Swackhamer 1992). Using this assessment after standard lecture-based instruction clearly demonstrates that lecturing fails to bring most students to a level of concept mastery or a deep understanding of Newtonian physics and that "only lecture" reinforces "only memorization" (Bollag 2007; Klymkowsky, Garvin-Doxas, and Zeilik 2003; Wood 2003). Rigorous research in physics classrooms comparing FCI results after lecturing to results after various active learning methods encouraged many physics educators to adopt interactive teaching. The findings in physics classrooms inspired others—including biologists

(Garvin-Doxas and Klymkowsky), chemists (Birk et al.), engineers (Griffin and Krause), and geneticists (Smith, Wood, and Knight 2008)—to develop analogous diagnostic instruments (Metz 2009). The data generated with concept inventories not only support specific pedagogical reforms but also increase educators' awareness of misconceptions based on students' prior knowledge.

Another method, Peer Instruction, has been studied in a variety of educational settings. In this student-centered approach, lectures are interspersed with short conceptual questions designed to reveal misconceptions related to prior knowledge as the questions actively engage students. Surveys of more than 700 instructors using Peer Instruction indicate learning gains (Fagen, Crouch, and Mazur 2002). When comparing the effectiveness of Peer Instruction in a two-year college with its effectiveness in a top-tier four-year research institution, Peer Instruction students with less background knowledge gained as much as students with more background knowledge (Lasry, Mazur, and Watkins 2008).

Inductive teaching methods are those in which an instructor first presents students with a specific challenge (such as experimental data to interpret, a case study to analyze, or a complex real-world problem to solve); then gives them time to recognize the need for facts, skills, and conceptual understanding; and, finally, provides appropriate instruction or helps students find the information on their own. This contrasts with deductive methods, in which an instructor teaches students appropriate theories and models, then does textbook exercises, and possibly never covers the real-world applications. Although some of the inductive methods do not result in improved academic achievement, as measured by content-based exams in chemical engineering courses, studies suggest the development of more positive student attitudes, a deeper approach to learning, greater retention of content, and enhancement of problem-solving and lifelong learning skills (Prince 2004; Prince and Felder 2007).

The University of Oregon developed Workshop Biology, an inquiry-based approach to teaching a general biology course for nonscience majors. The curriculum incorporates direct confrontation of students' misconceptions through concrete experiences; investigative activities during which students pose and attempt to answer their own questions; and an introduction to science in context. Detailed evaluation over several years demonstrated that Workshop students displayed dramatic improvement in conceptual learning and understanding of scientific reasoning, a greater appreciation of science and its role in their lives, and greater motivation and involvement in learning activities than did students in a similar course taught with a more traditional content-oriented lecture style. Students effectively learned content without sitting and listening to a lecture, did not need to know content before participating in inquiry, and displayed better decision-making skills when compared to students in the more traditional course (Udovic et al. 2002).

Evidence for How to Attract and Retain Science Majors

When inductive teaching is not used, the resulting failure to connect course content to the real world has been shown repeatedly to contribute to students' leaving the sciences (Seymour and Hewitt 1997; Kardash and Wallace 2001). Empirical data from chemical engineering classes indicate that encouragement of collaboration rather than competition enhances not only interpersonal skills but also academic achievement, positive student attitudes, and student retention in the major (Prince 2004). Peer Instruction decreases student attrition in introductory physics courses at both four- and two-year institutions (Lasry, Mazur, and Watkins 2008).

Initiation of the UTeach Program at the University of Texas at Austin doubled the number of secondary math and science teachers graduating from the university. Math and science majors experience secondary school teaching as early as their freshman years. Working with experienced teacher mentors, the undergraduates' teaching experience becomes progressively longer and more independent as they learn to design and teach inquiry-based lessons that develop critical-thinking skills. The pathway to teacher certification is streamlined to allow completion of both the bachelor's degree and teacher certification in four years (UTeach, University of Texas at Austin Natural Sciences). The methods modeled in this program are based on research about how teachers can best help secondary-school students learn science and math. They discourage rote memorization and instead emphasize hands-on exercises, teamwork, development of critical-thinking skills, and understanding of the scientific method (Brainard 2007).

Evidence of Greater Satisfaction Among Teachers

Science educators who write or speak about using student-centered pedagogy almost always mention its benefits to them as well as to their students. The active learning approach reignites educators' enthusiasm for teaching, gives them the pleasure of getting to know their students, allows them to look forward to entering the classroom each day, and provides a sense of accomplishment when their students achieve their learning goals. Such positive energy from the teacher cannot help but affect students' experiences in the science classroom.

Conclusions

Science education should focus less on memorization of vocabulary and facts and more on students' understanding and integration of scientific concepts; less on what students can repeat back in class and more on their long-term retention and ability to transfer their knowledge to contexts outside the classroom; and less on what instructors cover and more on teaching students to apply their knowledge. Teaching strategies that encourage students to become actively engaged in their own learning can produce levels of understanding, retention, and transfer of knowledge greater than those resulting from traditional lecture and laboratory classes (Boyer Commission on Educating Undergraduates in the Research University 1998; DeHaan 2005; Honan 2002; National Research Council 2000, 2003a, 2003b).

OUR STUDENTS' PORTRAYALS OF EFFECTIVE TEACHING

To build a learning partnership with our students, as I suggest in this book's title, we must listen as carefully to our students as we expect them to listen to us. As I read reports of several groups of scholars who asked students about what constitutes effective teaching, I was struck by the consensus among diverse populations of undergraduates.

In Richard Light's book (2001), students commented on the characteristics of their most meaningful classes and effective professors. Other authors focus specifically on students' reactions to science and mathematics courses and include the responses of students graduating with science, technology, engineering, and mathematics (STEM) majors, as well as those who took STEM courses but chose other majors (Kardash and Wallace 2001; Seymour and Hewitt 1997; Strenta et al. 1994; Tobias 1990, 1992; Treisman 1992).

I have organized into five categories students' opinions about what makes a course and its instructor effective or ineffective.

Faculty Attitudes Toward Teaching

Some students believe that STEM faculty dislike undergraduates, do not want to teach, do not value teaching as a professional activity, lack the motivation to learn to teach effectively, and are indifferent to students' academic concerns. They blame faculty preoccupation with research for these attitudes. Some students fault a faculty member's personal preferences, and others hold academia responsible due to its emphasis on research productivity as a major criterion for faculty tenure and promotion, as well as for institutional prestige.

Lack of adequate student-teacher feedback about what students are learning—or not learning—also reflects faculty indifference to students. Without dialogue, students feel powerless to influence the pace or depth of the course. A majority of students want more quizzes and short assignments, ideally with opportunities for revision.

Students characterize ineffective teachers as having no clear goals or organization for their courses, resulting in a poor fit between class materials, homework, and tests. Their lessons lacked preparation, logical sequencing, or coherence, and the teachers made little effort to check that students could follow the arguments or ideas.

The students unfavorably compare STEM faculty with those in non-STEM disciplines who more often treat teaching as an important aspect of their professional duties and make an effort to do it well. Students consider changes in content and learning goals of science classes to be insufficient unless accompanied by changes in the way faculty members teach.

Interaction Among Students

Activities involving several other students—with or without a faculty member and directed toward accomplishing academic work—help build a collegial spirit. Some teachers organize cooperative learning groups in the classroom, and others simply ask students to form their own study groups that meet outside of class.

Several decades ago nearly every educator announced that homework should be done alone. Discussing problem sets or essay assignments was considered cheating. Today teachers increasingly encourage students to work together on homework assignments. Faculty can facilitate this by giving in-class activities or homework assignments so challenging or complex that the only way to get the work done is to collaborate. Students report that such tasks increase both their learning and their engagement with a class. In his research on minority mathematics students, Treisman (1992) identified and compared the interaction and study patterns of Asian Americans who did well in calculus with those of African Americans who performed poorly. A key difference was that Asian Americans formed small groups with whom they regularly studied outside class. Small-group work appears more important for the sciences than for any other field; Light (2001) observed that those who leave science majors rarely join study groups and instead work alone.

Classroom Teaching Techniques

Students stress that it is not *what* is taught in science classes that makes the classes difficult, but *how* the content is delivered. An emphasis on the memorization of facts at the expense of conceptual understanding is a weakness of many STEM courses. Faculty fail to make connections among concepts; do not illustrate the application of concepts; do not encourage discussion; give dull presentations; and fail to provide students with the sense of discovering things together. Students praise faculty who do not tell them what to think, but rather how to think creatively. Students want to be taught to deliberate like professionals in a particular discipline, and they prefer to use class time to accomplish tasks they could not complete on their own.

Class Size

Students emphasize small class size as an attribute of effective classes and state that small-group tutorials, small seminars, and one-to-one supervision are, for many, their best educational experiences. But students also stress the importance of introductory STEM courses and report that their decisions to leave a science major was influenced more by negative experiences in freshman science than by positive experiences in other fields. Unfortunately, introductory courses are often synonymous with large class sizes. Faculty can counteract these negative effects by forming small cooperative learning groups, even within a large enrollment course meeting in a lecture hall.

Grading Practices

Students hold negative opinions of a course that encourages competition among students by using grading practices that do not reflect what students feel they have accomplished. Assessment systems such as "grading on the curve" are viewed more as being geared to weeding out students than to encouraging all interested and talented students. Students with strong high school math and science backgrounds often avoid science classes in college because of heavy competition for grades. They may prefer courses with less grade competition, even if the courses have greater workloads.

FACTORS PROMPTING STUDENTS TO SWITCH FROM SCIENCE MAJORS

The sciences have the highest defection rates of all undergraduate majors, as well as the lowest rates of recruitment from other majors. For their book *Talking About Leaving: Why Undergraduates Leave the Sciences*, Seymour and Hewitt (1997) gathered data from both switchers and nonswitchers. Reasons for avoiding STEM majors or switching away from a science major echo students' descriptions of ineffective courses. Poor teaching by faculty contributed to one-third of all switching decisions and was the third most common explanation for leaving a STEM major: 90% of switchers cited poor teaching, and 75% of nonswitchers complained about the quality of teaching. Additional grounds for avoiding science majors were lack or loss of interest in the disciplines; a non-STEM major offering a better or more well-rounded education; lack of peer study support; preference for the teaching approach in non-STEM classes; poor teaching by teaching assistants; and communication problems with foreign teaching assistants.

The widely quoted insights of Sheila Tobias, who was educated in history and literature, contribute to our understanding of why intelligent and motivated students experience difficulties in mathematics and science and what we as educators and administrators can do to prevent the loss of potential talent from these disciplines (Tobias 1990, 1992, 1993). Tobias also documents the role that teaching methods play in discouraging interest in science majors and careers among both women and men.

The climate of the typical STEM classroom has a greater negative effect on women. Rates of persistence in STEM majors are significantly lower for females than for males (Strenta et al. 1994; Tobias 1990). Although we know less about the college and graduate school experiences of the relatively small number of women who remain in STEM majors, we cannot blame gender imbalance on innate ability, as Lawrence Summers, past president of Harvard University, so infamously stated (Bombardieri 2005). Research on the cognitive abilities of males and females from birth to maturity lends no support to this claim. Some previous gender differences are now eliminated or reversed: A generation ago far more men than women attended college, and of those in college, a greater proportion of men than women majored in biology, medicine, mathematics, economics, or accounting. Just as these century-old discrepancies had social causes, so undoubtedly do today's disparities—more men than women continue to major in physics and engineering (Spelke 2005).

A study of 5,320 students entering four highly selective postsecondary institutions examined possible causes for the disproportionate departure of women from science majors. A smaller proportion of women (35%) than men (49%) were initially interested in science. Of those initially interested, only 60% of both sexes stayed in science, with smaller proportions of women (48%) persisting than men (66%). Students who remained science majors stated that their classes were structured to be too competitive; there were few opportunities to ask questions; and professors were relatively unresponsive, not dedicated, and not motivating. Students who left science generally were more attracted to other fields, but many shared the criticisms of overcompetitiveness and inferior instruction, along with the view that the work was too difficult. Except for perceived competitiveness, women did not rate their classroom experiences as being more unpleasant than men did (Strenta et al. 1994). College women's distaste for aggression and competition among fellow students is also supported by other researchers (Manis et al. 1989).

If STEM faculty continue blaming the exodus from their disciplines on students' inability to cope with hard classes, then they will never consider attrition a solvable problem. By maintaining this mind set, educators will continue to structure introductory courses to weed out students, rather than design them to encourage talented students who previously have been ignored. Such faculty attitudes also dissuade students who persist in the majors from sharing their concerns. Light (2001) suggests that to attract and keep more students in the sciences, educators should design their courses to de-emphasize competition for grades, structure classroom activities to provide opportunities for interaction among the students and faculty members, and encourage small study groups to meet outside formal classes.

WHAT LECTURE-FREE TEACHING CAN ACCOMPLISH FOR SCIENCE

The United States today has an urgent need for science educators and researchers to replace retiring professionals and to meet the requirements of a society increasingly more dependent on science and technology. Equally important is the need for a more scientifically literate citizenry able to function in a technologically complex world, not only by understanding scientific concepts and new discoveries but also by making informed decisions in their personal lives and in the voting booth. I believe that fundamental reform of science teaching methods can simultaneously address these issues.

The scientific community benefited during the post-Sputnik period from an increase in both material resources and citizen support. But concomitant reforms of science education consisted mainly of altering course materials and adding teaching enhancements; these are not factors that contribute to students' deciding for or against science careers.

My interest in pedagogical reform was stimulated in part by my previous research on gender equity in math and science education (Wood 1997; Wood and Brown 1997). Through reading, observing high school students in single-sex math classes, interviewing high school girls who participated in both mixed-sex and all-female math classes, and personally experiencing science classes as an undergraduate at a women's college, I became aware of differences in teaching methods and the classroom climate when only females are present.

In the early 1990s I visited The SummerMath Programs at Mount Holyoke College, the Smith College Summer Science and Engineering Program for High School Girls, and the all-female math class in my own rural Maine community. In these I observed the successful use of cooperative learning with high school girls. I attended a powerful workshop by Myra and David Sadker, who together worked to eliminate gender bias from America's schools (Sadker and Sadker 1995). I tried some suggested techniques in my own mixed-sex college classrooms and witnessed a more effective learning environment for all students, not just females. My two areas of scholarly activity intersected: I reread books I had originally discovered when researching gender equity and found them equally relevant to reforming science education.

A recent publication affirmed these connections by strongly supporting the principles of "feminist pedagogy" that consider *how* students are taught in addition to *what* they are taught (Association of American Colleges and Universities 2008; Kuh 2008). Traditional science pedagogy puts females and members of other underrepresented groups at a distinct disadvantage, especially in the important introductory-level college science classes. Large class size, competitiveness among students, the expectation that students will study alone, and a lack of nurturing relationships with faculty all contribute to turning these students away from STEM majors. In the past efforts to increase the confidence and success of underrepresented groups in math and science have rarely considered that the teaching methods themselves are at fault.

As Seymour and Hewitt wrote so eloquently (1997, 314):

> Even if we knew how to teach girls to be more independent in their learning style, we must first consider whether it is desirable to change the collective identity of one gender group so they can more easily be fitted into educational settings which reflect the socialized learning styles of the other gender. Furthermore, some aspects of the learning environment in which women feel most comfortable—particularly cooperative, interactive and experiential learning contexts—are also congenial to many young men, and encourage the development of skills and attitudes which have increasing value in occupational and social contexts beyond academe. For those faculty questioning the need for institutional change, the "problem of women" may need to be reframed. Moving pedagogy from a focus on teaching to a focus on learning, and from selecting for talent to nurturing it, will disproportionately increase the persistence rate of able women in S.M.E. [science, math, engineering] majors. It also promises to reduce the loss of able male students.

We need reform in science education, and we need it now. The reform must grow out of collaboration among educators at all levels. The educators, in turn, need to listen to what their students say about classroom methods that work for them. If we truly want to increase the number of science majors and create a more scientifically literate society, we must tap resources that have been ignored in the past: We need to engage not only the type of students who have always been successful with traditional lecture and note-taking but also those who respond better to different modes of teaching. We need to include Tobias's "second tier" (1990) in an expanded potential talent pool by responding to considerable data recommending that we replace lectures with more interaction among students; memorization with conceptual understanding; and cookbook-style laboratories with inquiry-based exercises. Such recommendations are based on scientific evidence, and when educators respond to this evidence they are "teaching science scientifically" (DeHaan 2005). Unfortunately, on a majority of campuses the instructor as information-delivering lecturer remains the standard. This model is not likely to attract more students to science careers or help citizens become more scientifically literate.

A reinvigoration of science teaching at research universities will not only engage more students in science but also can stimulate the creativity of their instructors: Gilbert Lewis's invention of the electron dot system occurred as he taught introductory chemistry at the University of California, Berkeley (Lewis 1916). When faculty invite students to question what and how they are learning, the instructor is forced to rethink his or her approach to both teaching and research problems and can experience greater personal satisfaction as a professor (Cech 2003).

Far more has been written about teaching reform than the typical educator has the time or energy to read or absorb, much less to adapt for a class. Teachers are often overwhelmed by the district, state, and federal policies and standards to which they are expected to conform. My hope is that this book will provide science educators with the tools to gradually transition to more effective and satisfying ways of teaching.

REFERENCES

Association of American Colleges and Universities (AAC&U). 2008. Rethinking scientific pedagogies. *On Campus With Women* 37 (2). *www.aacu.org/ocww* (accessed November 18, 2008).

Birk, J., B. Jenkins, R. Bauer, S. Krause, and M. Pavelich. Chemistry concept inventory. *www.foundationcoalition.org/home/keycomponents/concept/chemistry.html.*

Bloom, B. S., ed. 1956. *Taxonomy of educational objectives: The classification of educational goals. Handbook 1: Cognitive domain.* New York: Longman.

Bollag, B. 2007. A top physicist turns to teaching. *Chronicle of Higher Education* 53 (23): A08.

Bombardieri, M. 2005. Summers' remarks on women draw fire. *Boston Globe,* January 17. *www.boston.com/news/local/articles/2005/01/17/summers_remarks_on_women_draw_fire* (accessed December 20, 2008).

Bonwell, C. C., and J. A. Eison. 1991. *Active learning: Creating excitement in the classroom.* ASHE-ERIC Higher Education Report No. 1. Washington, DC: The George Washington University, School of Education and Human Development.

Boyer Commission on Educating Undergraduates in the Research University. 1998. Reinventing undergraduate education: A blueprint for America's research universities. *http://naples.cc.sunysb.edu/Pres/boyer.nsf.*

Brainard, J. 2007. Texas offers a model for training math and science teachers. *Chronicle of Higher Education* 54 (17): A8.

Cech, T. R. 2003. Rebalancing teaching and research. *Science* 299 (5604): 165.

Crowe, A., C. Dirks, and M. P. Wenderoth. 2008. Biology in bloom: Implementing Bloom's taxonomy to enhance student learning in biology. *CBE—Life Sciences Education* 7:368–381.

DeHaan, R. L. 2005. The impending revolution in undergraduate science education. *Journal of Science Education and Technology* 14 (2): 253–269.

Fagen, A. P., C. H. Crouch, and E. Mazur. 2002. Peer Instruction: Results from a range of classrooms. *Physics Teacher* 40:206–209.

Garvin-Doxas, K., and M. Klymkowsky. Building the biology concept inventory. *http://bioliteracy.net/Readings/papersSubmittedPDF/Garvin-Doxas%20and%20Klymkowsky.pdf.*

Griffin, R., and S. Krause. Materials concept inventory. *www.foundationcoalition.org/home/keycomponents/concept/materials.html.*

Handelsman, J., D. Ebert-May, R. Beichner, P. Bruns, A. Chang, R. DeHaan, J. Gentile et al. 2004. Scientific teaching. *Science* 304 (5670): 521–522.

Hestenes, D., M. Wells, and G. Swackhamer. 1992. Force concept inventory. *Physics Teacher* 30:141–158.

Honan, W. H. 2002. *New York Times Education.* 2002. Whither college lectures? Maybe right out the door. August 14.

Kardash, C. M., and M. L. Wallace. 2001. The perceptions of science classes survey: What undergraduate science reform efforts really need to address. *Journal of Educational Psychology* 93 (1): 199–210.

Klymkowsky, M. W., K. Garvin-Doxas, and M. Zeilik. 2003. Bioliteracy and teaching efficacy: What biologists can learn from physicists. *Cell Biology Education* 2:55–161.

Kuh, G. D. 2008. *High-impact educational practices: What they are, who has access to them, and why they matter.* Washington, DC: Association of American Colleges and Universities.

Lasry, N., E. Mazur, and J. Watkins. 2008. Peer Instruction: From Harvard to the two-year college. *American Journal of Physics* 76 (11): 1066–1069.

Lewis, G. N. 1916. The atom and the molecule. *Journal of the American Chemical Society* 38:762–785.

Light, R. J. 2001. *Making the most of college: Students speak their minds.* Cambridge, MA: Harvard University Press.

Manis, J. D., N. G. Thomas, B. F. Sloat, and C. D. Davis. 1989. *An analysis of factors affecting choices of majors in science, mathematics, and engineering at the University of Michigan.* CEW Report No. 23. Ann Arbor: University of Michigan Center for the Education of Women.

Mazur, E. 2009. Farewell, lecture? *Science* 323 (5910): 50–51.

Metz, A. M. 2009. Quantitative assessment of student learning in large undergraduate science classrooms: Approaches and caveats. In *College science teachers guide to assessment,* eds. T. R. Lord, D. P. French, and L. W. Crow, 15–30. Arlington, VA: NSTA Press.

Mount Holyoke College. SummerMath Program. *www.mtholyoke.edu/proj/summermath.*

National Research Council (NRC). 2000. *How people learn: Brain, mind experience and school.* Expanded ed. Washington, DC: National Academy Press.

———. 2003a. *Evaluating and improving undergraduate teaching in science, technology, engineering, and mathematics.* Washington, DC: National Academies Press.

———. 2003b. BIO 2010: Transforming undergraduate education for future research biologists. Washington, DC: *National Academies Press. www.nap.edu/catalog.php?record_id=10497#toc.*

Prince, M. 2004. Does active learning work? A review of the research. *Journal of Engineering Education* 93 (3): 223–231.

Prince, M., and R. Felder. 2007. The many faces of inductive teaching and learning. *Journal of College Science Teaching* 36 (5): 14–20.

Sadker, M., and D. Sadker. 1995. *Failing at fairness: How our schools cheat girls.* New York: Touchstone.

Seymour, E., and N. M. Hewitt. 1997. *Talking about leaving: Why undergraduates leave the sciences.* Boulder, CO: Westview Press.

Smith, M. K. , W. B. Wood, W. K. Adams, C. Wieman, J. K. Knight, N. Guild, and T. T. Su. 2009. Why peer discussion improves student performance on in-class concept questions. *Science* 323 (5910): 122–124.

Smith, M. K., W. B. Wood, and J. K. Knight. 2008. The genetics concept assessment: A new concept inventory for gauging student understanding of genetics. *CBE—Life Sciences Education* 7:422–430.

Smith College. Summer Science and Engineering Program for High School Girls. *www.smith.edu/summerprograms/ssep/index.php.*

Spelke, E. S. 2005. Sex differences in intrinsic aptitude for mathematics and science? A critical review. *American Psychologist* 60 (9): 950–958.

Strenta, A. C., R. Elliott, R. Adair, M. Matier, and J. Scott. 1994. Choosing and leaving science in highly selective institutions. *Research in Higher Education* 35 (5): 513–547.

Tobias, S. 1990. *They're not dumb, they're different: Stalking the second tier.* Tucson, AZ: Research Corporation.

———. 1992. *Revitalizing undergraduate science: Why some things work and most don't.* Tucson, AZ: Research Corporation.

———. 1993. *Overcoming math anxiety.* Revised and expanded ed. New York: W. W. Norton.

Treisman, U. 1992. Studying students studying calculus: A look at the lives of minority mathematics students in college. *College Mathematics Journal* 23 (5): 362–372.

Udovic, D., D. Morris, A. Dickman, J. Postlethwait, and P. Wetherwax. 2002. Workshop Biology: Demonstrating the effectiveness of active learning in an introductory biology course. *BioScience* 52 (3): 272–281.

University of Texas at Austin Natural Sciences. UTeach. *http://uteach.utexas.edu.*

Wood, B. S. 1997. All-female mathematics classes: An opportunity for classroom teachers and researchers to collaborate. *New England Mathematics Journal* 30 (1): 10–16.

Wood, B. S., and L. A. Brown. 1997. Participation in an all-female Algebra I class: Effects on high school math and science course selection. *Journal of Women and Minorities in Science and Engineering* 3:265–277.

Wood, W. B. 2003. Inquiry-based undergraduate teaching in the life sciences at large research universities: A perspective on the Boyer Commission Report. *Cell Biology Education* 2:112–116.

PART I

The Steps to Lecture-Free Teaching

Chapter 3

The Chronology of Course Design

Step 1   Consider the unique situation of the course you are preparing to teach.

Step 2   Determine the learning goals for the course.

Step 3   Create formative and summative assessments that provide feedback about the learning goals to both you and your students.

Step 4   Choose a teaching strategy that accomplishes the learning goals, responds flexibly to feedback from the assessments, and maintains coherence in the course.

Step 5   Develop in-class activities and homework assignments that achieve the learning goals, include formative assessments, and support the teaching strategy.

Step 6   Decide on a grading system for the semester.

Step 7   Assemble a topic schedule, with clearly indicated dates of in-class and laboratory activities, tests, and due dates for homework assignments.

Step 8   Use the course textbook and your previous lecture notes to create content outlines of topics and important terms you want students to know and understand.

Step 9   Compose a detailed course syllabus that describes features in Steps 1 through 8 and emphasizes the learning partnership between the students and you.

Step 10   Organize the topic schedule, syllabus, content outlines, in-class and laboratory activity worksheets, and formative assessments in a loose-leaf binder called *The Coursepack* that students will bring to each class meeting.

Step 11   On the first day of class, construct heterogeneous cooperative learning teams of four or five students.

Step 12   Use class time to answer student-generated questions and to lead activities and laboratory exercises that contribute to concept comprehension.

Step 13   Enjoy the unpredictable! Keep your mind and eyes open for new teaching techniques and activities that augment the cohesiveness of your course, support your learning goals, and stimulate a dialogue between you and your students.

Many books and articles guided my journey to Lecture-Free Teaching. Other books, discovered late in my reform process, demonstrate how the authors of those publications and I uncovered similar flaws in the traditional pedagogy and traveled different routes to transform our teaching, yet ended with solutions that share many characteristics (Fink 2003; McManus 2005; Wiggins and McTighe 2006). The books are affirming in their parallels to my chronology of course design, but at the same time the authors offer differences that may be helpful to some readers. Fink's and McManus's intended audience is college instructors, whereas the primary audience for Wiggins and McTighe is K–12 teachers. But my 13 steps for course design, as well as theirs, can be adapted to teaching in a wide range of disciplines and grades.

Step 1: Consider the unique situation of the course you are preparing to teach.

Whether you are planning changes in a class you have previously taught or designing new curricula, there are always conditions you cannot alter. In *Creating Significant Learning Experiences: An Integrated Approach to Designing College Courses*, Fink (2003) lists six situational factors to consider when planning a course.

The first situational factor is "Specific Context of the Teaching/Learning Situation." This category includes the number of students enrolled in the class; whether the course is for high school students in a particular grade or is an introductory, upper-level, or graduate course at a college or university; the length and frequency of the class meetings; the time of day and days of the week for class meetings; whether the classroom is a large lecture hall, a smaller classroom, a laboratory, or a seminar room; and the type and arrangement of seats and tables within that room.

Each condition can either enhance or detract from your ability to engage your students effectively. For example, enrollment numbers affect how many cooperative learning teams I build on the first day of class and how many students compose each team (Step 11). If the course is introductory, I consider that students will vary in their preparation for the course; if the course has prerequisites, I consider materials the students are expected to know. The length and frequency of class meetings affect the types of formative assessments and activities that I plan (Steps 3 and 5) to ensure that students can comfortably complete the tasks during class, with time for reflection and closure. Early morning classes and those that meet on Friday afternoons are undesirable for college students; different criteria apply for secondary school schedules. Type and size of the classroom and seating arrangement often are factors over which the educator has little control, but these variables can present an opportunity for creative use of space.

A hallmark of Lecture-Free Teaching is flexibility, and I try to be adaptable when responding to the factors mentioned. However, as I gain experience and confidence teaching outside the lecture mode, I become more adept at persuading colleagues and administrators that changes in the length and

 STEP

frequency of my class meetings, as well as the arrangement of the classroom seats, enhance student learning. If we ever build a new classroom building, I will lobby for flexible seating to facilitate communication among students working in cooperative learning groups. But factors that cannot be changed will always exist and must be considered when designing a course.

Fink next describes "Expectations of External Groups," a factor particularly relevant to secondary school science educators who are constrained by district and state curriculum standards and lists of required content. At the college level an institution may dictate course or curriculum learning expectations, as might a professional accreditation organization. The catalog description of the course, often written by several educators who teach the same course, must be taken into account. When designing my courses, I consider how to meet these expectations in creative ways with my lecture-free pedagogy, remembering that science content can be delivered by a variety of methods.

The third situational factor is the "Nature of the Subject." A science course typically combines learning factual content with acquiring physical skills (such as using a microscope). Science is dynamic, lending itself to the exploration of changes and controversies. Such characteristics can be used to a science educator's advantage in a lecture-free format. I use the laboratory component to help students understand and apply the facts. Similarly, changes and controversies inherent in scientific disciplines can be shaped into discussions, debates, case studies, and other methods of reinforcing the content.

The fourth factor involves "Characteristics of the Learners," which include the current life situations of the students; the personal or professional goals they have for the course and their reasons for enrolling; their prior experiences, knowledge, skills, and attitudes about the subject; and their learning styles. This situational factor is challenging for me because of the heterogeneity of learners at my institution. I strive to present a course that is rigorous but at the same time accessible to students with poor preparation and study skills. Many of the undergraduates I teach are older than the traditional college student, and they often have considerable family and work responsibilities. Some students live on campus, and others commute long distances each day. Negative attitudes about required science and mathematics courses abound. Students may have been told they have a particular learning style or "don't test well," making them resistant or lacking in confidence when confronting certain types of teaching or assessment techniques. Accommodating dissimilar students can be challenging, but the variety inherent in Lecture-Free Teaching improves my chances of creating an appropriate learning environment for all. Construction of learning teams on the first day of class (Step 11) randomly groups students of differing abilities and interests and engages them in cooperative teaching and learning that potentially benefits all of them.

The fifth factor, "Characteristics of the Teacher," is probably the category most familiar to us as we design our courses, but at the same time it is the most difficult to change. We should contemplate our familiarity with and attitude toward the subject; whether the subject is within or outside our comfort zone; and our beliefs, values, strengths, and weaknesses as teachers and learners. All

STEP

of these characteristics vary widely among teachers, of course, but they also can be different for a single educator depending on the course he or she is designing. Each time I plan a course for the upcoming semester, I re-evaluate my personal characteristics related to this course. As my experience teaching a course increases, I sometimes recognize there is more to a subject than I originally appreciated. For the past two decades I have taught an undergraduate course in genetics, which is such a rapidly changing field that, in some ways, I feel less confident about my knowledge now than I did a few years ago. This creates new challenges when designing and preparing for this course.

Finally, Fink discusses the "Special Pedagogical Challenge." By this he means the special situation that challenges both students and teacher to create a meaningful and successful learning experience. An example would be the fact that my introductory science courses are primarily taken by students who are required to complete two science courses to graduate. They may believe they have no interest in the subject, and they also may lack confidence in their ability to do well. This is where creative use of Lecture-Free Teaching can help engage a reluctant student and reduce his or her anxiety.

Keep in mind that even if you teach several sections of the same course at the same school during the same semester, the situational factors can vary among those sections and necessitate changes in how you design and teach each section. We have all had instances where the morning section of a class runs smoothly and is enjoyable to teach, but the afternoon session leaves you feeling frustrated and incompetent. It is easy to blame this on a couple of less-than-cooperative students in the class, but paying attention to differences in other situational factors can lead to more successful and satisfying class meetings, saving you both time and emotional energy.

Step 2: Determine the learning goals for the course.

Too often as we plan a course, we begin by listing major content topics derived from the textbook's chapter titles—our goal is to cover those topics. When I first began teaching, senior faculty members who previously taught the courses handed me their syllabi, and I used their content topics as "my goals."

It wasn't until one summer when I sat down with a book called *The Course Syllabus: A Learning-Centered Approach* (Grunert 1997), now in its second edition (O'Brien, Millis, and Cohen 2008), that I articulated the true purpose of each of my courses, not only to myself but also to my students. My current learning-centered approach goes well beyond having students learn a body of content. Instead, my goals are more akin to those of a liberal education: I consider how to help my students change their views of the world significantly; how to foster an interest in the discipline that will continue beyond the date of the final exam; how to prepare students to make effective choices in the voting booth and become citizens of the world; and how to help them acquire thinking skills they can apply to other life endeavors. The box "Examples of Course

 1 STEP
 2 STEP
 3
 4
 5
 6
 7
 8
 9

10

11

12

13

Learning Goals" lists course learning goals for three different types and levels of college courses.

For help identifying and ranking one's instructional goals, I recommend the Teaching Goals Inventory, a self-assessment devised by Angelo and Cross (1993). Comprehensive descriptions of how to formulate learning goals are provided in both *Understanding by Design* (Wiggins and McTighe 2006) and *Creating Significant Learning Experiences* (Fink 2003).

Examples of Course Learning Goals

For General Biology I (Biology 112)

1. Students will use written and oral communication, with terms associated with major topics in biology, to convey what they have learned, both to me and to their peers.
2. Students will apply knowledge to situations they have not yet experienced.
3. Students will use the scientific process to make observations, form hypotheses, design and conduct experiments, analyze results, and discuss conclusions.
4. Students will apply knowledge to make personal and ethical decisions.
5. Students will interact with peers in a cooperative learning team.

For Human Nutrition (Biology 300)

1. Students will apply nutrition facts to make practical dietary choices. They will demonstrate this skill individually and in collaboration with members of their cooperative learning teams.
2. Students will write a detailed and complete nutritional assessment (based on diet and physical activity) of their assigned service-learning partner.
3. Students will make effective dietary choices for themselves, their family, and their friends.
4. Students will practice scientific thinking skills that can be applied in other life endeavors.
5. Students will locate reliable sources of nutritional information and use them to make appropriate dietary decisions.

For Science Seminar (Biology/Environmental Studies 489)

1. Students will become familiar with the structure of professional science writing by reading examples of primary research papers, scientific dialogues, and case studies.
2. Using guidelines, students will choose topics appropriate for an original case study written in each of several case study styles.
3. By participating in weekly homework assignments, class discussions, and oral presentations, students will use the case study method to demonstrate the process of scientific inquiry.

STEP

4. Students will locate, read, and interpret scientific data during in-depth investigations of current scientific topics.
5. Students will logically defend or counter a position proposed by their chosen topics.
6. Students will follow a rubric to write a comprehensive and original case study that includes factual information from primary scientific literature, thought-provoking discussion questions, and teaching notes that describe how the case should be presented to a participating audience.
7. In an oral presentation, students will familiarize the audience with background information, present their case study stories, put participants into discussion groups to answer case questions, and facilitate discussion of the research questions.
8. Throughout the semester, students will offer constructive criticism of their classmates' case study ideas, manuscripts, and oral presentations.

Step 3: Create formative and summative assessments that provide feedback about the learning goals to both you and your students.

Partway through a decade of pedagogical reform, I realized that my assessments needed to better reflect my learning goals. I previously relied on summative assessments to measure and document student learning. I promptly returned graded tests and assigned papers and gave students time during class to ask questions about them, but there was no real opportunity or incentive for them to correct their errors or misconceptions. I observed many students taking a quick glance at their grade without bothering to read the comments and corrections I had painstakingly written in the margins.

I originally anticipated completing the circle of my pedagogical reform by modifying my summative assessments, but after reviewing the extensive assessment literature, I realized I could not use summative assessments effectively without first introducing formative assessments, during which students practice the skills needed to achieve the learning goals for each course. Students come to class with prior knowledge and possible misconceptions that affect their interpretations of new knowledge. In-class formative assessments, usually ungraded and often completed within a cooperative learning team, can dispel misconceptions and contribute to new, more accurate learning. Formative assessments provide information throughout the teaching and learning process to both my students and me so that I can adjust my instruction in ways that help students correct misunderstandings before they attempt a test or assignment on which they will be graded. This collaboration reinforces the learning partnership and is both a goal and a consequence of Lecture-Free Teaching.

STEP

STEP

A Daily Formative Assessment: The Murkiest Point

This formative assessment occurs at the end of every class meeting. As students depart, they hand me a small paper on which they have written their name and at least one point from the day's class that they found either confusing or interesting. To have his or her attendance recorded, a comment or question about the day's class must be submitted. I receive timely information about the effectiveness of my teaching and whether or not activities were useful, confusing, or interesting. At the beginning of the next class I respond to the "murkies." This assessment requires no teacher preparation, minimal class time, and a few minutes to review. With large class enrollment, a work-study student can record attendance and organize the questions. If used correctly, "murkies" provide valuable feedback to both students and educator, strengthening their partnership of learning.

I suggest that formative assessments be a part of every class meeting and take a variety of forms. Some assessments require almost no preparation and very little time to administer daily, such as the Murkiest Point (see above), or weekly, such as Genetics Problem Sets (see below). More elaborate assessments are effectively embedded in an in-class or homework activity designed to teach a content topic, such as Inheritance of ABO Blood Typing in Humans (Appendix C-1).

Excellent resources exist for easily locating a variety of appropriate assessments. A book for educators representing all disciplines is *Classroom Assessment Techniques: A Handbook for College Teachers* (Angelo and Cross 1993). *College Science Teachers Guide to Assessment* (Lord, French, and Crow 2009) is useful for both the educational researcher and the classroom educator and covers a variety of topics, including validation of assessment survey instruments, assessment of learning outcomes, forms of assessment, how-to assessment practices, and tips to enhance assessment in the college science classroom. A series of books with detailed instructions for formative assessment probes is designed for K–12 science educators, but can be adapted for use in postsecondary classrooms (Keeley 2008; Keeley, Eberle, and Dorsey 2008; Keeley, Eberle, and Farrin 2005; Keeley, Eberle, and Tugel 2007; Keeley and Tugel 2009).

A Weekly Formative Assessment: Genetics Problem Sets

Problem solving is an essential skill for mastery of genetics. Most genetics textbooks include a large collection of end-of-chapter problem sets, making it easy for an instructor to choose ones representative of the style and scope of questions for an upcoming test. Weekly problem sets assigned for homework can be an effective formative

STEP

assessment; the challenge is to motivate the students to devote sufficient individual effort while encouraging them to work in study groups. Grading problem sets not only contradicts the purpose of formative assessments, but also requires a lot of time for the teacher. On the other hand, if homework is purely voluntary, few students are disciplined enough to complete it each week. My compromise is to assign problems at the end of each week (based on that week's content) and have them due at the first class meeting the following week. The beginning of that class is reserved for answering questions about specific homework problems. Immediately after answering questions, I collect the problem sets and grade them for completeness only. After class I post solutions on Blackboard. This assessment gives students and me prompt feedback on concept comprehension, provides me a measure of whether students are investing sufficient time on problem solving, and serves as an opportunity to clear up misconceptions about the previous week's content.

To ensure that students devote appropriate effort to ungraded assessments, you must respond promptly to the results with meaningful feedback. If questions on the Murkiest Point are not answered at the beginning of the next class, if weekly problem sets are not reviewed and collected, if in-class exercises are not discussed to reveal confusion, then students will not take these activities seriously. Each time you teach, ask yourself what you would like your students to be able to do at the end of the day's instruction, and then design an assessment that will determine if they can do it. As you discover whether your students have achieved the day's learning goals, your students will become aware of their own misconceptions and move down the path of independent learning. Involve your students in the phases of your teaching reform by explaining changes you have made or will make in response to assessment results.

The best summative assessments require a demonstration of skills and knowledge practiced during formative assessments by asking students to apply them to novel situations. At the end of Appendix C-2 is an appropriate test question based on an inquiry-based laboratory. Graded tests, papers, and group assignments should not only quantify student learning but also enhance that learning. Occasionally, a student will tell me excitedly that while taking a test, he or she thought about a concept in a different way and finally understood it. When that occurs, I know that I have stumbled on an effective evaluation of significant learning. I strive to have all of my assessments accomplish this.

STEP

Step 4: Choose a teaching strategy that accomplishes the learning goals, responds flexibly to feedback from the assessments, and maintains coherence in the course.

When I began incorporating active learning into my teaching repertoire, I gave too little consideration to a teaching strategy. One stated goal in my sabbatical application was to "incorporate at least one active learning exercise into each of my lectures." The result was a sometimes disjointed class meeting comprising activities that were relevant to content topics but not always providing a smooth transition from one topic to the next. As I gained experience in Lecture-Free Teaching, I created teaching strategies that supported the learning goals by encouraging students to prepare before each class meeting. One of my primary responsibilities is to demonstrate connectedness among content topics and in-class activities.

Although my teaching strategies depend somewhat on specific learning goals for a particular course, I generally provide detailed content outlines to guide students through their textbook reading and note-taking before each class meeting (Step 8). Rather than using class time for lecturing, I begin by answering questions e-mailed to me about the textbook reading, as well as the Murkiest Point questions submitted at the end of the previous class (Chapter 7). Next come in-class activities designed to expose misconceptions stemming from prior knowledge or textbook readings. These activities allow me not only to correct students' misunderstandings before it is too late but also to give students opportunities to practice skills they will need for summative assessments. Lecture-free does not mean that I never stand in front of the class and share factual information. I often give what could be described as mini-lectures, but these are in direct response to student questions or confusion, rather than being short presentations I plan in advance to follow a prescribed schedule during a class meeting.

Students taking notes before each class on an outline of content topics and important terms effectively substitutes for my giving a lecture. Students' notes are derived from reading their textbooks and ensure that they are informed of content I expect them to know, just as a lecture would. Although a student must be organized and disciplined to accomplish this reading and note-taking in advance, I experience greater success with this strategy than with anticipating that my lecture will inspire students to do the reading afterward, as promoted by others (Lord 2007). Occasionally reviewing notes students have (or have not) made on their outlines gives me a tangible method to guide better study methods. Reinforcing learning during class is a more efficient use of time and also motivates students to attend class because they know I will not use class time to review what they could simply read on their own. My job is to convince students that preparing for and participating in class leads to better comprehension of concepts and, ultimately, saves them time (Chapter 6).

STEP 4

A consistent teaching strategy for all of my courses is cooperative learning (Chapter 12) that begins in the first 15 minutes of the first class meeting of the semester (Chapter 10). Many studies validate the effectiveness of cooperative learning (Lord 2001), and I have fully embraced this method. A detailed discussion of cooperative learning takes place in Part III of this book.

I avoid predictability in the structure of class meetings. An element of surprise keeps both my students and me engaged; curiosity as students anticipate an upcoming class is an incentive for regular attendance. My teaching is an amalgamation of a variety of instructional strategies created and perfected by other educators (Chapters 10–16). Although I admire each of these strategies, they become tedious if used exclusively week after week. I combine them in ways that create variety while challenging me to maintain coherence within and between class meetings. An examination of sample topic schedules in Appendix A-1–6 demonstrates that some topics are introduced by a laboratory exercise, whereas others conclude with one; some content lends itself to using a case study; sometimes learning teams work together for the entire class meeting; sometimes individuals give presentations; and sometimes formative assessments dominate the class period.

Possible connections are always on my mind as I read journals such as *The American Biology Teacher* and *Journal of College Science Teaching*. When I see a good idea for a specific activity or a laboratory exercise with potential for one of my courses, my first consideration is determining how well the activity will integrate into the class. I strive to use activities that reinforce and expand on previous experiences so that the early activities become the base on which students build comprehension of more complex topics.

The course syllabus that I distribute in General Biology I (Appendix A-8) describes several writing assignments, including a scientific report of a laboratory investigation. Because I make liberal use of case studies (Chapter 15), the first class meeting is an ideal time to present this instructional strategy, while at the same time introducing students to cooperative learning within their newly formed teams (Chapters 10 and 12). During a recent semester I chose an introductory case study that not only is inherently interesting to students but also acquaints them with the scientific process and models the structure of their upcoming scientific reports.

"Cell Phone Use and Cancer: A Case Study to Explore the Scientific Method" (Parilla 2006) is among hundreds of case studies published by the State University of New York at Buffalo on the peer-reviewed website of the National Center for Case Study Teaching in Science. After volunteers assume roles of different characters and read the case aloud, I hand each learning team copies of five different news articles about research on cell phone use and cancer. Each team member reads at least one of the short articles and summarizes it for the team. The group discusses differences among the headlines of the five articles, analyzes the scientific methodology described, and compares results and conclusions. Based on these articles from the lay press, the learning team offers suggestions for improvement of the scientific study. At the end of the

STEP

exercise, I give students the original research article (Lönn et al. 2004) on which each of the shorter articles was based so they can compare information presented by the lay press with the publication by the scientists. Many students have never seen an article in the primary literature. For homework they read the article, and at the next class we review how the scientific process was followed and how the journal article models their own future scientific reports.

By the end of the first week of the course, students have experienced two components of my teaching strategy—cooperative learning and the case study—and have acquired skills and knowledge they will apply throughout the semester. Each time they begin an inquiry-based lab exercise or participate in a case study, this learning is reinforced.

Step 5: Develop in-class activities and homework assignments that achieve the learning goals, include formative assessments, and support the teaching strategy.

Years ago I decided that one of my goals was to develop my students' scientific reasoning skills, but I did not yet appreciate that my courses displayed a disconnect between teaching strategies and learning goals. After a series of content-laden lectures, I created test questions that required students to apply factual information to solve novel problems. My students, not surprisingly, could not make the leap and performed poorly on these questions. I realized that my instructor-centered strategy encouraged memorization of facts, but my test questions asked students to apply those facts in new ways. Today I enjoy designing activities that allow students to simultaneously learn and understand content.

Journals are a great source of ideas for in-class and homework activities. Like many people, my husband and I subscribe to more periodicals than we have time to read. They accumulate, partially read, on the kitchen counter, the living room coffee table, and bedside tables until, during a break between semesters, I devote several days to intense reading and then recycle the ones I will never have a chance to read. But two journals that I read promptly and cover-to-cover are *The American Biology Teacher* and *Journal of College Science Teaching*. I make the time for these journals because I am fearful I will miss a suggestion I could use immediately. In those two publications I find ideas for in-class activities and homework assignments for nearly all of the courses I teach. A comprehensive list of science education journals is available on the National Center for Case Study Teaching in Science website, from the State University of New York at Buffalo. Journals for educators in agriculture, anthropology, biology, chemistry, dentistry, engineering, environmental studies, geography, geology, mathematics, nursing, pharmacy, physics, psychology, statistics, and veterinary medicine are described on the site.

Topical journals, along with books and online sources, provide appropriate ideas for every discipline and age group. Increasingly, I do not use an activity as originally presented by its author but rather adapt it to more closely

STEP 4

STEP 5

fit my learning goals. Often, after I lead an activity, I ask my students to suggest ways to improve it for the next time I teach the course. Sometimes an article inspires my own idea for a completely different learning activity, such as the new way in which I used "sock chromosomes," described below.

Genetics lends itself particularly well to learning by manipulating models. Over the years my students have used paper, popsicle sticks, pipe cleaners, Twizzlers, and beads on a string to represent chromosomes. Several different articles (Chinnici, Neth, and Sherman 2006; Oakley 1994; Stavroulakis 2005) suggest using socks to demonstrate mitosis, meiosis, and karyotyping, all of which I have done.

I recently took ingredients from those previously published articles to create my own recipe for an entirely new use of sock chromosomes. When I lead hands-on workshops, I begin the session just as I do the first class meeting of a semester: I randomly divide participants into cooperative learning teams of approximately four people, using one of my methods for accomplishing this while at the same time introducing students to content (Wood 2007, 2009). For a workshop at a national conference of biology educators, I wanted to challenge participants with something more than I would students on the first day of an introductory course. At a local discount store I bought numerous "homologous pairs" of socks (socks of the same size and style, but with different colors or patterns). As the workshop participants gathered, they passed around a large bag in which I had mixed all of the single socks. After each person had reached into the bag and selected one sock, I asked everyone to search the room until they located their "sister chromatid." After finding "her" (or him!), they would work together to find their "homologous pair," then form a tetrad by sitting together, and finally become a four-person learning team for the workshop session.

As I stressed in Step 4, activities should contribute to the cohesiveness of the curriculum. The instructor should also avoid too many different activities during one class meeting. When first using active learning, I feared that activities would conclude too quickly, leaving me with extra time during which I would be forced to lecture or (heaven forbid!) dismiss class early. Although I often have extra activities ready to go, I rarely use them and instead reserve time at the end of the class meeting for closure and reflection on the activity's connection with previous and future topics. My change to fewer, longer class meetings each week provides this important conclusion time because I do not spend time getting the class "warmed-up" on multiple days of the week (Chapter 8).

I always look for elements that tie the entire course together and that I can use to reinforce earlier material while building on the foundation. My goals are to connect all of the course strands during class meetings near the end of the semester and to create appropriate comprehensive questions for the final exam.

STEP

Step 6: Decide on a grading system for the semester.

A useful book called *Effective Grading: A Tool for Learning and Assessment* (Walvoord and Anderson 1998) includes several grading models. A commonality among them (including my own, which I describe later in this chapter) is that the grading system communicates the instructor's values and goals for the course.

To determine a course's grading system, I list all of the tests, assignments, and other factors that will contribute to the semester grade. Then I return to my previously determined learning goals (Step 2) to be sure everything listed reflects those goals. To assign points to each item, I consider the comparative value I place on each aspect of the course. Rather than starting with a specific number of course points to divide among the assessments, I allot points to each test or assignment, starting with the one that contributes the most (for example, 100 points for a comprehensive final exam or a major paper), and then assign fewer points to the others based on their relative contribution toward accomplishing the learning goals. Finally, I total the number of points for the list of assessments (Appendix B-1). The student receives a letter grade according to the percentage of total possible points earned.

The list of graded tests and assignments, along with their point distribution, is in the course syllabus. The relative number of points conveys to students the value I place on each category of assessment so they can determine the time and effort they should invest in each. Too often students spend an excessive amount of time on a task that does little to help them achieve the learning goals.

I believe a student who does well on a comprehensive final exam has acquired the skills and knowledge that I have assessed on earlier topic tests. If a student earns a solid C or better on the comprehensive final, I drop the lowest previous test score when calculating his or her course grade. The purpose is to motivate students to maintain their effort through the end of the semester. The policy gives students another chance to understand the material, this time with the perspective of an entire semester of learning. I generally wait until midterm (which immediately precedes the last day to withdraw from a course at my university) to announce this opportunity. The intentional delay deters students from slacking off for most of the semester, mistakenly thinking they can make it up at the end. Furthermore, I do not want to encourage students for whom there is no hope of passing to remain in the course after the withdrawal deadline because they believe they can somehow ace the final. I want them to realize that although the final exam represents a substantial component of the course grade, it is just one element; dropping a single low grade does not erase an entire semester of poor performance.

Once you draft a grading system, you need to confirm that it truly reflects how you value each component of the course. For example, you may want to be sure that a student who actively participates in class but has not achieved other learning goals will not inappropriately inflate his or her grade through vigorous class participation. Or perhaps you value participation so much that a participative student who would ordinarily get a D now gets a C. If student

STEP

performance on written, individual tests best reflects your learning goals, then the grading system must demonstrate this. If a final project is as important as the combined tests, then possible points for the final project should be equal to total test points.

My grading system is easily modified to include extra credit points by simply adding extra credit to an individual's earned points without adding points to the possible total points. For example, learning-team members may earn a few extra credit points during test review activities (Chapter 12). I occasionally offer extra credit points when students attend a relevant public lecture if they submit a short reflective essay about the experience. I maintain extra credit points as separate categories in the grade record, rather than adding on points to a particular test, because I want students to have accurate information about their performance on a test.

Avoid potential pitfalls when incorporating extra credit points by making certain you do not place too much relative value on them. Students should not be able to pass a course because they accumulated extra credit points. If I offer extra credit points for participating in an event outside of class time, some students complain that this is unfair because they have a schedule conflict. I point out to them that another student's extra credit points do not subtract points from their grade; they can use the time not spent on extra credit work to do better on the regular assignments.

I have no need to modify my grading system for penalties because the only official penalty I have is for late submission of work, for which I subtract one point (usually from 30 or 35 possible points) for each day an assignment is late. I emphasize this policy both in the syllabus and verbally, thereby avoiding subjective decisions about giving extensions. Students rarely request extra time to complete a paper or argue with me about it. They make their own decision about whether it is worth it to turn in something late—another lesson in assuming responsibility.

I never grade on the curve because this emphasizes competition among students and undermines my goal of cooperative learning. If many students perform poorly on a particular test, I look for flaws in questions and sometimes eliminate them from test grade calculations. If just a couple of students correctly answer a flawed question, I can add extra points to their grade. I announce to the class how I have done this, rather than using a curving formula.

Step 7: Assemble a topic schedule, with clearly indicated dates of in-class and laboratory activities, tests, and due dates for homework assignments.

As students enter the classroom on the first day of the semester, I hand them a topic schedule (notice that I do not call it a lecture schedule!). The topic schedule depends on elements I describe in Steps 1 through 6, so it is created after the completion of these steps. But since content outlines, the syllabus,

STEP

STEP

and coursepack organization depend on the topic schedule, construction of this latter element must precede Steps 8 through 10.

The layout of the topic schedule affects students' interpretations of their responsibilities during the semester. I needed several years of trial and error before finalizing a template that eliminates confusion. I try to limit my topic schedules to the front and back of an 8½- × 11-inch paper, with the first half of the semester on one side and the second half on the other. The order of column headings on my table format is important: Listing homework assignments in the far left column underscores that students should complete the homework before the scheduled class, which may be the reverse of the order to which they are accustomed. An example of a typical topic schedule for General Biology I is in Appendix A-1, followed by examples of topic schedules for five other courses (Appendixes A-2, A-3, A-4, A-5, and A-6).

Although I avoid exceeding the length of a double-sided sheet of paper, I include as much detail as I can to reduce verbal reminders about upcoming assignments. The responsibility is shifted to the students when they adopt the habit of checking the topic schedule several times each week. My obligation is to stay on schedule as much as possible and to promptly notify students of changes. My previously described policy (Step 6) of deducting one point for each day an assignment is late also contributes to students' taking more responsibility and is an effective method for receiving assignments in a timely fashion.

My university uses Blackboard, an online course-management system that permits easy communication with students enrolled in a course and provides links to a variety of course information. Although I post topic schedules on Blackboard as well as on my web page, I distribute a hard copy (three-hole punched so that it can be inserted in the coursepack) on the first day of class to better explain how the course is organized and what I expect from the students. The topic schedule is most useful if kept in the front of the coursepack, which contains content outlines and worksheets (Step 10).

Step 8: Use the course textbook and your previous lecture notes to create content outlines of topics and important terms you want students to know and understand.

Content outlines ensure that a course includes necessary and appropriate factual material and that students are informed about the sections of textbook chapters that I consider most important. In other words, content outlines substitute for a lecture: Many of my content outlines are derived from past lecture notes, so they include exactly the same topics about which I would lecture. Student note-taking on outlines *before* class replaces student note-taking *during* lectures. By guiding students through the chapters of the text, content outlines free class time for in-class activities that help students better comprehend and apply scientific information and uncover misconceptions or confusion based on prior knowledge or from reading the textbook.

STEP

On the first day of class I explain to students how to use the content outlines provided in their coursepacks. I also explain this in the syllabus for each course in the section "How to Succeed" (Appendix A-8).

An example of a content outline is included in Appendix A-7. I format content outlines with four spaces between each term and concept to allow adequate room for note-taking as students read the assigned textbook chapter. This sample outline relates to other examples in this chapter: Students take notes on Outline 10: Genetics to prepare for Week 9 class meetings indicated on the sample topic schedule for General Biology I (Appendix A-1); these meetings include participation in the in-class activity Inheritance of ABO Blood Typing in Humans (Appendix C-1).

Placing outlines with related in-class activities in a coursepack supports my teaching strategy goal of maintaining coherence (Step 4). As indicated in the General Biology I topic schedule, the sample Genetics outline follows two previous weeks of learning about DNA replication and cell reproduction. The first part of Outline 10 links these earlier topics to new terms that students need to understand and use during their study of genetics. The part of the outline about genotype and phenotype prepares students to participate in the in-class activity on ABO blood types. Several weeks later in the semester, students review and apply what they learned about these blood groups to understand immunology and ABO/Rh blood typing in humans.

Step 9: Compose a detailed course syllabus that describes features in Steps 1 through 8 and emphasizes the learning partnership between the students and you.

As discussed in Step 2, I did not truly understand the purpose and value of a well-designed syllabus until I read *The Course Syllabus: A Learning-Centered Approach,* now in its second edition (O'Brien, Millis, and Cohen 2008). As the authors explain, a comprehensive learning-centered syllabus not only describes what the instructor will cover but also is an important resource to support learning and intellectual development. Composing such a document requires substantial thought and analysis; a syllabus evolves each time you teach a course to a different set of learners. The process of articulating learning goals, assessments, teaching strategies, activities, grading practices, and content helps you develop and teach a better course.

The syllabus often is the first communication between you and your students. When carefully conceived, it can demonstrate effectively your beliefs about education, your values concerning the content and structure of the course, and your expectations for students and what they can expect from you. A well-written syllabus can minimize misunderstandings throughout the semester. An example of a course syllabus for General Biology I is in Appendix A-8.

Traditionally, faculty use the first day of class solely to distribute and review the syllabus. Before the semester begins, I alert students via e-mail that they will begin learning content on the first day of class and that this

meeting will last for the full class period (frequently almost three hours for my combined lecture/laboratory courses). Although I distribute both the topic schedule and the syllabus as students enter the classroom on that first day, I immediately engage students in an activity (Step 11) that not only introduces them to some course content but also sends the message that attendance is important at all class meetings and that our time together will be used for learning that cannot occur outside class.

Although I may discuss key sections of the syllabus, I mention several times that the first assignment is to read the syllabus carefully. This is also listed as homework on the corresponding topic schedule. Those students who comply will find a surprise extra credit opportunity on the final page of the syllabus. At the beginning of the second class I announce how many students took advantage of this, thereby reinforcing the importance of students' taking responsibility for their own learning.

My syllabus is generally six single-spaced pages (in addition to two pages of topic schedule), and all eight pages are designed to be a resource for the entire semester. The syllabus provides not only practical information about the course but also more general information (such as learning goals, teaching techniques, assignments, and the grading system), always emphasizing the students' responsibility for their own learning and the ongoing partnership between the students and me.

Step 10: Organize the topic schedule, syllabus, content outlines, in-class and laboratory activity worksheets, and formative assessments in a loose-leaf binder called *The Coursepack* that students will bring to each class meeting.

I have developed coursepacks for each course I teach and modify them as an important part of my preparation for an upcoming semester. Students buy coursepacks in the campus bookstore as one of their required texts. This arrangement not only saves my department money by eliminating the need to copy handouts, but I also believe that purchasing even a modestly priced coursepack increases students' commitment to the course. In addition, with all course materials in their possession from the first week of the semester, students can plan ahead and know exactly what they will miss if absent.

Most important, with a coursepack students can view the structure of the entire semester. Demonstrating coherence is a critical part of my teaching strategy (Step 4), and over the years I have become more skilled at choosing appropriate activities so that individual class meetings not only have a theme and make smooth transitions between activities but also allow students to experience connections among the content topics. Having all of the semester's course elements in chronological order in a single loose-leaf notebook underscores these links.

Each time I lead a workshop on Lecture-Free Teaching, someone suggests that rather than requiring students to purchase hard copies, I post each week's

STEP

STEP

coursepack material online. Although it is true that assembling coursepacks makes my preparation for an upcoming semester more intense, I believe there is a distinct advantage to having all of the course materials in a binder that is brought to every class meeting. I number coursepack pages consecutively, making it convenient to ask students to turn to a particular page during class or to refer to previous or future exercises to emphasize connections among content topics. Students own their coursepacks, and if a student loses his or her coursepack, she or he must buy another copy—another way of encouraging students to take responsibility for their own learning. And, of course, I never need to worry that they forgot to print needed materials for an in-class activity from the online source. The meat of every coursepack is the content outlines (Step 8) on which students take notes while reading an assigned chapter.

Step 11: On the first day of class, construct heterogeneous cooperative learning teams of four or five students.

The first day of class is, in many ways, the most important class meeting of the semester. Investing time and effort to plan an interesting, well-organized day can create a positive classroom climate that lasts the entire semester. The first class is your opportunity to set the stage for constructive interpersonal relations among the students and between you and your students.

Goals for my first class meeting include having students

- understand the benefits of my Lecture-Free Teaching methods,
- experience how the course is structured and what is expected of them,
- learn some course content,
- begin to feel comfortable with their classmates and to develop a rapport with me, and
- understand their responsibility for the success of the course.

My method for building heterogeneous learning teams initiates work toward all of these goals within the first 15 minutes of the semester. In Chapter 10, I describe how for each course I design a different organizational concept by which students form cooperative learning teams of four or five students with whom they will work on in-class and homework activities for the semester (Wood 2007, 2009).

Because of previous negative experiences, some students are reluctant to work in groups. Explaining to them, at the outset, the proven benefits of teamwork and also how I will monitor, evaluate, and assess contributions of team members (Chapter 12) starts them off with a more positive attitude about what may be an unfamiliar or uncomfortable learning tool. The theme of the team-building activity introduces factual content that is reiterated throughout the semester, so this exercise is much more than an icebreaker (Appendix C-4).

STEP

STEP

I believe in the power of words and that your choice of words affects listeners' or readers' perceptions and expectations of what you want to communicate. For years I talked to students about forming cooperative learning groups, an important instructional strategy first promoted in the 1980s (Johnson and Johnson 1989; Johnson, Johnson, and Smith 1991). Now I prefer the expression *learning teams* (Michaelsen, Knight, and Fink 2004). This term is meaningful to my many sports-minded students and describes a supportive interaction among students that ultimately benefits everyone.

Step 12: Use class time to answer student-generated questions and to lead activities and laboratory exercises that contribute to concept comprehension.

I invite students to communicate promptly with me about course content they do not fully understand. There are several different ways to accomplish this:

- E-mail me questions before 7:00 a.m. on the class day
- Write the Murkiest Point at the end of a class meeting (Murkiest Point box, p. 27)
- Call or visit me in my office
- Use the time-honored method of raising one's hand during class

The first thing I do at a class meeting is respond to "murkies" from the previous class, as well as to any questions I received via e-mail. In the syllabus I explain that if I receive no questions or requests for additional explanation of a topic, I assume everyone in the class understands both the previous and new material. I then proceed with the scheduled in-class activity or laboratory exercise. As I describe in Step 4, I sometimes give what could be described as mini-lectures, but these are in direct response to student questions or confusion.

During a semester I employ a variety of instructional strategies, described in detail in Part III of this book: inquiry-based laboratories resulting in scientific reports; writing by students; cooperative learning, including Peer Instruction, Problem-Based Learning, and test review sessions; Team-Based Learning; service-learning; case studies; and student-led teaching models. As discussed in Step 5, a plethora of classroom-tested activities for science students at all levels is available in journals, books, and online sources. I keep in mind that what I have the students do during class should increase their understanding and give them practice applying factual knowledge related to the day's topic. With Lecture-Free Teaching one cannot predict exactly how long a planned exercise will take, so I reserve time for clarification and closure at the end of every class.

Class time should be used for learning that students cannot accomplish alone outside the classroom. Students in Light's (2001) study reported that classes in which a professor simply repeats what they have just read or could easily read in a textbook are not a good use of their time. Similarly, Tobias

STEP

STEP

(1990) found that in-class activities, laboratory exercises, videos, and guest lectures will not be taken seriously by students unless test questions and homework assignments reflect these experiences.

Step 13: Enjoy the unpredictable! Keep your mind and eyes open for new teaching techniques and activities that augment the cohesiveness of your course, support your learning goals, and stimulate a dialogue between you and your students.

Although the unpredictability of leading a lecture-free class may be unsettling at first, I encourage you to embrace the energy that accompanies this pedagogy. Flexibility and responsiveness to what happens during each class meeting with each unique group of students are the keys to the success of my methods.

I began my teaching reform by gradually incorporating others' ideas about which I had read or heard. As I gained experience and confidence, I used more of my own ideas, and now I am sometimes surprised by my creativity. An everyday experience or conversation can suggest an ideal in-class activity or laboratory investigation. I am increasingly bold about trying something completely new, but afterward I ask students to reflect on what we have done and tell me whether it was helpful to them, if I should repeat it with future students, and their recommendations for improving the activity.

Honest feedback from students is vital. We ask our students to take risks in their learning, and we must do the same. My hopes are that as we develop rapport and mutual respect, students feel more like equal participants in the process and that we truly engage in the learning partnership referred to in the subtitle of this book.

REFERENCES

Angelo, T. A., and K. P. Cross. 1993. *Classroom assessment techniques: A handbook for college teachers*. 2nd ed. San Francisco: Jossey-Bass.

Chinnici, J. P., S. Z. Neth, and L. R. Sherman. 2006. Using "chromosomal socks" to demonstrate ploidy in mitosis and meiosis. *American Biology Teacher* 68 (2): 106–109.

Fink, L. D. 2003. *Creating significant learning experiences: An integrated approach to designing college courses*. San Francisco: Jossey-Bass.

Grunert, J. 1997. *The course syllabus: A learning-centered approach*. Bolton, MA: Anker Publishing Company.

Johnson, D. W., and R. T. Johnson. 1989. *Cooperation and competition: Theory and research*. Edina, MN: Interaction Book Company.

Johnson, D. W., R. Johnson, and K. A. Smith. 1991. *Active learning: Cooperation in the college classroom*. Edina, MN: Interaction Book Company.

STEP

STEP

Keeley, P. 2008. *Science formative assessments: 75 practical strategies for linking assessment, instruction, and learning.* Arlington, VA: NSTA Press.

Keeley, P., F. Eberle, and C. Dorsey. 2008. *Uncovering student ideas in science, vol. 3: Another 25 formative assessment probes.* Arlington, VA: NSTA Press.

Keeley, P., F. Eberle, and L. Farrin. 2005. *Uncovering student ideas in science, vol. 1: 25 formative assessment probes.* Arlington, VA: NSTA Press.

Keeley, P., F. Eberle, and J. Tugel. 2007. *Uncovering student ideas in science, vol. 2: 25 more formative assessment probes.* Arlington, VA: NSTA Press.

Keeley, P., and J. Tugel. 2009. *Uncovering student ideas in science, vol. 4: 25 new formative assessment probes.* Arlington, VA: NSTA Press.

Light, R. J. 2001. *Making the most of college: Students speak their minds.* Cambridge, MA: Harvard University Press.

Lönn, S., A. Ahlbom, P. Hall, and M. Feychting. 2004. Mobile phone use and the risk of acoustic neuroma. *Epidemiology* 15 (6): 653–659.

Lord, T. R. 2001. 101 reasons for using cooperative learning in biology teaching. *American Biology Teacher* 63 (1): 30–38.

———. 2007. Teach for understanding before the details get in the way. *Journal of College Science Teaching* 36 (6): 70–72.

Lord, T. R., D. P. French, and L. W. Crow, eds. 2009. *College science teachers guide to assessment.* Arlington, VA: NSTA Press.

McManus, D. A. 2005. *Leaving the lectern: Cooperative learning and the critical first days of students working in groups.* Bolton, MA: Anker Publishing Company.

Michaelsen, L. K., A. B. Knight, and L. D. Fink, eds. 2004. *Team-Based Learning: A transformative use of small groups in college teaching.* Sterling, VA: Stylus.

Oakley, C. R. 1994. Using sweat socks and chromosomes to illustrate nuclear division. *American Biology Teacher* 56 (4): 238–239.

O'Brien, J. G., B. J. Millis, and M. W. Cohen. 2008. *The course syllabus: A learning-centered approach.* 2nd ed. San Francisco: Jossey-Bass.

Parilla, W. V. C. 2006. Cell phone use and cancer: A case study to explore the scientific method. National Center for Case Study Teaching in Science Case Collection. *www.sciencecases.org/cell_phone/cell_phone.asp.*

Stavroulakis, A. 2005. Meio-socks and other genetic yarns. *American Biology Teacher* 67 (4): 233–238.

Tobias, S. 1990. *They're not dumb, they're different: Stalking the second tier.* Tucson, AZ: Research Corporation.

Walvoord, B. E., and V. J. Anderson. 1998. *Effective grading: A tool for learning and assessment.* San Francisco: Jossey-Bass.

Wiggins, G., and J. McTighe. 2006. *Understanding by design.* 2nd ed. Upper Saddle River, NJ: Pearson Education.

Wood, B. S. 2007. Learning biology while constructing cooperative learning groups: The first 15 minutes. *American Biology Teacher* 69 (6): 330.

———. 2009. Learning science while constructing learning teams. *Journal of College Science Teaching* 38 (5): 28–32.

Chapter 4

The Feedback Loop

I read the book *Making the Most of College: Students Speak Their Minds* (Light 2001) with some trepidation. After devoting a decade to transforming my courses, I was curious about what students believe enhances their learning—and was relieved to recognize my teaching methods in their descriptions of effective instruction. This validation, of course, was due to neither coincidence nor my prescience. Rather, the changes I had made were in response to both my perception of successes and failures in my classroom and valuable feedback from my students.

As described in the steps to Lecture-Free Teaching (Chapter 3), with my course design, I first identify learning goals and then use assessments to determine whether students have achieved these goals. My teaching strategy is flexible enough to respond to information gleaned from formative and summative assessments. Sometimes my response occurs immediately after an assessment, sometimes at a later class meeting, and sometimes when I teach the course during a future semester. I develop in-class activities and laboratory exercises to accomplish the learning goals, support the flexible teaching strategies, and incorporate both formative and summative assessments. This sequence forms a powerful feedback loop.

This feedback loop brings to mind how we use the scientific process to solve a problem. First, we ask a question based on our observations or background research; from these observations we construct a hypothesis. We test the hypothesis with an experiment by analyzing the resulting data and drawing a conclusion. Feedback in the form of a conclusion either supports our hypothesis or necessitates stating a new hypothesis, proceeding again through the steps, and assessing the new information. Each time we repeat the feedback loop, we hopefully move closer to answering the original question.

If we apply the scientific process to Lecture-Free Teaching, the most important question instructors ask is: Are my students achieving the learning goals I created? The hypothesis in this process is the teaching strategy we design with specific in-class and laboratory activities. For the experiment, we follow the activities with formative and summative assessments. Once we complete our experiment and examine the data derived from the assessments, we conclude whether or not we have support for the hypothesis. If not, we devise a new hypothetical teaching strategy and repeat the steps of the feedback loop, each time getting closer to a teaching strategy that will accomplish the learning goals.

Be forewarned: Not all of the feedback you receive will be what you want to hear. As I described in Chapter 3, among my formative assessments are the daily "murkies" in which students describe the murkiest or most interesting point. Once students understand that you invite opinion, they freely dispense it. Receiving feedback and responding to it does not mean that you automatically do what the students want you to do, nor should you create easier tests if students perform poorly and complain that the tests are too hard. An appropriate response to negativity may be a more thorough explanation of the proven value of your teaching methods and of effective ways to study for your course.

You have to mean it when you tell students you want both positive and negative feedback on your pedagogy because with Lecture-Free Teaching, students become increasingly comfortable with supplying this feedback both during class and on your end-of-semester evaluations. If your self-esteem depends on consistently flattering student evaluations, this teaching style is not appropriate for you. I find that although the written comments on end-of-semester evaluations are candid, the quantitative scores about my courses remain high. I optimistically interpret this to mean that most students are appreciative of my efforts to improve my teaching and of our learning partnership.

Workshop Biology professors at the University of Oregon (discussed in Chapter 2) also use feedback to inform their teaching. The creators of Workshop Biology classify the reactions of most students to their transformed pedagogy as "critically appreciative" (Udovic et al. 2002). They report that a significant subset of students expresses frustration and discomfort with the atypical demands of the course. Rather than attributing this to laziness, the educators believe the students do not understand that opinions expressed in science require substantiation. Because the kind of thinking the instructors demand often is outside students' previous experiences, the students do not yet value learning that goes beyond memorization and regurgitation. These educators used feedback from students—as do I—to modify their approach, but stressed the need to help students adjust to new expectations rather than lowering the standards for the courses.

Years ago, as I describe in Chapter 3, when I initially decided that critical thinking was one of my learning goals, I did not yet appreciate the disconnect between these learning goals and what students were doing as they sat in the classroom listening to me talk for 50 minutes. After a series of content-heavy lectures, I posed test questions that required them to analyze, synthesize, or evaluate. Students performed poorly on such questions because my then-inflexible teaching strategy did not respond by linking assessment results to how students spent their time during class. In addition, class meetings did not provide opportunities for ungraded formative assessments so that students and I could correct misconceptions before a graded summative assessment. In other words, I failed to complete the feedback loop.

The steps I have taken toward Lecture-Free Teaching exemplify the levels of thinking in Bloom's taxonomy of educational objectives (1956), a system articulated by a group of educational theorists more than a half century ago that still has meaning for postsecondary science educators today (Bissell and Lemons 2006; Cheesman 2009a, 2009b; Crowe, Dirks, and Wenderoth 2008; Lord 2009). Bloom's taxonomy consists of six categories of learning: knowledge, comprehension, application, analysis, synthesis, and evaluation. The first two categories require no critical thinking skills but are essential to accomplish the last four, which involve the higher-order thinking that characterizes critical thought.

The learning levels of Bloom's taxonomy can be envisioned as a hierarchical triangle with an element of a lower level that provides the foundation for an element in the next level (Lord and Baviskar 2007). In this model the first level, knowledge, forms the wide base of the triangle. With my course design, students acquire factual knowledge by using the content outlines to guide their preparatory reading of assigned chapters. For the second level, comprehension, students take notes on the content outlines by explaining terms and concepts in their own words. Application, the third level, occurs with in-class activities and laboratory exercises in which students apply factual knowledge and comprehension to situations they have not encountered before. Level four, analysis, is accomplished with formative assessments that challenge students to explain facts and determine how constituent parts of the material relate to one another; students answer questions in collaboration with their learning team to achieve this level. During synthesis, students make connections among elements of the other learning levels; synthesis may occur, for example, as students design and conduct a scientific experiment to test their hypothesis. Finally, evaluation occurs when students employ elements from all of the underlying levels to construct an argument for or against an opinion, or to determine the quality of information. This last level can be accomplished by justifying one's answers on a multiple-choice test, critiquing a book or journal article, participating in a case study, or writing a scientific report about an experiment designed and conducted by students.

If a course is structured to follow Bloom's hierarchy of learning, students experience fewer problems answering exam questions that require higher-order thinking because they have actively participated in their own learning; shared information about their preconceptions with their instructor; corrected misunderstandings based on prior knowledge; and practiced thinking critically during class meetings. Using the feedback loop, both students and educator evaluate students' progress toward comprehension and make changes accordingly.

Feedback from me to my students, as well as from my students to me, drives Lecture-Free Teaching and inspired the subtitle for my book—*A Learning Partnership Between Science Educators and Their Students*. When Lecture-Free Teaching incorporates the feedback loop, the method can truly succeed.

REFERENCES

Bissell, A. N., and P. P. Lemons. 2006. A new method for assessing critical thinking in the classroom. *Bioscience* 56 (1): 66–72.

Bloom, B. S., ed. 1956. *Taxonomy of educational objectives: The classification of educational goals. Handbook 1: Cognitive domain.* New York: Longman.

Cheesman, K. L. 2009a. Alternative forms of assessment for the college science laboratory. In *College science teachers guide to assessment*, eds. T. R. Lord, D. P. French, and L. W. Crow, 49–54. Arlington, VA: NSTA Press.

———. 2009b. Writing/using multiple-choice questions to assess higher-order thinking. In *College science teachers guide to assessment*, eds. T. R. Lord, D. P. French, and L. W. Crow, 35–41. Arlington, VA: NSTA Press.

Crowe, A., C. Dirks, and M. P. Wenderoth. 2008. Biology in bloom: Implementing Bloom's taxonomy to enhance student learning in biology. *CBE—Life Sciences Education* 7:368–381.

Light, R. J. 2001. *Making the most of college: Students speak their minds.* Cambridge, MA: Harvard University Press.

Lord, T. R. 2009. Practices that jeopardize bona fide student assessment. In *College science teachers guide to assessment*, eds. T. R. Lord, D. P. French, and L. W. Crow, 137–145. Arlington, VA: NSTA Press.

Lord, T., and S. Baviskar. 2007. Moving students from information recitation to information understanding: Exploiting Bloom's taxonomy in creating science questions. *Journal of College Science Teaching* 36 (5): 40–44.

Udovic, D., D. Morris, A. Dickman, J. Postlethwait, and P. Wetherwax. 2002. Workshop Biology: Demonstrating the effectiveness of active learning in an introductory biology course. *BioScience* 52 (3): 272–281.

Chapter 5

Customized Course Design: Science Seminar

When I first began to modify my teaching, the steps I now recommend for course design had not yet evolved. But when given the opportunity to plan a new course, I find using my chronological steps is logical, effective, and easy. This chapter illustrates the adaptability of my steps to Lecture-Free Teaching (Chapter 3) by describing how I designed and taught a new course in the seminar format, rather than transforming a course previously taught primarily by lecture.

Science Seminar (Biology/Environmental Studies 489) is a writing-intensive course open to junior and senior students with a major or minor in a science discipline and to teacher education majors with concentrations in science. The University of Maine at Presque Isle catalog describes Science Seminar generically to allow flexibility for the different professors who teach the class:

> In this writing intensive course students will learn how to choose an appropriate scientific topic for a research project; will complete weekly written and/or oral assignments designed to improve science writing and presentation skills; will submit a final manuscript in a form suitable for publication in a peer-reviewed journal; and will present their final product in a public forum. Each week students will participate in both peer-evaluations and discussions of their assignments. (University of Maine at Presque Isle catalogue course descriptions)

For Step 1 of the Chronology of Course Design (p. 22), I considered the unique situation of the course I was preparing to teach in terms of the situational factors discussed in Chapter 3. The "Specific Context of the Teaching/

Learning Situation" (p. 22) for Science Seminar was its design as an upper-level seminar that would enroll relatively few students. I chose to meet with students three hours per week in a classroom with tables arranged in a U-shape so that we could face one another during seated discussions; this formation allowed one person to stand in the open part of the U during an oral presentation. The "Expectations," according to the catalog description, were that students would write a major paper and present it to an audience, so the "Nature of the Subject" included cognitive, written, and oral presentation skills. Although the requirement that students be junior or senior science majors or minors decreased heterogeneity in the "Characteristics of the Learners," students represented different science disciplines and arrived with varying skill levels. As for "Characteristics of the Teacher," I use case studies liberally in every course I teach (Chapter 15) and also co-wrote a published case study (Hoese, Gibber, and Wood 2002), so it was logical for me to design the Science Seminar around writing a case study in science. The "Special Pedagogical Challenge" is the history of the seminar: Some students found the former course a significant hurdle in their final semester of college. My challenge was to design a course that prepared students more effectively for the rigors of the final project.

For Step 2, I identified the course learning goals as those listed on p. 25 for Science Seminar. To complete Step 3, which involves creating formative and summative assessments, I designed a progression of in-class activities and homework assignments to prepare students gradually for the final paper and oral presentation. An important contribution to this gradual preparation is that the grading criteria and rubrics (Appendixes B-2, B-3, B-4, and B-5) are used not only by me as the instructor for summative assessments but also by seminar classmates to critique one another's ideas and presentations, as described in the learning goals in Chapter 3. The assessments include frequent practice with both writing and oral presentations and a great deal of constructive feedback during each week's meeting.

For Step 4, I chose a teaching strategy that took advantage of my experience as both a leader and a writer of case studies in science. My atypical textbook choice, *Start With a Story: The Case Study Method of Teaching College Science* (Herreid 2007), is actually written for science educators rather than students. The first time I taught the seminar, participants applauded the book choice, because they found it a refreshing change from the didactic textbooks in their other science courses and quite appropriate for wrapping up their undergraduate careers. I used the text for weekly reading assignments listed on the topic schedule (Appendix A-6), as well as for examples of the different styles of case studies to discuss during class. Both the students and I supplemented the cases in the book with many others from the National Center for Case Study Teaching in Science Case Collection, at the State University of New York at Buffalo.

My teaching strategy includes the following:

- During the first part of the semester students complete homework readings and participate in case study exercises that introduce them to different case study styles. Students practice creating their own ideas for an appropriate topic and story outline for case studies representing each of the styles, as described in the grading criteria in Appendix B-2.

- Each week's homework readings, class discussions, and oral presentations contribute to students' preparation to use the case study method to write a clear and comprehensive manuscript on a specific science research topic of their choice and then to present the case orally to an audience of faculty members and students at the end of the semester.
- Students meet with me in class for approximately 45 hours during the semester and work on their projects outside the scheduled class time. Class meetings are used for instruction, experiencing case studies, student presentations, discussion, and critique by peers and me.
- Students base their written papers and oral presentations on explicit written grading criteria and receive appropriate and prompt feedback on the written and oral work from both their peers and me, as described in the grading criteria for an original dialogue, in Appendix B-3; grading criteria for a one-hour oral presentation of a case study chosen from the National Center for Case Study Teaching in Science Case Collection, in Appendix B-4; and grading criteria for their final project, an original case study that includes an oral presentation and teaching notes, in Appendix B-5.
- Students revise drafts of at least two of the major written assignments after a required consultation with a Writing Center tutor.

After I completed Steps 1 through 4, the remaining steps of course design fell naturally into place. The in-class assignments and homework activities, grading system (Appendix B-1), topic schedule (Appendix A-6), and syllabus were straightforward once I had determined the learning goals, assessments, and teaching strategies. Because of the seminar nature of the class, I did not create content outlines or organize a coursepack, although these elements can be added easily in the future if I decide they would be useful. The class enrollment was small enough that permanent cooperative learning teams were inappropriate; instead, students formed temporary teams with various classmates to work cooperatively on case study questions. Class time was filled with individual presentations and critiques of one another's work. Peer evaluation was a vital part of the course; sometimes we all made comments and gave suggestions orally following a presentation. I also asked students to first practice using a grading rubric on a case study presented by me and then to regularly complete grading rubrics for their peers without my ever seeing them. This way their opinions helped classmates improve without influencing my grading of the final product. Students indicate that this is a particularly valuable exercise for both the presenter and the person completing the evaluation.

A sampling of comments from end-of-semester student evaluations validates the success of my adapting the chronology of course design to this upper-level seminar:

> I have enjoyed this class very much. It is one of the best classes I have taken at [college]. It gives students a chance to use critical thinking skills instead of memorizing. I

also liked combining writing with science. The different backgrounds of the students kept things interesting with many different topics. —Emily, Biology major

I really enjoyed taking this course. In addition to learning the subject material about using case studies in science, I learned a lot about science in general. —Laura, Elementary Education major

This method is great for teaching . . . .
—Neal, Secondary Education major

I structured my seminar so that students could gradually build the foundations they needed to write and present original case studies. Johnson and Smith (2008) report on their own similar attempt to modify a previously unsuccessful approach to teaching undergraduate science and nonscience majors how to complete semester-long, hands-on science research projects. In their initial version of this class, Johnson and Smith simply provided students with the objective, told them to select a topic, and had them conduct research. This open-ended approach produced disappointing results. They redesigned the course to build what they call a "scaffolding" and were able to successfully strike a balance between cookbook instructions and an unstructured, open-ended approach. Scaffolding consists of careful determination of learning goals, assessments to give students grounding in what it means to think scientifically, a teaching strategy that included appropriate in-class exercises and discussions, preparatory homework and lab events, and clearly identified milestones. As in my Science Seminar, this foundation increased student confidence and the quality of final projects.

The Chronology of Course Design that I describe in Chapter 3 can guide an educator in a step-by-step fashion to course reform. However, the sequence is flexible enough to allow creative adaptations to formats such as a seminar or independent research while still adhering to sound principles of effective course design.

REFERENCES

Herreid, C. F., ed. 2007. *Start with a story: The case study method of teaching college science.* Arlington, VA: NSTA Press.

Hoese, W. J., J. Gibber, and B. Wood. 2002. Gender: In the genes or in the jeans? A case study on sexual differentiation. National Center for Case Study Teaching in Science, Case Study Collection. *www.sciencecases.org/gender/gender.asp.*

Johnson, M., and M. Smith. 2008. Designing appropriate scaffolding for student science projects. *Journal of College Science Teaching* 37 (2): 24–29.

University of Maine at Presque Isle. Catalogue course descriptions. *www.umpi.edu/files/catalogue/course-catalogue.pdf.*

PART II

The Rhythm of the Semester

Chapter 6

Getting Ready

STUDENT PREPARATION

Educators who have taught lecture-based courses—especially one with large enough enrollments that student absences or lack of class participation go unnoticed—have experienced disappointment with the sporadic nature of student preparation before class. Most of us encourage our students to complete specific readings before class meetings, as explained in our course syllabi; we believe that even a modicum of familiarity with concepts and their terminology makes the lesson more meaningful. But informal observations as well as formal studies indicate that students seldom read the suggested pages beforehand, especially if they expect you to cover the necessary information during a lecture. Often they never get to the reading at all.

Educators representing a variety of disciplines attribute the rarity of student preparation before lecture-based classes to both negative incentives for completing the preclass reading and a lack of positive incentives for preparing ahead of time. A recent study suggests that faculty behavior enables noncompliance with reading assignments. Although educators value reading as an important part of the academic experience, many students do not understand the purpose of assignments that provide background information. A disadvantage of the lecture method is that students are not always sure how assigned reading enhances or even relates to the lecture. Students feel frustrated when instructors spend a significant amount of time merely reviewing or summarizing material they were asked to read before the class, and they are likely to begin skipping the preparation step altogether (Brost and Bradley 2006).

The creators of Peer Instruction (discussed more fully in Chapter 12) acknowledge that their method is effective only if students prepare for class by reading the textbook. The instructors provide guidelines for thinking about each reading assignment, but Crouch and Mazur (2001) recognize that even the best students need incentives to complete these preparations. After trying a variety of techniques, the incentive that Crouch and Mazur found most effective is a three-question web-based assignment due before each class. All three questions are free response. The first two concern topics the instructors consider to be difficult aspects of the assigned reading. The third question is similar to what I require in my "murkies" at the end of each class meeting (as discussed in Chapter 3). Students are asked to describe what they found most confusing about the reading or, alternatively, what they found most interesting. They receive credit based on effort rather than correctness (Crouch and Mazur 2001). Such preclass questions and my postclass "murkies" not only encourage students to prepare and pay attention during class but also guide instructor preparation.

Another science professor (Klionsky 2001/2002) has students purchase his lecture notes from an on-campus copy service and uses the textbook as a supplementary source of information. Students have six to eight pages of lecture notes to read before each class, rather than a lengthy textbook chapter. Each topic is preceded by an outline to help organize the material, and the syllabus contains guideline questions for each topic. The incentive to read even this minimal volume of material is that course grades are based entirely on quizzes (no midterms or final), and half of the grade is based on quizzes about material in the lecture notes, given at the beginning of each class. Still another science professor stopped expecting students to read material ahead of time and instead views his job as introducing the topic during a lecture in a way that stimulates students to use the textbook to clarify information. His challenge is to provide follow-up objectives for the lesson after the students initially hear the information from the instructor (Lord 2007).

Cooperative Learning (Chapter 12) and Team-Based Learning (Chapter 13) can also encourage before-class preparation by students. Proponents of Team-Based Learning (Michaelsen, Knight, and Fink 2004) recommend creating conditions that foster both individual and group accountability: By designing a course in a way that allows student performance to contribute to students' grades, instructors motivate the students to prepare for and participate fully in activities during class. In *Team-Based Learning: A Transformative Use of Small Groups in College Teaching*, the authors provide a list of possible solutions to the problem of persuading students to complete preclass reading. For example, they suggest preparing a reading guide with questions students should be able to answer, allowing each team to ask one question of the instructor before a preclass quiz, and creating an audio "walk-through" of the text to guide individual study before class (Michaelsen, Knight, and Fink 2004, p. 218).

Similar suggestions are made by science educators who promote teaching with case studies (Chapter 15), an instructional strategy that sometimes incorporates cooperative learning or Team-Based Learning. A self-contained case supplies factual information as the case unfolds and requires no advance preparation. Other cases include preclass quizzes or graded group assignments that call for participation by all group members. For long-term cases, students submit a product days or weeks after the assignment has been given. For the case study method to truly address the student-preparation problem, the case study must stimulate a student's interest to learn more, or there must be some sort of reward-and-punishment system (Herreid 2007). A benefit of this method is that students are less likely to view a case study as an inconsequential add-on to the usual class; instead, they will consider it an integral part of the learning experience.

Student preparation before each class is vital to the success of Lecture-Free Teaching because taking notes on the content outlines while reading the assigned textbook chapters in fact substitutes for taking notes during a lecture (Chapter 3, Step 8). The design of my in-class activities assumes that students have read the chapters, and these activities serve as formative assessments to inform both my students and me of student misconceptions based on prior knowledge or misunderstanding of the readings.

The content outlines not only provide guidelines for reading and interpreting information in textbook chapters but also list factual information for which students are responsible. This is equivalent to an instructor lecturing about the information he or she considers most important, but it is probably more effective because students can read the chapter at their own pace and choose a time to read when they are most alert. As others have pointed out, if material that students need to learn is in a textbook, they will probably learn more efficiently from reading than from listening to you discuss the material during a lecture (McKeachie 1999). Listening to a lecture certainly does not prevent distortion of new information based on prior knowledge and misconceptions. However, for students to take notes that will guarantee their understanding of the material, they often require incentives from the instructor. I continue to try various inducements without placing an untenable grading burden on myself. An obvious solution is to collect each outline and grade it for completeness and quality of the notes. Without teaching assistants to help me with this task, I cannot do this regularly. Also, when I do grade outlines, I must promptly return them for the students to use.

Currently, I collect the first outline at the beginning of each semester to give students feedback on appropriate outline notes and to be sure they fully understand that reading and notes should be completed before the appropriate class. Completing homework before a topic is covered in class is a novel and sometimes confusing concept for many. In the weeks that follow I periodically collect outlines without advance notice and try to schedule this on a day when learning teams will work independently for part of the class period so that I can grade and return the outlines before students leave the classroom. To emphasize that this assignment is most useful if completed *before* the class, I am unyielding in my policy of never accepting late submissions. I have considered having students submit outlines electronically in advance of each class, but this would quickly become too time-consuming unless I had a qualified teaching assistant, who at my school would be another undergraduate. In some classes I permit students to bring their coursepacks with completed outlines to use during tests. This does not, however, prevent last-minute "cramming" of information into the outlines, thereby negating the value of preparing before class.

Another incentive is the regular opportunity for students to ask questions about outline topics they did not understand as they read a chapter (Chapter 3, Step 12). I encourage students to e-mail me specific questions about an outline before 7:00 a.m. on the day of class. I take as much time as necessary at the start of the class to answer these questions, which is, in effect, giving a mini-lecture in response to students' questions. The difference between what I do and what other educators do is that my mini-lectures are a direct reply to students' questions, rather than a short presentation I plan in advance to follow a prescribed schedule during the class. Receiving questions in advance gives me the opportunity to organize them and their answers and to determine if they will be answered instead by one of the activities I have planned for that day. These questions reveal potential problem areas or possible misconceptions. Students are less shy about sending an e-mail question that I will answer without using their names than they are about raising their hands during class. If students take advantage of this, they not only learn something by constructing questions but also have the opportunity to listen to my mini-lecture that directly answers their queries. Posing a question requires active participation by a student because he or she cannot simply ask me to explain the information in Outline 6, Part B; I require the student to have done enough background reading to be able to formulate an articulate, specific question. Taking the time to answer the question reinforces inquisitiveness. The entire process should lead to better comprehension than does students' passively taking lecture notes they intend to ponder sometime in the future (perhaps in the wee hours of the morning on the day of a test).

In general students appreciate the coursepack with its outlines, even if it means taking more responsibility for their own learning. What follows are some excerpts of comments I solicited from students who have taken more than one course from me:

> I think that the outlines were very useful. They allowed me to stay on track during the class, decreasing the risk of getting behind in the reading. —Darren

> Getting used to the outlines was a bit of a challenge. Some outlines have followed the chapters, while other have skipped around. The main concept behind the idea, however, is one that works. It takes the guesswork out of trying to decide which of the material is most important and which of the material is just "filler." The outlines also help keep you organized. However the 4 spaces is sometimes not enough space, so I like to also keep some loose-leaf in my coursepack to write down some of the example problems which we cover in class. —Hannah

I think the outlines in the coursepack are a great idea. They help by narrowing down the chapter to concepts and terms the INSTRUCTOR feels are important. Many students have trouble taking notes independently from text because it can be hard to decide which things are important when faced with so much new information. Knowing what the professor believes is important while reading the chapter really helps so that you can pay attention to things that (a) are relevant, (b) you'll need to know later to apply new concepts, and (c) to know what's coming on a test! I also think that it's a great substitute for lecture so that more time during class can be devoted to the learning activities, because those are the things that really help me understand the material. —Kristie

As I explain in the syllabus of every course I teach, my test and exam questions require the same higher-order thinking skills that students practice during in-class assignments and laboratory activities. For each test, I encourage students to bring a one-sided 8½- × 11-inch paper on which they have written what they consider the most important content from their outline notes. This not only guides their preparation for an upcoming test but also reinforces what I have already told them: My test questions ask them to apply what they have learned in class, rather than to regurgitate memorized facts. Students tend to refer to these as "cheat sheets," but I quickly correct them by saying that they are in fact "honesty sheets," which becomes our nickname for this preparatory assignment.

Perhaps the most effective thing I do is to explain carefully (and repeatedly) to students that the most efficient use of their time is to familiarize themselves with factual material *before* each class so they can apply this information during in-class activities to gain understanding and long-term retention of concepts. To convince them, I must ensure that each class meeting offers students something that can be obtained neither by reading the textbook nor by listening to a lecture. If class time predictably provides such experiences, students are motivated to prepare in advance. My responsibility is to choose in-class activities that do, in fact, depend on advance preparation. Also, graded assessments must be based on what happened during the class rather than on a regurgitation of memorized facts. This requires careful design of both activities and assessments—the creative and, for me, the most enjoyable aspect of Lecture-Free Teaching.

A poorly prepared student soon learns that cramming for an exam by memorizing assigned content does not result in the necessary comprehension of concepts. Being ready to participate during class is an important part of preparation. Since changing to Lecture-Free Teaching, I have noticed improved attendance, increased attentiveness during class despite the nearly three-hour length, and active participation by nearly 100% of the students—all satisfying observations to make from the front of the classroom.

INSTRUCTOR PREPARATION

Instructor preparation for Lecture-Free Teaching is every bit as important as student preparation before class, even for a veteran educator who has taught the same course for many years. To prepare successfully for a lecture-free course, one must shift the focus from crafting a series of informative, entertaining monologues to designing every class meeting to support the learning goals.

Because I no longer have lecture notes sitting in front of me, I must reserve adequate time before each class meeting to carefully review factual content for the day's topic, paying particular attention to areas that are fuzzy for me or to those topics I anticipate will trigger the most confusion among students. But much of my preparation occurs long before the beginning of the semester. As described in Chapter 3, as I design a course I create formative and summative assessments that provide information about progress toward the learning goals. My preparation must also ensure that assessments and in-class activities not only connect to each other but also reward students appropriately for advance preparation. Many instructors schedule graded quizzes for the beginning of each class period to encourage students to read the text and attend class, but I believe this does not foster true comprehension and long-term retention. My goal is to construct a course in such a way that participation in well-designed learning activities becomes the incentive for reading the assignments and being present in class.

A reasonable question from a potential lecture-free teacher is, how much more time will I need to invest? I would be disingenuous if I claimed that I spend less time preparing for a lecture-free class; I would be equally dishonest if I told students that my courses are "easier" for them. But as I gained experience and confidence using these methods, the process became so intuitive—and the time spent so enjoyable—that I am unaware of the extra hours.

The originators of Peer Instruction (Crouch and Mazur 2001; Mazur 1997) find or create five new "thought" questions for each 90-minute class and explain to their students that they want them to learn to "critically reason" about physics, not to merely memorize equations. As described in the section on student preparation, these physics professors also use web-based assignments to motivate their students to do the assigned reading in advance of each lecture. Teaching this way requires considerable instructor preparation but not the usual volumes of lecture notes—it is a modification of how one spends time preparing for a course.

I concur with the recommendations of proponents of Team-Based Learning (Herreid 2007; Michaelsen, Knight, and Fink 2004):

- Start with some basic changes, and add sophistication over time.
- Implement your changes in one course at a time.
- Start with a course that already has as many advantages as possible: a subject familiar to you, a moderate number of students, at least a 75-minute time slot for class meetings, or a classroom

without significant physical barriers to having students work face to face in groups.

I have converted previously taught courses and also have developed new courses to be lecture-free. For new courses, time and effort outlays were similar to what they would be when preparing a semester of lectures. To change previous lecture courses, I transformed my lecture outlines into content outlines for student coursepacks. The major efforts were designing formative and summative assessments to reflect the higher-order thinking I now expected, choosing an appropriate teaching strategy, and locating and adapting in-class assignments and homework activities. As noted by Knight and Wood (2005), the extra time and effort required to design and teach an interactive class are considerable when transforming an existing lecture course, but preparing to teach a class for the first time may not require much more effort than would a semester's worth of lectures.

A significant difference is that I no longer arrive in the classroom with lecture notes in hand, ready to lead a class meeting that is almost completely predictable. Instead, I prepare by reviewing factual content and considering connections to the activities that I have planned for the day. I organize and sometimes research answers to questions I gathered from students either via "murkies" or e-mails sent. The answers are planned to avoid redundancy and enhance links to the day's class structure so that my responses are helpful both to the students who pose the questions and to the rest of the class. I must strike a balance between replying to all questions and preventing underprepared students from commandeering class discussions.

The instructor must anticipate an open classroom in which students may challenge their own and your ideas, as well as one in which you and your students truly get to know one another. For me, the intellectual stimulation comes from not knowing precisely which path each day's class meeting will take. My comfort level is much higher if I am well prepared for the day's topic, but preparedness does not equal total control over what occurs during the class period, as it did when I gave a perfectly choreographed lecture.

I disagree with those who have said to me that this teaching method would not be feasible for an inexperienced teacher. In my Science Seminar, described in Chapter 5, those who initially participate in case study exercises as students easily assume the role of leaders of case studies for their presentations. I believe that as more high school and college faculty begin to use participative methods, the newly minted educators will naturally prepare for and teach their classes as they have been taught—which is, after all, what we have always done.

REFERENCES

Brost, B. D., and K. A. Bradley. 2006. Student compliance with assigned reading: A case study. *Journal of Scholarship of Teaching and Learning* 6 (2): 101–111.

Crouch, C. H., and E. Mazur. 2001. Peer Instruction: Ten years of experience and results. *American Journal of Physics* 69 (9): 970–977.

Herreid, C. F. 2007. The Boy Scouts said it best: Some advice on case-study teaching and student preparation. *Journal of College Science Teaching* 37 (1): 6–7.

Klionsky, D. J. 2001/2002. Constructing knowledge in the lecture hall: A quiz-based, group-learning approach to introductory biology. *Journal of College Science Teaching* 31 (4): 246–251.

Knight, J. K., and W. B. Wood. 2005. Teaching more by lecturing less. *Cell Biology Education* 4:298–310.

Lord, T. 2007. Please don't read the text before coming to lecture. *Journal of College Science Teaching* 37 (1): 52–54.

Mazur, E. 1997. *Peer Instruction: A user's manual.* Upper Saddle River, NJ: Prentice-Hall.

McKeachie, W. J. 1999. *McKeachie's teaching tips: Strategies, research and theory for college and university teachers.* 10th ed. Boston: Houghton Mifflin Company.

Michaelsen, L. K., A. B. Knight, and L. D. Fink, eds. 2004. *Team-Based Learning: A transformative use of small groups in college teaching.* Sterling, VA: Stylus.

Chapter 7

Communicating

During the first class meeting of the semester, I explain to my students our respective responsibilities in a lecture-free course. I particularly emphasize the importance of frequent communication among all of us and describe the various opportunities for accomplishing this. The partnership of learning will not succeed without this regular exchange.

For each method below, communication must be two-way. Encourage students to relay concerns, questions, and misunderstandings to you, and then respond in a way that convinces them that these are meaningful exercises. You must promptly read and consider students' messages and then reply in more than a perfunctory fashion. If a student conveys a valid criticism that indicates you should make a mid-semester modification, you should, in fact, do this if at all possible, and let students know that you changed in response to their suggestions. If you decide against an adjustment, you should explain why. Some educators fear that by admitting the need for improvement, they will lose the respect of their students. However, I believe this behavior enhances mutual respect, both between students and instructor and among the students themselves. Mutual respect is vital to the success of any partnership.

E-MAIL

In all of my syllabi (see Appendix A-8 for an example) the first section is called "How to Find Me" and lists my office location, hours that I am usually available in my office, my phone number, and how to reach me via the electronic methods described in this chapter. Since I began Lecture-Free Teaching, students have become more comfortable with informal communication during class, and this has led to their more frequently initiating face-to-face meetings in my office. But e-mail continues to be a popular method and, if used correctly, works well.

As I explained in Chapter 6, as students prepare for an upcoming class by reading the text and taking notes on content outlines, I invite them to e-mail me specific questions before 7:00 a.m. on the day of the class. This invitation should be an incentive to complete the outline preparation in advance because I take as much time as necessary at the beginning of each class meeting to answer any questions I received. I tell students that when I receive no questions, I assume that everyone read the chapter and understood the information perfectly, and I will proceed with the day's activities without clarification of factual material. I cannot claim that every student sends me questions indicating that they have attempted to understand the day's reading assignment; there is wide variation among individual students and also from semester to semester. But by carefully reading these e-mails, I not only gather specific questions to answer in class but also receive feedback about potential problem areas or misconceptions in the day's topic, and then I can adjust my teaching accordingly.

Your responsibility as an instructor is to promptly reply to any e-mails. You must bring every question to class, even if only to explain that it is a question beyond the scope of the course, to tell students what page in the text contains the answer, or to report that the day's activity will answer the question. Any other e-mails must also receive a prompt electronic response from you. We have all experienced the frustration of writing e-mails and never hearing back: Did they ignore your e-mail? Were they offended by it? Did the e-mail get filtered by their software program? Even when you are extremely busy, it is imperative to take a few seconds to let the student know you received the communication, that it matters to you, and that you will respond as soon as possible or during class.

WEB PAGE OR ONLINE COURSE-MANAGEMENT SYSTEM

For years I have maintained a web page through which students can access course information and use a link to e-mail me. I am not a heavy user of technology, but the online course-management system (Blackboard) adopted by my university has enhanced the ease with which my students and I communicate. Not only can I make the usual course information readily accessible, but I can e-mail either individual students or the entire class, post announcements and assignments, create links to online journal articles, and send students scanned documents. I also use Blackboard to post grades so that individuals can view test and other assessment results as soon as I post them. A student can compare his or her score on an assessment with the range of scores or the average score for the entire class, and can also determine his or her grade percentage at a certain point in the semester. Blackboard and other online systems (some of them with free public access) offer many other communication services, most of which I have yet to explore. In the future I will use a communication network for members of a cooperative learning team.

THE MURKIEST POINT

In *Classroom Assessment Techniques* (1993), Angelo and Cross describe the Minute Paper as the technique used most often and by more college teachers than any other in their book. For this simple method the teacher stops class two or three minutes early and asks students to write answers to two questions: "What was the most important thing you learned during this class?" and "What important question remains unanswered?" Students submit these as they leave the classroom, and the instructor obtains important feedback on student learning.

Even easier is their Muddiest Point, for which the teacher asks students to jot down a quick response to one question: "What was the muddiest point in _____?" The blank in the question could be a lecture, discussion, homework assignment, or laboratory exercise. Faculty invest little time to obtain a lot of information about which elements are most confusing for students.

A similar method I use at the end of every class meeting is something I've termed the Murkiest Point (nicknamed by my students as "murkies"). As I describe in Chapter 3, at the end of each class meeting students take a few minutes to respond to either "What was the murkiest point today?" or, if the student understood everything perfectly, "What was the most interesting point today?" Some students may respond to both. To provide students with an incentive to consistently submit a murky, I use the murkies to record attendance; otherwise, some students will zip up their backpacks and promptly depart at the formal conclusion of the class, skipping this important opportunity for communication. I try to read the murkies as soon as possible to gain feedback on the success of each class meeting while the events are fresh in my mind. At the beginning of the next class, I clarify topics about which any student expressed confusion. I generally do not use the student's name when I respond to a question because I want to avoid having the student feel self-conscious about asking what he or she may perceive as a stupid question—a common cause for reticence during class. Students depend heavily on this method of communication and often remind me if I forget to distribute the pad of paper at the beginning of the class period. They also want to ensure that their attendance is duly noted!

An important aspect of each method above is encouraging students to think about the big picture: "What concept remained confusing at the end of the class?" "What concept did you understand most clearly today?" Through your teaching methods, you should underscore the central themes of a topic. The murkies are a way to determine whether you succeeded on a particular day.

FORMATIVE ASSESSMENT

A series of four volumes titled *Uncovering Student Ideas in Science* (Keeley, Eberle, and Dorsey 2008; Keeley, Eberle, and Farrin 2005; Keeley, Eberle, and Tugel 2007; Keeley and Tugel 2009) together offers 100 formative assessment probes for K–12 science teachers. A companion to this series is *Science Formative Assessment: 75 Practical Strategies for Linking Assessment, Instruction, and Learning* (Keeley 2008). The authors define summative assessment as a way to document and measure the extent of student achievement. This type of assessment contrasts with formative assessment, which is used to gather information about student learning throughout the teaching and learning process. With formative assessment a teacher can modify instruction and correct misconceptions. However, federal, state, and district mandates for greater accountability have tilted the emphasis on assessment toward the summative side, with more and more standardized testing of K–12 students resulting in marginal gains in achievement (Keeley, Eberle, and Farrin 2005).

At the college level exclusive use of traditional summative assessments perpetuates grades as the main objective of class participation. With appropriate use of formative assessment, on the other hand, teachers determine what their students think and know while there is still time to change the outcome. Studies have shown that with formative assessment, there is improvement in science learning, particularly among low-performing groups of students (Seymour and Hewitt 1997).

In the past I maintained a conventional and narrow view of assessment, considering it primarily a means of assigning a grade. I still grade tests and assignments, of course, but I now refer to those as summative assessments. Ungraded assignments and exercises, submitted either formally or informally, are formative assessments. In some ways they are even more important than the summative assessments because they encourage students to change their preconceptions or learning methods, and the feedback gives me the opportunity to alter how I present course content. In the broadest sense, the "murkies" I describe in the previous section are formative assessments.

I have always devoted considerable time to grading tests and papers by annotating them with comments and corrections, hoping that students will learn from their mistakes and do better on the next summative assessment. Too often I observed students walk up to my desk on the day I return a test, quickly look at their grades, and return the tests without reading my notations or even examining which questions they missed. I realized that students did not consider the summative assessment part of their learning experiences; the tests were behind them and there was nothing they could do to change or improve their grades. On the other hand, every so often, students would tell me that while taking the test they had a sudden insight and understood a previously confusing concept. How could I get all of my test questions to accomplish this? That is impossible, of course, but with generous use of ungraded, formative assessments throughout the semester, I am moving in that direction.

I generally use an ungraded formative assessment for a topic that has historically been problematic for my students and me. I look back in the margins of my teaching notes to see where I jotted notes to myself about something I need to improve, I review the most frequently missed test questions, or I examine end-of-semester student evaluation comments from the last time I taught a course. In other words, when I choose a formative assessment, I have a definite learning goal in mind (Appendix B-1). I use the information I gather to respond immediately and possibly redirect students' learning before they encounter a graded summative assessment. I also use the data to improve my own teaching of a concept.

Research supports the benefits of this two-way communication with students. Teacher-centered activities such as lecturing do not contribute to awareness of student thinking or understanding for either the educator or students. In contrast, effective formative assessment probes not only engage students in content topics and stimulate in-class discussions but also provide valuable insights on teaching and learning (Irving 2007).

DUE DATES

Under the category of communicating, I consider it my duty to provide students with timely and consistent information about their responsibilities as course participants. This advance planning requires time and effort as I prepare for an upcoming semester, but the reward is a predictable structure that teaches students the importance of time management and being accountable for their own learning.

Within the detailed syllabi and topic schedules I provide both electronically and as a hard copy, I explain and list due dates for each part of an assignment (including drafts) for the entire semester. Because I give so much advance notice—this information is provided on the first day of the semester—I state clearly that I deduct one point from the assignment's total points for each day that it is submitted late. The assignment can be something as simple as telling me the title of the books they are going to read and review (Chapter 11) or something as complex as a final nutritional assessment of a service-learning partner (Chapter 14). In each case the students decide whether it is worth it to take an extension. I may discuss with them the pros and cons, but the final decision is theirs. Communicating this information is important because it shifts the responsibility for completing work on time to each student and eliminates my possibly subjective decisions about late submissions.

As in any successful partnership, regular and frequent communication is vital. Individual students will find the various methods of communication more or less comfortable, so instructors should be sure to provide a variety of ways to share feedback. Remember that not only do students have the responsibility to communicate to you their concerns, but you also have a responsibility to respond promptly to questions and to provide results of formative and summative assessments.

REFERENCES

Angelo, T. A., and K. P. Cross. 1993. *Classroom assessment techniques: A handbook for college teachers.* 2nd ed. San Francisco: Jossey-Bass.

Irving, K. E. 2007. Formative assessment improves student learning: Teaching science in the 21st century; Part seven in a series. *NSTA Reports* 18 (7): 6–8.

Keeley, P. 2008. *Science formative assessment: 75 practical strategies for linking assessment, instruction, and learning.* Arlington, VA: NSTA Press.

Keeley, P., F. Eberle, and C. Dorsey. 2008. *Uncovering student ideas in science, vol. 3: Another 25 formative assessment probes.* Arlington, VA: NSTA Press.

Keeley, P., F. Eberle, and L. Farrin. 2005. *Uncovering student ideas in science, vol. 1: 25 formative assessment probes.* Arlington, VA: NSTA Press.

Keeley, P., F. Eberle, and J. Tugel. 2007. *Uncovering student ideas in science, vol. 2: 25 more formative assessment probes.* Arlington, VA: NSTA Press.

Keeley, P., and J. Tugel. 2009. *Uncovering student ideas in science, vol. 4: 25 new formative assessment probes.* Arlington, VA: NSTA Press.

Seymour, E., and N. M. Hewitt. 1997. *Talking about leaving: Why undergraduates leave the sciences.* Boulder, CO: Westview Press.

Chapter 8

Erasing Lecture-Laboratory Boundaries

The most common criticism of college students who both remain in and switch from science majors concerns the relationship between science lecture and associated laboratory classes. Not only do students complain that the lab topics do not reliably relate to lecture topics, but they also note the disproportionately small amount of academic credit earned for lab courses in relation to the large amount of time they require in class and for homework (Seymour and Hewitt 1997). I agree with this comment and add that traditional methods for assigning credit to lecture and lab, along with the fact that laboratories are often taught by someone other than the regular professor, marginalizes the laboratory in both students' and professors' minds rather than affirming the value of this hands-on experience. If comprehension of science content is significantly enhanced when concepts are connected to inquiry experiences (as documented by several reports cited below), then the conventional structure of lecture and laboratory instruction is the antithesis of what it should be.

Such problems are not limited to postsecondary education. Despite widespread promotion of developmentally appropriate lab investigations for students of all ages and ability levels, laboratory experience is often an add-on rather than an integral part of K–12 instruction (National Science Teachers Association 2004, 2007a, 2007b). Inquiry-based laboratories are typically disconnected from the flow of science lessons in U.S. high school classrooms (National Research Council 2006). Even Advanced Placement (AP) laboratory exercises used in many high schools tend to be "cookbook" rather than inquiry-based (O'Connell 2008).

Many college science faculty perceive significant obstacles to providing inquiry experiences for all students. These educators often have a restricted conception of inquiry and limited knowledge of how to incorporate it into the undergraduate science curriculum. They narrowly define scientific inquiry to be participation in independent laboratory research, and most schools do not have the resources to offer such experiences to every science student. An effective substitute is modification of lab exercises and other classroom activities to require students to use the kind of thinking that characterizes research as they develop a deeper understanding of science and scientific inquiry.

Although cookbook-style laboratories can develop some aspects of scientific reasoning and may boost interest in science, they have little effect on helping students truly understand concepts. Recent studies demonstrate that inquiry-based, hands-on laboratory teaching increases comprehension of complex biological concepts compared to the standard or "cookbook" formats (Rissing and Cogan 2009). Standard laboratory exercises often are limited in scope and focused on mechanical procedures rather than meaning. As described by the Boyer Commission on Educating Undergraduates in the Research University (1998), the difference between cookbook and inquiry-based labs is authenticity. The commission's analogy is the difference between watching a live sporting event and seeing something replayed on TV where the final outcome is already known. If we want students to learn to play the game of research, we have to let them onto the field. Whether a laboratory experience is in fact superior to listening to a lecture or watching a demonstration by the teacher depends on the extent to which understanding of concepts and problem-solving procedures is emphasized (McKeachie 1999).

If cooperative learning groups (Chapter 12) complete inquiry-based lab exercises and other assignments within the context of a course, then students interact with their team members, their instructor, and other learning teams. All these activities contribute to a collegial spirit among participants, model the scientific process, and stimulate excitement about science. The results of the work of Udovic et al. (2002) provide evidence that inquiry-oriented activities help students construct a better understanding of fundamental scientific concepts and improve their ability to use the information to solve unfamiliar problems. Other studies report that in disciplines such as physics, teaching problem solutions by going through a routine series of steps during class is not an effective way to develop students' understanding (McKeachie 1999).

With practice an educator can incorporate inquiry into any situation in which questions are posed and students attempt to solve problems in groups during class. Buck, Bretz, and Towns (2008) developed a rubric to quantify the level of inquiry for a particular exercise. They describe six characteristics to evaluate the degree of student independence and then define five levels that indicate the extent to which a lab investigation provides directed guidance to students in terms of the six characteristics. Each level denotes a specific form of inquiry. Their rubric is useful for assessing one's current laboratory exercises and also for modifying them to be increasingly inquiry-based.

During my decade of science teaching reform, I gradually erased lecture-laboratory boundaries by weaving all elements together into an inquiry-based course design (Wood 2009a, 2009b). This style of instruction is not only more engaging for students but also models how real science is done. Others have evaluated similarly integrated science courses for education majors (Edgcomb et al. 2008) and zoology and botany courses at a large research university (Burrowes and Nazario 2008). Their data demonstrate increased academic achievement, conceptual understanding of science content, and ability to apply scientific process skills. When full integration of lecture and lab is impractical, other methods can effectively incorporate inquiry into large lecture courses (Herreid 2007; Pukkila 2004).

I believe that if preservice teachers experience rigorous, inquiry-based activities within their regular college science courses (not just in their science teaching methods classes), they will naturally use this pedagogy once they are responsible for their own classrooms. Requiring college students to design and conduct their own experiments develops laboratory skills that prepare future teachers to effectively and safely lead lab exercises. Edgcomb et al. (2008) report an increase in students' confidence in their ability to teach science after completing their integrated lecture-laboratory courses.

When liberated from a step-by-step list of laboratory exercise instructions, I observe my own students growing increasingly comfortable in the lab setting. Although I closely supervise them, students take control of their own experiments: They choose and find appropriate supplies on the laboratory shelves and, when the exercise is complete, carefully wash and put away glassware and equipment. If undergraduate science instructors consistently model inquiry-based labs, future K–16 science educators will more easily employ these methods.

Beyond benefiting students who will become educators or researchers after graduation, "scientific literacy is best served when students are engaged in inquiry" (National Research Council 1996). Scientific inquiry is a powerful way to improve understanding of science content. Students learn how to make observations, ask questions, state hypotheses, design and conduct investigations, collect evidence from several sources, examine data and develop explanations for the data, and communicate or defend conclusions about whether or not the original hypothesis is supported. Increasing numbers of science educators observe that participating in real scientific investigations enhances students' attitudes toward science, their motivation for learning, and their conceptual development in the discipline. I strongly recommend incorporating this pedagogy into all science instruction, particularly introductory courses. If hands-on laboratory exercises are impossible, virtual problem-solving environments can provide an analogous experience (DeHaan 2005).

As I describe in Chapter 1, my original goal for reforming my teaching methods was simply to lead some sort of active learning exercise during every class meeting. I began by adapting ideas of others and later designed some activities of my own. But with the inclusion of in-class activities, my students and I felt rushed, and the topics lacked coherence when activities ended abruptly without adequate closure or had to be completed at home or during the next class meeting. In response I changed "lecture" sessions from 50 minutes three times per week to 75 minutes twice a week.

Ultimately, I erased the arbitrary boundary between lecture and laboratory. In contrast to the customary weekly schedule of three 50-minute lectures plus a three-hour laboratory at a different time of the week, sometimes with an instructor other than me, my classes now meet with me alone in the laboratory twice a week for two approximately three-hour sessions. I am gradually replacing instructor demonstrations and cookbook-style laboratory exercises with inquiry-based activities. In their cooperative learning teams (Chapter 12), students apply the scientific process to develop hypotheses and then design and perform experiments. My formative and summative assessments complement and reinforce the inquiry-based approaches.

AN INQUIRY-BASED COURSE DESIGN

For General Biology I, the semester's first activity provides a foundation for the inquiry-based laboratory exercises in which students will participate during the next 15 weeks. The initial class meeting is an ideal time to introduce the use of case studies (Chapter 15), with students working in their newly organized cooperative learning teams (Chapter 10). An introductory case about possible health risks attributed to cell phone use (as discussed in Chapter 3) is inherently interesting to students and acquaints them with the scientific process and the structure of their future scientific reports of laboratory investigations, shown in Appendix B-7. I intentionally avoid the term *lab report* to differentiate what I expect for this writing assignment from what they may have produced as high school students after completing a cookbook-style laboratory exercise.

During Week 2 of the semester, learning team members examine the General Biology I Topic Schedule (Appendix A-1) for dates of the four or five lab exercises I identified as inquiry-based. Each student on a team chooses a different exercise for which he or she will write the scientific report. During a recent semester, students investigated diffusion and osmosis, enzyme activity, photosynthesis versus cellular respiration in plants, fermentation in yeast, and eutrophication. Before the date scheduled for each exercise, I expect students to have completed the assigned textbook reading. Guided by my written and verbal instructions, they first practice relevant laboratory procedures. Then each team chooses from a selection of subtopics to investigate. They decide on and state a hypothesis, after which they design and perform an experiment to test the hypothesis. The experiment must be one that can be accomplished during the time allotted using supplies and equipment available in the laboratory or on campus. In the case of the eutrophication lab (Appendix C-3), we traveled to nearby ponds and lakes to collect water samples. Although students complete each investigation as a team and all team members are responsible for participating in laboratory procedures and understanding related concepts, only one student from each team writes the scientific report for a specific investigation, and he or she is graded individually on this report, as described in Chapter 11.

For investigations scheduled near the beginning of the semester, I provide extra guidance in the written laboratory exercise instructions. As the semester progresses, students gain more confidence and expertise and take increasing responsibility for choosing materials and methods. Appendix C-2 includes instructions for a laboratory exercise called Beano and Lactaid: Enzymes at the Grocery Store, which is scheduled for one-third of the way through the semester and follows the content outline in the coursepack titled Cellular Energy and Enzymes. Appendix C-3 includes an example of instructions for a laboratory exercise, Eutrophication, that is scheduled for the semester's final class meetings. Before the lab, a guest speaker describes her research on the effects of chemical fertilizers applied to surrounding farmlands on local bodies of water. The lab instructions follow the content outline in the coursepack called Humans Impacting the Environment.

To help students write their individual scientific reports, I instruct students to carefully follow the Scientific Report of Laboratory Investigation Scoring Rubric (Appendix B-7). An important step in this process is taking a draft report to the campus Writing Center for a peer tutor consultation. The greatest benefit of this requirement is teaching students to write a first draft and then revise it after critique by someone unfamiliar with the topic, a procedure often followed by scientists before they submit a manuscript for possible publication.

During the semester each student on a learning team writes one scientific report about a different laboratory investigation. At the University of Maine at Presque Isle, professors teach and grade everything; we have no teaching assistants or lab managers. An advantage of students taking turns writing the team's scientific report is that when the class performs a laboratory investigation, I do not receive a multipage report from every student in the class but just one from each learning team. Students have about 10 days following an investigation to submit the scientific report, which counts for a substantial number of points (Appendix B-1).

During the laboratory, I supervise learning teams by wandering around the room, briefly stopping to listen to or interact with each team. Sometimes they barely acknowledge my presence because they are so engaged in the processes of discussing their hypothesis, designing an experiment with appropriate controls, examining their data to determine whether they support the hypothesis, and discussing how future experiments could be conducted to improve the collection of data or to test new hypotheses. The individual scientific reports are generally a more polished, higher quality product than the smaller-scale lab reports I assigned in the past. I believe that the sense of ownership of the experiment encourages increased individual and team effort.

An unexpected and important outcome of inquiry-based learning is the equitable allocation of responsibility among the team members. I have no need to formally assign tasks to each student within a team. The student who chose to write a particular scientific report spontaneously assumes the role of principal investigator, has a vested interest in the success of the investigation, and oversees all aspects of the experiment. Furthermore, with the clear and specific list of grading criteria, each student has advance knowledge of my expectations and can work relatively independently to write the scientific report.

Because learning teams may use different sets of equipment and supplies, students are generally responsible for collecting their own materials from the laboratory shelves and cabinets, correctly washing the glassware, putting away supplies and equipment, and cleaning their lab tables for the next class. Although I am always present and emphasize safety as I closely supervise experimental procedures, I observe another unexpected benefit of increased independence and responsibility for students: a marked decrease in their apathy. All students become comfortable in the laboratory environment and grow more competent as they conduct experiments safely and efficiently.

A valuable lesson that is initially difficult for students to accept is that their experiments do not have to "work." Although I urge them to state a hypothesis they believe will be supported by the experimental data, I reassure them that discovering an incorrect hypothesis or a flawed experimental design can produce more significant learning than delivering predicted results. Students soon realize they can write a meaningful scientific report and may, in fact, create a more interesting discussion section following unanticipated findings.

Finally, it is important to reserve time at the end of the laboratory session for each learning team to share their experimental designs and results with the entire class. This discussion underscores their shared experiences, gives them a chance to make suggestions and comments to other teams, and helps build a collegial spirit within the class.

EVIDENCE FOR POSITIVE EFFECT OF INQUIRY-BASED COURSE DESIGN

Two recently published studies corroborate the effectiveness of my methods. Moore (2008) reports a strong correlation of lab attendance with students' academic performance in introductory science courses and concludes that higher rates of laboratory attendance may be due to the fact that labs often are more interactive than lectures. I have also observed more consistent attendance since I combined "lectures" and laboratories.

Burrowes and Nazario (2008) describe a three-way comparison of the effectiveness of a big lecture course (110 students) with a separate lab taught by a teaching assistant; a small lecture course (32 students) with a separate lab taught by a teaching assistant; and what the authors call a "seamless course," which is an integrated lab-lecture (32 students) similar to my design. They analyze student learning, students' attitudes toward biology, and students' perceptions of both the botany and the zoology courses they studied.

Their results strongly support my premise that a combined lecture-laboratory course more effectively engaged students in the process of science and improved learning while developing scientific process skills.

Voluntary comments made on the end-of-semester evaluations almost unanimously support the combined lecture-laboratory. Students often suggest that *all* science classes at the university be taught this way. A sample of written comments from students in my General Biology I course (a class for both majors and nonmajors that also fulfills part of the general education curriculum science requirement) includes the following:

> I really enjoyed this class. I found the discovery-based learning model of this class to be a very good form of teaching. I found that I was able to retain more and made the material covered easier to relate to. I would welcome other classes structured in a similar fashion, especially science courses.

> I've *never* had a science class that I have been able to feel like I knew what was going on. This teaching style has helped me to understand the concepts being studied. I wish that I could have had this kind of exposure to science at an earlier age. It might have made a difference in my chosen career.

> Overall I *learned* a lot this semester. I stress learned over memorized.

> I learn better through hands-on work.

> I was worried about the different teaching style, but I have found that I have a better understanding of the material and can apply it to different situations. This has been my most challenging class, but also my most rewarding.

> I enjoy the unique style of teaching. Having a variety of ways to learn keeps me interested . . .

> I am completely impressed with how you applied the new teaching method to this class. It is inspiring as a future teacher.

Removing the arbitrary boundary between lecture and laboratory and incorporating inquiry-based laboratory exercises are two powerful ways to improve the effectiveness of a science course previously taught using traditional lectures and cookbook-style laboratories. Many students report that the three-hour class period goes by more quickly than a traditional 50-minute lecture. As the teacher, I find it satisfying to hear the buzz of animated conversations within learning teams as the students plan and perform their own experiments.

REFERENCES

Boyer Commission on Educating Undergraduates in the Research University. 1998. Reinventing undergraduate education: A blueprint for America's research universities. *http://naples.cc.sunysb.edu/Pres/boyer.nsf*.

Buck, L. B., S. L. Bretz, and M. H. Towns. 2008. Characterizing the level of inquiry in the undergraduate laboratory. *Journal of College Science Teaching* 38 (1): 52–58.

Burrowes, P., and G. Nazario. 2008. Promoting student learning through the integration of lab and lecture: The seamless biology curriculum. *Journal of College Science Teaching* 37 (4): 18–23.

DeHaan, R. L. 2005. The impending revolution in undergraduate science education. *Journal of Science Education and Technology* 14 (2): 253–269.

Edgcomb, M., S. L. Britner, K. McConnaughy, and R. Wolffe. 2008. Science 101: An integrated, inquiry-oriented science course for education majors. *Journal of College Science Teaching* 38 (1): 22–27.

Herreid, C. F. 2007. "Clicker" cases: Introducing case study teaching into large classrooms. In *Start with a story: The case study method of teaching college science*, ed. C. F. Herreid, 221–226. Arlington, VA: NSTA Press.

McKeachie, W. J. 1999. *McKeachie's teaching tips: Strategies, research and theory for college and university teachers*. 10th ed. Boston: Houghton Mifflin Company.

Moore, R. 2008. Research and teaching: Are students' performances in labs related to their performances in lecture portions of introductory science courses? *Journal of College Science Teaching* 37 (3): 66–70.

National Research Council (NRC). 1996. *National science education standards*. Washington, DC: National Academy Press.

———. 2006. *America's lab report: Investigations in high school science*. Washington, DC: National Academies Press.

National Science Teachers Association (NSTA). 2004. NSTA position statement: Scientific inquiry. Arlington, VA: NSTA. *www.nsta.org/about/positions/inquiry.aspx*.

———. 2007a. NSTA board revises statement on lab investigations. *NSTA Reports* 18 (7): 3, 5.

———. 2007b. NSTA position statement: The integral role of laboratory investigations in science instruction. Arlington, VA: NSTA. *www.nsta.org/about/positions/laboratory.aspx*.

O'Connell, D. 2008. An inquiry-based approach to teaching: Photosynthesis and cellular respiration. *American Biology Teacher* 70 (6): 350–356.

Pukkila, P. J. 2004. Introducing student inquiry in large introductory genetics classes. *Genetics* 166:11–18.

Rissing, S. W., and J. G. Cogan. 2009. Can an inquiry approach improve college student learning in a teaching laboratory? *CBE—Life Sciences Education* 8:55–61.

Seymour, E., and N. M. Hewitt. 1997. *Talking about leaving: Why undergraduates leave the sciences*. Boulder, CO: Westview Press.

Udovic, D., D. Morris, A. Dickman, J. Postlethwait, and P. Wetherwax. 2002. Workshop Biology: Demonstrating the effectiveness of active learning in an introductory biology course. *BioScience* 52 (3): 272–281.

Wood, B. S. 2009a. Erasing lecture-laboratory boundaries: An inquiry-based course design. In *Inquiry: The key to exemplary science*, ed. R. E. Yager, 177–190. Arlington, VA: NSTA Press.

———. 2009b. Inquiry-based labs: The scientific report. In *College science teachers guide to assessment*, eds. T. R. Lord, D. P. French, and L. W. Crow, 111–114. Arlington, VA: NSTA Press.

PART III

The Instructional Strategies

Chapter 9

Learning From One Another

Many people before me have published books and articles that describe instructional strategies to successfully engage students in the classroom and bring about long-term, meaningful learning. Some of these educators inspired me when I first began my pedagogical reform (Allen and Stroup 1993; Bonwell and Eison 1991; Grunert 1997; Johnson, Johnson, and Smith 1991; Mazur 1997; Meyers and Jones 1993; Silberman 1996). Others that I have read more recently affirm my conviction that lecturing is not the most effective way to teach (Angelo and Cross 1993; Bain 2004; Duch, Groh, and Allen 2001; Fink 2003; Herreid 2007b; Knight and Wood 2005; Light 2001; Mazur 2009; McManus 2005; Michaelsen, Knight, and Fink 2004; Seymour and Hewitt 1997; Tagg 2003; Walvoord and Anderson 1998; Weimer 2002; Wiggins and McTighe 2006).

Science educators often perceive their disciplines as being uniquely content driven; they believe that the nature of what they are expected to accomplish during a semester is quite different from that of educators representing other branches of knowledge. When an instructor in the humanities, business, or even psychology proposes an instructional strategy, some science educators immediately reject it as impractical for their classrooms. Many fail to recognize the similar concerns and frustrations we all face and refuse to see the relevance of ideas conceived by someone not in their specific fields.

Most of my college teaching experience has been at an institution with a small, multidisciplinary faculty, providing me with the opportunity to have frequent and close contact with colleagues teaching diverse subjects. We argue and compromise at faculty meetings, serve on committees together, occupy offices on the same corridor, and socialize in one another's homes. I learn much from these co-workers, many of whom participated in the faculty discussion groups on active learning and classroom assessment that I have led in the past (and describe in Chapter 19). I have equally benefited from regular communication with K–12 educators through university–high school partnerships in my community and as part of my professional organization memberships. All of these interactions reinforce that there is much about teaching that we can share with one another.

Because scientists are skeptical by nature, they often are reluctant to try a new pedagogy. Like students who bring misconceptions based on prior knowledge to our courses, many science educators have the misconception that students will learn effectively only what we tell them in class (Knight and Wood 2005). But there is solid evidence supporting active learning in the science classroom in a variety of disciplines—including, but not limited to, anatomy and physiology, chemical engineering, dental education, endocrinology, general biology, organic chemistry, and physics (Herreid 2007a). What we lack are data defending the traditional lecture.

In recent years more science educators are addressing the issues of dissimilar learning styles among their students. We are beginning to realize that we must teach the *process* of learning in addition to teaching the facts. By varying our instructional strategies, we respond to the fact that some methods work better than others for students with different learning styles. Even more significantly, we can teach the process of learning at the same time that we teach the facts. Comprehension is enhanced when we offer several ways to learn.

People have known for hundreds of years that they remember what they see and do. A 2,000-year-old proverb attributed to Confucius states, "I hear and I forget. I see and I remember. I do and I understand." Data by Stice (1987) support this simple proverb: Engineering students remember 10% of what they read, 26% of what they hear, 30% of what they see, 50% of what they see and hear, 70% of what they say, and 90% of what they say as they do something.

In an attempt to increase student success in the physical sciences, Dubetz et al. (2008) implemented a system of multiple education reforms in general chemistry courses to satisfy the diverse learning styles of their students. Their nine categories of reform were course structure, administration of a diagnostic exam, course website, group problem solving, weekly quizzes, assigned homework problems, practice exams, guided-inquiry experiments, and supplemental instruction. They report that reforms significantly improved grades, decreased attrition, and accounted for positive feedback from students as well as from faculty in affected programs, such as nursing. Group problem solving, weekly quizzes, practice exams, and supplemental instruction had the greatest effect. The authors believe the success of the pedagogical reforms is due to reaching diverse learning styles by incorporating multiple methods and to using active learning strategies.

Lecture-Free Teaching is an amalgamation of the instructional strategies I will discuss in this section. In the chapters that follow I describe each method and provide examples of how to apply it to subjects considered content driven. Because embracing variety while maintaining coherence is an important feature of my pedagogy, I sometimes employ a more flexible structure for a strategy than do those educators from whom I heavily borrow ideas and techniques. Along the way I add my own flavor and bring new ideas to the classroom setting. Although there are a lot of similarities in the designs of courses I teach, there are also facets unique to each one. Comparisons can be made among the examples of topic schedules that I provide in Appendix A.

Although I devote separate chapters to most instructional strategies, there is considerable overlap among them, and the shared elements affirm their common strengths. Most are in fact hybrids of several methods. For example, although the title of Chapter 12 is "Cooperative Learning," small-group collaboration is the underpinning of everything I do in Lecture-Free Teaching. Within the first 15 minutes of the first class of the semester, I build cooperative learning teams (Chapter 10), and these permanent groups of students work together to improve their writing (Chapter 11), participate in Team-Based Learning (Chapter 13), prepare for and complete service-learning projects (Chapter 14), solve problems in case studies (Chapter 15), and learn from student-led teaching models (Chapter 16). Only for organizational purposes do I place instructional strategies in separate chapters.

Science educators teaching in different parts of the country and the world, at different types of institutions, in classrooms of different sizes, and to various demographics report striking similarities in the pressures they experience: students who complain that science is too difficult or boring, students who leave science majors or never consider them in the first place, economic demands from institutions to do more with less in the classroom, and colleagues who look askance at novel pedagogies. Through a process similar to convergent evolution, many of us have individually adopted teaching strategies that overlap with and resemble one another in important ways. We have responded to similar environmental pressures by moving away from traditional lecture-based instruction.

REFERENCES

Allen, R. D., and D. J. Stroup. 1993. *Teaching critical thinking skills in biology.* Reston, VA: National Association of Biology Teachers.

Angelo, T. A., and K. P. Cross. 1993. *Classroom assessment techniques: A handbook for college teachers.* 2nd ed. San Francisco: Jossey-Bass.

Bain, K. 2004. *What the best college teachers do.* Cambridge, MA: Harvard University Press.

Bonwell, C. C., and J. A. Eison. 1991. *Active learning: Creating excitement in the classroom.* ASHE-ERIC Higher Education Report No. 1. Washington, DC: The George Washington University, School of Education and Human Development.

Dubetz, T. A, J. C. Barreto, D. Deiros, J. Kakareka, D. W. Brown, and C. Ewald. 2008. Multiple pedagogical reforms implemented in a university science class to address diverse learning styles. *Journal of College Science Teaching* 38 (2): 39–43.

Duch, B. J., S. E. Groh, and D. E. Allen, eds. 2001. *The power of Problem-Based Learning: A practical "how to" for teaching undergraduate courses in any discipline.* Sterling, VA: Stylus.

Fink, L. D. 2003. *Creating significant learning experiences: An integrated approach to designing college courses.* San Francisco: Jossey-Bass.

Grunert, J. 1997. *The course syllabus: A learning-centered approach.* Bolton, MA: Anker Publishing Company.

Herreid, C. F. 2007a. Assessment and evaluation of the case study process. In *Start with a story: The case study method of teaching college science,* ed. C. F. Herreid, 401–403. Arlington, VA: NSTA Press.

———, ed. 2007b. *Start with a story: The case study method of teaching science.* Arlington, VA: NSTA Press.

Johnson, D. W., R. T. Johnson, and K. A. Smith. 1991. *Active learning: Cooperation in the college classroom.* Edina, MN: Interaction Book Company.

Knight, J. K., and W. B. Wood. 2005. Teaching more by lecturing less. *Cell Biology Education* 4:298–310.

Light, R. J. 2001. *Making the most of college: Students speak their minds.* Cambridge, MA: Harvard University Press.

Mazur, E. 1997. *Peer Instruction: A user's manual.* Upper Saddle River, NJ: Prentice-Hall.

———. 2009. Farewell, lecture? *Science* 323 (5910): 50–51.

McManus, D. A. 2005. *Leaving the lectern: Cooperative learning and the critical first days of students working in groups.* Bolton, MA: Anker Publishing Company.

Meyers, C., and T. B. Jones. 1993. *Promoting active learning: Strategies for the college classroom.* San Francisco: Jossey-Bass.

Michaelsen, L. K., A. B. Knight, and L. D. Fink, eds. 2004. *Team-Based Learning: A transformative use of small groups in college teaching.* Sterling, VA: Stylus.

Seymour, E., and N. M. Hewitt. 1997. *Talking about leaving: Why undergraduates leave the sciences.* Boulder, CO: Westview Press.

Silberman, M. 1996. *Active learning: 101 strategies to teach any subject.* Boston: Allyn & Bacon.

Stice, J. E. 1987. Using Kolb's learning cycle to improve student learning. *Engineering Education* 77 (5): 291–296.

Tagg, J. 2003. *The learning paradigm college.* Bolton, MA: Anker Publishing Company.

Walvoord, B. E., and V. J. Anderson. 1998. *Effective grading: A tool for learning and assessment.* San Francisco: Jossey-Bass.

Weimer, M. 2002. *Learner-centered teaching: Five key changes to practice.* San Francisco: Jossey-Bass.

Wiggins, G., and J. McTighe. 2006. *Understanding by design.* Expanded 2nd ed. Upper Saddle River, NJ: Pearson Education.

Chapter 10

The First Day of Class: Learning Science While Constructing Cooperative Learning Teams

The first day of class is an important opportunity to introduce yourself and your teaching methods in ways that create a favorable classroom climate. Investing considerable thought and effort into structuring an effective first class meeting pays rich dividends in the form of positive learning experiences for the entire semester.

My first mission is to communicate to students that class time is valuable and that the purpose of class meetings is to accomplish tasks they cannot complete on their own. To model how you will use class time and to demonstrate your expectation that students will take responsibility for their learning, do not use the first day simply for attendance and distribution of a topic schedule and syllabus, or even for detailed explanations of this course information. Careful reading of these documents is something that students can and should do independently. I hand out these important resources as soon as students are seated in the classroom, but rather than going through each of them, I explain the importance of placing the information prominently in the front of their coursepacks and referring to the materials throughout the semester. I describe key elements of the topic schedule and syllabus only in the context of the day's activities, and pepper the first class meeting with reminders that the first assignment is to carefully read the syllabus (also listed as the first homework assignment on the topic schedule).

Those who heed my reminders before the second class meeting are rewarded with three extra credit points, as described in Chapter 3, Step 9. As the second class meeting begins, I announce how many students began the semester with extra credit points for completing that first assignment. Those who neglected to read the syllabus look puzzled and then begin flipping through the pages of their topic schedule and syllabus. I have sent the message that students are responsible for thoroughly reading handouts and material in the coursepack and for completing assignments on the topic schedule before each class.

After distributing the topic schedules and syllabi on that first day of class, my next task is to construct heterogeneous cooperative learning teams in which students will work for the entire semester (Chapter 3, Step 11). Finally, depending on the time scheduled for each class period, I introduce students to at least one of my instructional strategies by having them participate, as a team, in an appropriate activity.

BUILDING THE TEAMS

Substantial evidence for the effectiveness of cooperative learning is detailed in Chapter 12. Among those who regularly use cooperative learning, the consensus is that groups or teams should be heterogeneous so that students experience diverse perspectives. Science educators recommend several methods for achieving this mix. Lord (2004) randomly assigns biology lecture students to groups on the first day of class and reorganizes any nonheterogeneous groups a week or two later. Jensen, Moore, and Hatch (2002) randomly assign human anatomy and physiology students to dissection groups before the first day of class and ask groups to establish their identity by selecting a scientific term from their text for their group's name. Crowe and Hill (2006) ensure random grouping for a semester-long independent research project for upper-division science electives by having students draw playing cards or numbers out of a hat. French (2004) assigns permanent student groups alphabetically in large-enrollment introductory science courses. In a large lecture hall he assigns them alphabetically to seat numbers, and in the laboratory they work in groups of three or four. Before the second organic chemistry class of the semester, Dinan (2006) creates four-person learning teams by examining students' academic records; his selections maximize group diversity in terms of academic ability, gender, race, personality, and other characteristics he observes during activities on the first day of class.

Allowing students to self-select group members has disadvantages. Although the students may prefer this method, claiming they know with whom they can work well or share similar schedules, such groups are more likely to support a friend who is a "free rider" and does not contribute appropriate effort

(Michaelsen, Knight, and Fink 2004). Also, students who do not know other class members may feel left out when placed in a group by default.

In contrast to the ideas described above, my method for constructing cooperative learning teams not only is random but also introduces students to course content within the first 15 minutes of the first class meeting (Wood 2007, 2009). Because they, in effect, build their own teams, students never complain that my method is biased, and generally they are content to remain in their original groups for the entire semester.

After students enter the classroom on the first day and are seated comfortably with their friends, I ask them to take a copy of the topic schedule and syllabus from the stacks being passed around the room, after which I announce that they now have to move. Unbeknownst to students, I have written a different set of words on the back of each syllabus. The following is an example of what I say next to a class of approximately 20 students, but an adaptation of this technique is equally effective in a larger-enrollment lecture class:

> On the back of your syllabus is a word or words that will become familiar to you this semester. Every one of you has a different term that relates to the content of this course. You should now organize yourselves into four groups according to a larger concept associated with those words. Once you have identified your fellow cooperative learning team members, sit together in a position that fosters communication. Be prepared to explain why you are together and to describe the scientific characteristics of your team name. You may use your textbook, your coursepack, and your brain.

In Appendix C-4 is a list of possible words I write on the syllabi. When I ask students to use their terms to build the teams, I generally give no information beyond the statement above. If the task is especially challenging, I later offer hints.

After receiving verbal instructions, students begin to move around the room, communicating with their fellow students until they determine how to sort themselves. When a potential group thinks it has discovered the "formula," those students check with me, and I let them know by saying yes or no. Once one team has established itself, others usually, but not always, follow quickly. The group formed first is encouraged to help others.

For the rest of the semester each cooperative learning team sits together in an arrangement that facilitates discussion. In a classroom with fixed seating, a square shape works well with two students in front, two students behind, and the front two turning around in their chairs as necessary. Four or five students sitting in the same row or at the same table facing front does not work well because students at the ends may not be fully engaged in discussions. The following sections describe examples of organizational concepts that will become the names of the learning teams for each of five courses.

General Biology I

General Biology I is the first semester of a two-semester course for both majors and nonmajors. It introduces basic principles and levels of biological organization, from the cell to the organism to ecosystems. I use the four eukaryotic kingdoms as categories to construct cooperative learning teams. Listed below each kingdom in Appendix C-4 are the scientific names of possible organisms to write on each student's syllabus. These organisms are ones that students will learn about during the semester or that are simply familiar to people living in northern Maine. In parentheses are common names or a brief description of the organism. For the rest of the semester, teams call themselves The Protists, The Fungi, The Plants, and The Animals. While building teams, students learn something about binomial nomenclature, use the names of the eukaryotic kingdoms, and are introduced to organisms they will study throughout the semester.

Sciences I

Sciences I is the first semester of a two-semester sequence for nonscience majors. It introduces the scientific method and major unifying theories from physics and Earth sciences, with applications to real-world problems. I use four forms of energy as categories to construct cooperative learning teams. I do not include chemical energy because it is covered during the second-semester course, but it could be used to organize a fifth team. Listed below each of the four forms of energy in Appendix C-4 are possible words to write on each student's syllabus. For the rest of the semester, teams call themselves The Mechanical Energies, The Radiant Energies, The Electrical Energies, and The Nuclear Energies. While building teams, students learn there are several forms of energy and are introduced to terms associated with each form.

Sciences II

Sciences II is the second semester of a two-semester sequence for nonscience majors. It introduces major unifying theories from chemistry, biology, and the environmental sciences, with applications to real-world problems. I use the names of four of the families of the periodic table of the elements as categories to construct cooperative learning teams. Listed below names of the four families in Appendix C-4 are possible elements (and, in parentheses, their symbols) to write on each student's syllabus. For the rest of the semester teams call themselves The Alkali Metals, The Alkaline Earth Metals, The Halogens, and The Noble Gases. While building teams, students examine a periodic table, observe something about the organization of the table, learn that each element has a symbol or abbreviation, hear the names of a variety of elements, and understand that elements represented by students in their team are part of the same chemical family and share some characteristics.

Human Nutrition

Human Nutrition is a 300-level biology course that explores nutrients, human metabolism, energy balance, nutrition for fitness, and eating disorders. I use the three macronutrients and one or two of the micronutrients as categories to construct cooperative learning teams. Listed below three macronutrients and one micronutrient in Appendix C-4 are possible names of organic compounds that I write on each student's syllabus. These organic compounds are either classified as the specific type of macronutrient/micronutrient or are associated with that category. For example, the molecules listed under protein are essential amino acids because amino acid subunits are linked together to form proteins and are the nutrient referred to when discussing proteins. It is inappropriate to use the names of food items under the categories because foods generally contain several kinds of macronutrients and micronutrients—we commonly refer to bread as a carbohydrate when in fact it also contains protein, fat, and several micronutrients. For the rest of the semester teams call themselves The Carbohydrates, The Lipids, The Proteins, and The Vitamins; The Minerals is an appropriate fifth team. While building teams, students learn about macronutrients and micronutrients, as well as organic compounds in food, and are introduced to terms they will use throughout the semester.

Genetics

Genetics is a 300-level biology course that first explores molecular and then classical genetics. The categories I use to construct cooperative learning teams are more complex than for the other courses and consist of four different amino acids. On the backs of syllabi for just four students, I write the name of one of these four amino acids (in other words, the team name), with its standard abbreviation in parentheses. On the remaining students' syllabi, I write three bases of messenger RNA nucleotides that would be translated into each of these four amino acids, as listed in Appendix C-4. Students enrolled in Genetics have limited previous knowledge of the transcription of DNA to RNA, the translation of RNA to amino acids, and the genetic code, so organizing themselves into these groups is challenging. Once a few students discover a copy of the "genetic dictionary" in their textbook or coursepack, they quickly determine how to sort themselves. For the rest of the semester, teams call themselves The Glycines, The Leucines, The Threonines, and The Arginines. While building teams, students hear the names of several amino acids and all four bases of messenger RNA nucleotides, understand that codes are used to determine which messenger RNAs will be translated into specific amino acids, realize that most amino acids may be specified by more than one codon, and use a copy of the genetic code—something as important to modern biology as the periodic table of the elements is to chemistry. Because the semester begins with molecular genetics, students apply this newly acquired knowledge almost immediately.

BONDING THE TEAMS

Immediately after team formations, I ask students to write the following information on note cards: their names, places of birth, high schools attended, where they live now, how the course relates to their majors, what they enjoy doing outside school and work, and one word to describe themselves. Students exchange cards with someone on their team whom they do not already know and briefly interview this person. Pairs of students then take turns introducing each other to the rest of the class and me. Before they begin, I demonstrate the format by introducing myself. In a larger class, or one with limited class time, introductions could occur just within the teams. Not only do team formation and introductions serve as effective icebreakers, but they also set an important precedent for students to talk to each other and to speak to the entire class. Even the most reluctant students benefit from having to do this in a nonthreatening situation in which they do not have to worry about giving the wrong answer. I believe that this short oral presentation on the first day of class encourages participation for the remainder of the semester.

In my longer class periods I follow peer introductions with an activity, such as a case study (Chapter 15) or laboratory exercise (Chapter 8), that requires team members to work together. For my introductory science courses I typically choose a case study from the National Center for Case Study Teaching in Science Case Collection that not only familiarizes students with the case study method—one of my favorite teaching strategies—but also requires them to apply the steps of the scientific method (Bailey 2002; Holt 2002). In General Biology I, the case study on cell phone use and cancer described in Chapter 3, Step 4 (Parilla 2006) provides a foundation for upcoming inquiry-based laboratories. A straightforward laboratory exercise is another effective way to begin an upper-level class for which enrolled students already possess some laboratory skills. In Genetics, for example, each team extracts DNA from their choice of a fruit or vegetable by using ordinary household supplies and appliances (Carlson 1998).

ACCOMPLISHMENTS OF THE FIRST DAY OF CLASS

At the conclusion of the first class meeting students have formed cooperative learning teams and been introduced to words and concepts about which they will learn in more detail and in various contexts during the semester. Team members immediately begin to refer to themselves by the term representing their organizing concept and to develop an identity not only within their group but also with the individual words that I wrote on their syllabi. Throughout the semester, because both students and I refer to the groups by their team names, students are reminded of the four eukaryotic kingdoms, the different forms of energy, the families of the periodic table, the macronutrients and micronutrients, or the triplet codes for building proteins.

In addition students experience the flavor of my teaching methods and the value of using class time to learn course content through active participation. Just as important, each student has an informal conversation with at least one team member whom they did not know previously, meets four or five students with whom they will work for the rest of the semester, and begins to develop a learning partnership with their fellow students and me that will contribute to the course's success. When my technique works well, teams readily form a social bond and are eager to work together. Within a couple of weeks the sense of community extends beyond the learning group to encompass the entire class.

Although my method for constructing learning teams does not reliably result in heterogeneous groups with evenly distributed strengths, as recommended by those who believe the teacher should organize the teams (Michaelsen, Knight, and Fink 2004), students do perceive it as impartial because they participate in building the groups. My method generally avoids potential problems caused by having friends on the same team because students who choose to sit together as they enter the classroom do not end up in the same group: Before the class I organize the stack of syllabi so that the terms alternate among ones that belong to the different learning teams. As students pass the stack of papers, they usually take the syllabus on top. The method I describe in Chapter 3, Step 5, describing the use of sock chromosomes, also mixes workshop participants because, even if they anticipated what I was going to do, they have no time to look through the large bag of socks to locate a specific "sister chromatid" or "homologous pair."

A well-organized first class meeting fulfills goals that I articulated in Step 11 of Chapter 3 because students

- understand the benefits of Lecture-Free Teaching methods;
- experience the course structure and expectations;
- learn some course content;
- begin to feel comfortable among their classmates and to develop a rapport with me; and
- understand their responsibility for the success of the course.

REFERENCES

Bailey, C. T. 2002. Thinking inside the box. National Center for Case Study Teaching in Science Case Collection. *http://ublib.buffalo.edu/libraries/projects/cases/box/box1.html*.

Carlson, S. 1998. Spooling the stuff of life. *Scientific American* 279 (3): 96–97.

Crowe, M., and C. Hill. 2006. Setting the stage for good group dynamics in semester-long projects in the sciences. *Journal of College Science Teaching* 35 (4): 32–35.

Dinan, F. J. 2006. Opening day: Getting started in a cooperative classroom. *Journal of College Science Teaching* 35 (4): 12–14.

French, D. P. 2004. Tips for managing a large, active-learning class. In *Teaching tips: Innovations in undergraduate science instruction*, eds. M. Druger, E. D. Siebert, and L. W. Crow, 13–14. Arlington, VA: NSTA Press.

Holt, S. 2002. Love potion #10. National Center for Case Study Teaching in Science Case Collection. *http://ublib.buffalo.edu/libraries/projects/cases/pheromones/pheromones1.html*.

Jensen, M., R. Moore, and J. Hatch. 2002. Cooperative learning—Part II: Cooperative group activities for the first week of class; Setting the tone with group web pages. *American Biology Teacher* 64 (2): 118–120.

Lord, T. R. 2004. Increasing student accountability through collaborative work in the classroom. In *Teaching tips: Innovations in undergraduate science instruction*, eds. M. Druger, E. D. Siebert, and L. W. Crow, 26–27. Arlington, VA: NSTA Press.

Michaelsen, L. K., A. B. Knight, and L. D. Fink, eds. 2004. *Team-Based Learning: A transformative use of small groups in college teaching*. Sterling, VA: Stylus.

Parilla, W. V. C. 2006. Cell phone use and cancer: A case study to explore the scientific method. National Center for Case Study Teaching in Science Case Collection. *www.sciencecases.org/cell_phone/cell_phone.asp*.

Wood, B. S. 2007. Learning biology while constructing cooperative learning groups: The first 15 minutes. *American Biology Teacher* 69 (6): 330.

———. 2009. Learning science while constructing learning teams. *Journal of College Science Teaching* 38 (5): 28–32.

Chapter 11

Writing by Students

Following a decade of interviews with 1,600 Harvard seniors, Richard Light observed that the more writing required in a college course, the greater the students' levels of engagement. This positive correlation is greater than with any other course characteristic (Light 2001). Although many of my students enter college without the honed writing skills of a typical Harvard undergraduate, I find that with enough guidance and opportunities to revise, they can generate a written product of which they and I can be proud.

Every course I teach includes at least one major written assignment, including a draft revision. The first section of this chapter discusses peer reviews of drafts as a method to improve students' writing. Next, I describe a variety of assignments, for which samples of grading criteria or rubrics are provided in Appendix B. Because writing is an integral part of several other instructional methods, I also discuss it in some of the chapters that follow.

PEER REVIEWS OF DRAFTS: PROS AND CONS

As anyone who writes professionally can attest, having a colleague critique a draft is the best way to improve your writing. I try to establish in my students the habit of writing a first draft far enough in advance that they have time to respond to feedback and submit a better final product. The student who critiques a draft also benefits by considering factors relevant to his or her own writing.

Exchange Among Classmates

In the past I set a due date for a draft at least a week in advance of the deadline for the final paper and asked students to exchange drafts with members of their learning teams. They used my grading criteria sheet to evaluate their partners' papers and returned the draft and the criteria sheet at the next class meeting. The authors then had about a week to make revisions, polish the draft, and submit the final product to me. Potential problems included the author's tardiness in finishing the first draft; the peer reviewer's tardiness in completing the critique; uneven effort and skills of the peer reviewer; and the hesitancy of peer reviewers to make negative comments. The first two obstacles can be avoided by using class time to exchange papers and complete the critiques and the last hindrance by explaining in advance how suggestions for improvement will help a classmate. But differences in skill levels will always exist among students. When the critiques are done outside class, there are inevitably factors beyond the control of either the student or the teacher.

Writing Center

Fortunately, several years ago my campus developed a Writing Center staffed by specially trained peer tutors with whom students make appointments for individual 50-minute consultations on their drafts (University of Maine at Presque Isle Writing Center). Writing Center consultants are undergraduates representing a variety of majors who are not only skilled writers themselves, but whose preparation includes specialized coursework and training in how to tutor in writing. An English professor directs the Writing Center and supervises the tutors. The center offers consultations at all stages of the writing process: finding a topic, development, organization, revision, and editing. The tutors do not "fix" or proofread papers but instead work collaboratively with each writer to address concerns. When those concerns include grammar, usage, and mechanics, consultants assist writers in identifying and correcting errors and improving their own proofreading and editing skills.

For each written assignment I announce two due dates: the first for completion of a consultation on a draft at the Writing Center, and the second, at least a week later, for submission of the final product. For each day that either step is late, one point is deducted from total possible points for the paper—generally between 30 and 100 points (Appendix B-1). This policy effectively eliminates requests for extensions of the due date because the decision to be late is the student's choice. My goal for requiring a consultation at the Writing Center is not only to promote the practice of preparing an early draft but also to encourage students to use the Writing Center on occasions other than assignments for my courses. As with less formal exchange of drafts among students in a learning team, which I described earlier, the Writing Center tutors demonstrate variable levels of skill and rapport with students. Advance draft preparation and constructive feedback, however, are always valuable.

Calibrated Peer Review

Although I have no personal experience with the Calibrated Peer Review (CPR) (The Regents of the University of California 2001), this online program is used by some science educators. Instructors use assignments directly from an online library and are not required to grade student writing themselves. Every assignment entails several stages. First, each student submits text based on the assignment source material; next, he or she evaluates (using a rubric) several example texts called calibration essays and receives feedback on these evaluations; then he or she evaluates the written work of three peers, followed by an evaluation of his or her own submitted text; and finally, the student receives his or her own assignment results.

A recent study reported that approximately two-thirds of assignments from the CPR assignment library were designed to engage students in some type of critical thinking, but less than one-third promoted higher-order writing skills. The authors recommended cautious use of the current library, the creation of a CPR user manual (with detailed instructions for creating high-quality writing assignments), and the development of a new CPR library that would include only assignments previously reviewed by experts in critical thinking or writing pedagogy. The authors viewed this program as only a framework for delivering and managing assignments and believe that assignments should be designed by individual instructors to achieve specific learning outcomes that encompass higher-order cognitive and writing skills (Reynolds and Moskovitz 2008).

BOOK REVIEW

For every science course I teach—with the exception of Science Seminar—I explain to students on the first day of the semester that they will choose and read a book from a list I post online and write a review of the book according to grading criteria in their coursepack (Wood 2009c). For each course I compile a list of books that relate directly or indirectly to the course content and make sure that the campus library owns all of the books. Every student must choose a different book to avoid competition in borrowing the books, as well as to diversify the background information obtained from the books, which students subsequently share with their classmates. The books are generally scientifically significant and written for the educated lay public. I have selected books on the basis of reviews in periodicals such as *Discover Magazine, Journal of College Science Teaching, Science News, Scientific American, American Biology Teacher*, and the *New York Times Book Review*. Over the years I have requested that the library purchase these relatively inexpensive books, and so the library has amassed a variety of titles related to each course. The lists are lengthy and I have not read most of the books, though this is one of my retirement fantasies.

I encourage students to choose a book from the list that truly appeals to them. To facilitate this, I supply a brief description of each book, summarized from a longer review. Before I included this additional information, students often chose a book from near the beginning of the list (with most selections being by authors whose last names began with the first letters of the alphabet!). Or they would visit the library, locate some books on the list, and choose the one with the fewest number of pages. With descriptions, students are more likely to read a book that engages them.

Because book reviews abound on websites, I reduce the possibility of intentional or inadvertent plagiarism by creating grading criteria that ask students to discuss specifically how the book relates to course content and the appropriateness of the book for someone taking this class. I also clearly differentiate this book "review" from a book "report" that students may have written during their K–12 years. I tried providing students with a sample of an actual book review from one of the periodicals I listed on the previous page so that they would understand the nature and purpose of a book review. I discontinued this, however, because students then followed the structure of the sample review so carefully that their own writing lacked originality.

Three due dates for the book review project are for submitting the book's title to me after borrowing it from the library, completing a consultation on the draft at the Writing Center, and submitting the final review to me for grading. Appendix B-6 is an example of my book review grading criteria—this one for Sciences II. The book review is the first phase of the Environmental Action Project (Chapter 14; Appendix B-8), a major element of this course. The grading criteria for book reviews of other courses are similar, but with questions specific to those subjects.

SCIENTIFIC REPORT

In my General Biology I course students participate in four or five inquiry-based laboratory activities during the semester, as described in Chapter 8. At the beginning of each laboratory project, I introduce a specific protocol and instruct the students to practice the necessary skills. The coursepack information about the activity includes a list of available laboratory supplies and equipment. Each cooperative learning team then designs and conducts its own experiment on the assigned topic. Before conducting their experiment, a learning team must state a clear hypothesis and describe the proposed materials and methods so that I can approve the procedure in terms of both expedience and safety (Wood 2009a, 2009b).

All team members participate fully in the planning and execution of the experiment and are responsible for understanding relevant background information, as well as the meaning of their results. For each inquiry-based laboratory the team determines in advance which member will write the resulting scientific report. The author is graded individually on his or her report (Chapter 8). I emphasize adherence to the scientific method and provide guidelines for writing the report in the style of a peer-reviewed journal article (Wood 2009b). Several days before the final report is due, students review their drafts with a peer tutor in the Writing Center. Even in this introductory course for both majors and nonmajors, students become engaged in the scientific process and, by carefully following the criteria in the Scientific Report of Laboratory

Investigation Scoring Rubric (Appendix B-7), can generally produce high-quality papers. I intentionally avoid the term "lab report" to differentiate what I expect for this writing assignment from what they may have produced as high school students after completing a cookbook-style laboratory exercise. Students have about 10 days from the end of their experiment to complete the scientific report (including the consultation at the Writing Center).

SERVICE-LEARNING PROJECT REFLECTION

As I describe in Chapter 14, "Service-Learning," three basic steps are generally considered essential for effective service-learning and enhancement of student learning: preparation, participation, and reflection (Lott and Michelmore 1997). For reflection my students submit a major written assignment. I currently incorporate service-learning into two very different courses.

Sciences II is the second semester of a two-semester general education curriculum sequence. The goal of the service-learning component is to connect, in a meaningful and timely way, topics from both semesters. A detailed description of the entire project is in Chapter 14. The grading criteria for the written reflection are in Appendix B-8.

Human Nutrition (Biology 300) is required for athletic training majors and also serves as a nonlaboratory science course in the general education curriculum and as an elective for biology majors, so the enrolled students are heterogeneous. The goal of the service-learning component is to improve wellness among members of the campus community. A detailed description of the entire project is in Chapter 14, as well as in a previous publication (Wood 2003). A complete nutritional assessment of a volunteer service-learning partner constitutes a major written assignment and substitutes for a comprehensive final exam in the course. The project outline, grading criteria, and point distribution are in Appendix B-9.

LEARNING PORTFOLIO

Many educators use learning portfolios to augment student writing. Although I have yet to assign them in my own classes, I recognize their potential as an instructional strategy that provides feedback on teaching and learning activities, as well as serving as an opportunity for students to engage in self-assessment (Zubizarreta 2004). A learning portfolio encourages students to take responsibility for their own learning, a fundamental premise of Lecture-Free Teaching.

CASE STUDY

In Science Seminar, described in detail in Chapter 5, student-written case studies are the major course project, substituting for a comprehensive final exam. The Seminar is a one-semester course for junior and senior science majors and minors. More than half of the course grade is based on a series of papers and oral presentations, each with specific grading criteria to guide students' preparations and provide regular feedback during the semester (Appendixes B-2–5).

There are a variety of ways for instructors to incorporate writing into science courses. Each method can both reinforce and augment the factual content of the course and, at the same time, provide students with practice in written expression. Designing meaningful assignments along with detailed grading criteria or rubrics will not only enrich students' learning but also facilitate your assessments of the written products.

REFERENCES

Light, R. J. 2001. *Making the most of college: Students speak their minds*. Cambridge, MA: Harvard University Press.

Lott, C., and C. W. Michelmore. 1997. Learning through service: A faculty perspective. *Liberal Education* 83 (1): 40–45.

The Regents of the University of California. 2001. CPR: Calibrated Peer Review. *http://cpr.molsci.ucla.edu.*

Reynolds, J., and C. Moskovitz. 2008. Calibrated peer review assignments in science courses: Are they designed to promote critical thinking and writing skills? *Journal of College Science Teaching* 38 (2): 60–66.

University of Maine at Presque Isle Writing Center. *www.umpi.edu/programs/cas/english/writing-center.*

Wood, B. 2003. Improving wellness on campus: Service-learning in a human nutrition class. *Journal of College Science Teaching* 33 (2): 27–31.

Wood, B. S. 2009a. Erasing lecture-laboratory boundaries: An inquiry-based course design. In *Inquiry: The key to exemplary science*, ed. R. E. Yager, 177–190. Arlington, VA: NSTA Press.

———. 2009b. Inquiry-based labs: The scientific report. In *College science teachers guide to assessment*, eds. T. R. Lord, D. P. French, and L. W. Crow, 111–114. Arlington, VA: NSTA Press.

———. 2009c. Student-authored book reviews. In *College science teachers guide to assessment*, eds. T. R. Lord, D. P. French, and L. W. Crow, 115–116. Arlington, VA: NSTA Press.

Zubizarreta, J. 2004. *The learning portfolio: Reflective practice for improving student learning*. San Francisco: Anker Publishing Company.

Chapter 12

Cooperative Learning

Cooperative learning is an integral part of Lecture-Free Teaching and begins within 15 minutes of the first class meeting, with the construction of learning teams. Chapter 10 describes both my methods for creating groups (Wood 2007, 2009) and those of other science educators from a variety of disciplines and types of courses (Crowe and Hill 2006; Dinan 2006; French 2004; Jensen, Moore, and Hatch 2002; Lord 2004). The consensus is that groups should be heterogeneous because, within a diverse group, students have access to a variety of perspectives during the learning process. Most instructors randomly assign students to permanent groups that work together for the entire semester. When students work together in small learning teams to explain scientific information to one another or to use factual material to solve problems, they readily discover their own misconceptions based on prior knowledge or confusion about what they have read in the textbook.

THE VALUE OF COOPERATIVE LEARNING

Powerful evidence has existed for decades about the effectiveness of cooperative learning at all levels of education and in all disciplines (Johnson and Johnson 1989). With this instructional technique students work together in small groups on a learning task. The method has significant potential for teaching a class of diverse students, even when some students have special needs (Putnam 1998). Since Herreid (1998) first published his article "Why Isn't Cooperative Learning Used to Teach Science?" more science educators have successfully used this method, and for them its value is undisputed. A folder in my file drawer bulges with articles supporting cooperative learning; these studies report that with cooperative learning, students take more responsibility for their own learning, develop higher-order thinking skills, retain more information, are more satisfied with the class, and express positive attitudes about the subject matter.

In any education setting, individuals employ distinct learning styles. Goran and Braude (2007) suggest that although some students learn best through visual, auditory, or kinesthetic modes, cooperative learning activates yet another mode. They describe this fourth modality as social learning, during which students become active participants and more effectively acquire problem-solving skills.

Cooperative learning is well suited to a relatively small class size. But even in a large lecture hall setting, students in astronomy, biology, chemistry, and physics demonstrate increased engagement and conceptual understanding when the instructor leads collaborative activities during class (Adams and Slater 2002; Cooper 1995; Crouch and Mazur 2001; Klionsky 2001/2002; Mazur 1997). A veteran of many years of using cooperative learning, Lord (2001) summarized more than 300 articles by listing 101 reasons to use this pedagogy to teach high school and college science.

For the book *Making the Most of College: Students Speak Their Minds*, Light (2001) and his fellow researchers interviewed more than 1,600 Harvard undergraduates. Among other results, they found that how students study and do their homework assignments outside class is a far stronger predictor of engagement and learning than are the particular details of an instructor's teaching style. Students who study outside of class in small groups of four to six, even just once a week, benefit greatly. Earlier researchers also reported improvement in academic performance when science and math students formed learning groups outside class (Hufford 1991; Treisman 1992). In the past collaboration on homework assignments was considered a form of cheating. Now when professors assign homework, they may send the opposite message by encouraging cooperation among students as a way to enhance learning. Some science faculty restructure their homework assignments so they are actually designed for groups (Light 2001).

Finally, an important aspect of cooperative learning to explain not only to your students but also to administrators and colleagues who may look askance at your teaching techniques is that this method models how people interact in the workplace and, in particular, in the scientific research community. Unfortunately, national norms of science education favor competitive rather than collaborative learning. Competition interferes with normal social interaction between students and creates isolation, suspicion, and a protective attitude toward the acquisition of knowledge and skills. With cooperative learning, students discover that working together enhances comprehension, provides intellectual discussion, and offers the emotional support necessary to persist in a challenging course. College seniors almost universally cited collaborative learning strategies as an important way to address intrinsically difficult material (Seymour and Hewitt 1997). The skills acquired by students during small-group learning may not be measurable on a content-based test, but they are likely to be among the most beneficial and lasting.

THE STRUCTURE OF COOPERATIVE LEARNING GROUPS

Strategies for organizing groups of students vary among instructors, and even from week to week for a single instructor. A group may work together for a day, a week, or the duration of the course.

Informal Cooperative Learning Groups

What Herreid (1998) calls "informal cooperative learning groups" may be brief, lasting a few minutes or as long as one class period. One of my first exposures to cooperative learning was observing Peer Instruction during Mazur's introductory physics class at Harvard University (Crouch and Mazur 2001; Mazur 1997). Peer Instruction is a modification of the traditional lecture format, with 10- or 15-minute presentations by the instructor, immediately followed by a conceptual multiple-choice question called a ConcepTest displayed on a screen. The question probes students' understanding of the content just presented. Students have one or two minutes to report their individual answers to the question, along with their confidence levels, using a student response system (also known as a personal response system, or clicker). These handheld devices allow an instructor to collect individual responses from hundreds of students at once and instantly share a graphical display of the responses. Next, the instructor urges students to discuss their answers with students sitting nearby and to try to convince others of the correctness of their own answer. During this two- to four-minute discussion, the teacher moves around the classroom to listen to the animated conversations among students. Finally, he or she again polls students for their individual answers (which may have changed as a result of the discussion). Using the student response system in a large lecture class not only keeps students engaged in course material but also is an effective formative assessment, giving an instructor immediate feedback on any discrepancy between his or her expectations of learning and what students actually understand.

When I first began using Peer Instruction, my college did not own clickers, so I devised a low-tech method that I still prefer. In the front of each student's coursepack I place five index cards, each a different color. The cards are hole-punched so that the set can be kept in the coursepack's three-ring binder, readily available during class. Before using Peer Instruction for the first time in a semester, I ask students to write a letter of the alphabet on each card according to my instructions (for example, *A* on orange; *B* on blue; *C* on yellow; *D* on green; *E* on pink).

I occasionally—not during every class—display on a large screen at the front of the classroom a conceptual multiple-choice question with up to five choices for a single correct answer. The questions are based on content assigned for students to prepare before class or material covered during class. All questions require higher-order thinking skills—application, analysis, synthesis, or evaluation (Bloom 1956). I ask students to take a couple of minutes to independently choose what they consider the correct answer. When I give a signal, students simultaneously raise their colored index cards to display their chosen answers. I then tell students to look at the color of the cards held up around the room, find someone who answered differently from them, and pair with that student to convince that student of his or her chosen answer. After as much as five minutes of discussion, students vote again. Unless the vote is unanimously correct, I call on various students to justify their choices until we have determined both the correct answer and the reason it is correct. In Appendix C-5 are examples of questions that could be used sequentially for Peer Instruction during a single class period. Answering and discussing these questions would ascertain students' ability to apply what they have just learned for homework and in class about the inheritance of ABO blood types (Appendix C-1).

Although my colored index card method stimulates the same animated discussions I observed in Mazur's lecture hall, I cannot obtain or save the instant numerical data. I do, however, receive a colorful display of students' comprehension of concepts and am able to respond to misconceptions immediately. But most important, the students can look around the room, see how their peers answered a question, and then pair for discussion with someone who has different thoughts about the answer than they do. This benefits not only a student who is initially confused but also a student who attempts to explain a concept to a classmate. Mazur's method was designed to improve instruction in a large lecture course, whereas I use my modification in a smaller classroom, but our techniques are interchangeable. This similarity was affirmed by a comparison of clickers to cards that concluded that Peer Instruction with clickers does not provide any significant learning advantage over low-tech flash cards (Lasry 2008). Another study of clickers versus cards reported that student achievement increased when clicker answers were graded compared to card answers that were ungraded (Freeman et al. 2007).

Continuing research on Peer Instruction offers more support for this informal collaborative learning by demonstrating its effectiveness in both a two-year college and a top-tier four-year research institution. Peer Instruction benefits students with both higher and lower levels of background knowledge and decreases student attrition in introductory physics courses at both types of institutions (Lasry, Mazur, and Watkins 2008). Also, peer discussion enhances concept understanding, even when none of the students in a discussion group originally knows the correct answer (Smith et al. 2009).

Formal Cooperative Learning Groups

Herreid's formal cooperative learning groups are larger groups that work together for anywhere from one class period to several weeks. For example, students may divide into temporary debate teams to research and argue the pros and cons of a controversial scientific topic. I occasionally use temporary groups when teaching a smaller class such as a seminar because I want students to experience working with different combinations of students during the semester. Student presenters organize groups of various sizes when they lead case studies in Science Seminar (Appendix B-4) or teaching models in Genetics (Appendix B-10). I also use formal but temporary learning groups whenever I lead a Lecture-Free Teaching workshop (Chapter 3).

Cooperative Base Groups

Cooperative base groups work together for the entire semester. I describe how I build these groups in Chapter 10. Students work in their base groups to complete in-class activities (see below), participate in laboratory exercises (Chapter 8), work on problems posed by case studies (Chapter 15), and occasionally complete group homework projects. Often students voluntarily gather with members of their base groups to study outside class or work on problem sets. I believe that my use of learning teams during class encourages effective group work outside class as well.

THE DESIGN OF IN-CLASS ACTIVITIES

Effective use of small-group learning requires considerable thought on the part of the educator as he or she plans activities. Five elements described two decades ago by Johnson and Johnson (1989), and reiterated more recently by Herreid (1998), remain essential to successful implementation of cooperative learning:

- **Positive interdependence.** The assigned task should be complex or time-consuming so that it requires group members to work together to complete it (Knabb 2000).
- **Individual and group accountability.** The activity should be organized so that not only is the group held accountable but also each member is responsible for his or her contribution.
- **Face-to-face interaction.** Devoting class time to group work, rather than assigning group activities as homework, ensures opportunities for students to exchange resources, provide feedback to one another, and challenge one another's conclusions.

- **Interpersonal skills.** Students may not know how to work in groups effectively. During in-class activities the instructor should facilitate interactions by wandering through the classroom, observing groups at work, and providing help and suggestions as necessary.
- **Group processing.** Students should have opportunities early in the semester to assess how well their group works together and then make changes to improve the functioning. Crowe and Hill (2006) anticipate and frequently avoid conflict within groups by initially explaining group dynamics, conducting team-building activities, and using group contracts. For semester-long investigative labs, Phillips et al. (2007) schedule regular team meetings with lab mentors to discuss teamwork skills and concerns as well as scientific issues. To monitor team functioning and facilitate team communication, students complete a lab team performance evaluation early in the process to derail potential problems.

PROBLEM-BASED LEARNING (PBL)

Problem-Based Learning uses complex, real-world problems to motivate students to identify and research concepts and principles needed for possible solutions. Some educators consider Problem-Based Learning an independent instructional strategy worthy of its own chapter in this book. I use it for Lecture-Free Teaching as an amalgam of several teaching strategies—a blend of cooperative learning, service-learning (Chapter 14), and case studies (Chapter 15). My students work in small learning teams, combining their collective skills to acquire, communicate, and integrate factual information.

Problem-Based Learning was pioneered in the 1960s at McMaster University in Hamilton, Ontario, Canada, where the medical school's effective use of this nontraditional teaching method attracted widespread interest. This instructional strategy is well suited to small groups of medical students learning scientific concepts in the context of clinical cases as they work in a tutorial with a faculty facilitator. I first observed Problem-Based Learning at the School of Medicine at the University of Melbourne in Australia.

In the early 1990s science faculty at the University of Delaware adapted Problem-Based Learning to their introductory science courses. They subsequently helped colleagues in other disciplines use the method, and several science professors published a how-to guide for instructors considering this teaching method (Duch, Groh, and Allen 2001). The authors explain how to find or write PBL problems that challenge students appropriately. They also describe how to modify this technique for a college classroom with larger enrollments. The criteria for choosing suitable problems parallel and overlap with those used for any cooperative learning assignment:

- The problem must engage students' interest, motivate them to probe for deeper understanding, and relate to the real world as much as possible.
- The best problems require students to make decisions or judgments based on facts, information, logic, and rationalization. Problems often are given to students in multiple stages, which is similar to the Interrupted Case Method, during which data are given to students piecemeal and the problem-poser's remarks alternate with the problem-solver's remarks (Herreid 2007a).
- The problem should be complex enough that cooperation from all members of the group is necessary to work toward a solution. The group members should synthesize what they learned in a face-to-face discussion rather than dividing the parts among individuals who work independently to complete an assignment. In the latter procedure, students end up learning less, not more.
- The initial questions of a problem should be open-ended, based on previously learned knowledge, and controversial.
- The content objectives of the course should be incorporated into the problems. Previous knowledge should connect to new concepts and new knowledge should connect to concepts in other courses and disciplines. The questions should challenge students to develop higher-order thinking skills as defined by Bloom (1956).

PEER EVALUATION OF GROUP WORK

When I first assigned group projects, I struggled with how to evaluate group effort while assigning a fair individual grade to each member. With feedback from students who felt dragged down by a team member, I kept revising my assessment methods until I arrived at a simple one that is acceptable to the majority of my students and me.

Appendix C-6 is an example of my anonymous peer evaluation sheet. The complexity of this method comes when calculating points for each student: First, determine the average percentage contribution for each individual by adding the percentages assigned by peers to a team member and dividing by the number of peer evaluations from that team. Then, adjust the team project grade for individual team members according to their average ratings. An important addition to the evaluation is the requirement that if the stated percentage contributions are unequal, the evaluator must explain why, in writing, at the bottom of the evaluation sheet. That condition effectively eliminated low ratings for someone in the group whom the evaluator disliked and prevented inflation of an evaluator's own rating.

Other science educators ask students to periodically complete ratings to assess the general functioning of their cooperative learning group. The purpose is not to assign a grade for a specific group project, as in Appendix C-6, but rather to provide feedback to fellow group members while there is still an opportunity to make positive changes. One study of engineering students examined the validity of instructor concerns that team members may agree to give one another identically high ratings, give ratings based on gender or racial prejudice, or inflate their own ratings (Kaufman, Felder, and Fuller 1999). The authors used a peer rating form midway through the semester (which was shared and discussed with teammates) and again in the last week of the semester. The final ratings would be used to adjust average homework grades. The form consisted of nine descriptive terms (ranging from excellent to no-show) that were converted to a numerical equivalent by the instructor. Peer ratings correlated positively with average test grades, supporting the implication that responsible team performance benefits academic performance. Furthermore, none of the concerns mentioned above affected the results. The authors recommended providing students with more guidance and practice in assigning ratings, something other science educators have also found helpful.

Herreid (2007b, 2007c), for example, uses peer evaluations as a modifier of the group work score, which is analogous to what I do using the evaluation form in Appendix C-6. Each student uses a numerical scale to evaluate his or her teammates anonymously at the end of the course. In his grading schemes individual scores are worth about 75% of the grade and group work 25%, and he gives students a certain number of points to distribute among their teammates. He sets a lower limit on the peer evaluation score for a student to pass the course; students who do not achieve this minimum score will not pass the course. Herreid believes this requirement compensates for inadequate group contributions by students who are satisfied with a C or D effort for the semester. He also requires explanations, as I do, of low or high scores assigned to group members.

Herreid encourages students to work harder at getting along by having the groups do a practice peer evaluation one-third of the way into the semester, giving them the opportunity to correct problem situations by asking their group how they can improve. This method also gives the instructor a chance to intervene before it is too late. Herreid also finds it useful to have students evaluate their personal progress in teamwork during the early days of the course. He might ask them to write a list of characteristics that identify good and poor team members and to think about their own behavior in terms of these qualities. Sometimes he hands out profiles of fictional students and asks the groups to discuss what kind of evaluation they would give these individuals. Other times he asks students to use a numerical scale to rank how well their group is performing and to consider what they could do as individuals to improve the team's work. All of these techniques are ways to prevent chronic problems and promote positive attitudes about cooperative learning.

Crowe and Hill (2006) use peer evaluation questionnaires more specific to a project and also to a team member's contribution to the cooperative learning experience. Henderson and Buising (2000) assign a collaborative, peer-evaluated research paper in a large biochemistry course. This type of exercise not only reduces an instructor's heavy grading load in a high-enrollment class but, more important, teaches students to review the work of their peers, enhancing their own writing skills as a result. For evaluation of a semester-long, open-ended laboratory inquiry in General Biology, Phillips et al. (2007) ask students to complete a detailed lab team performance evaluation early in the process; they identify specific tasks their team does well, as well as what aspects of their performance they want to change.

I find that to promote positive teamwork, I can explain to students at the beginning of the course how sharing both positive and negative comments can help their classmates improve and succeed in the class. As explained in Chapter 5, my Science Seminar students regularly complete grading sheets for their peers without showing them to me, so their opinions can provide assistance without the possibility of influencing my evaluation of the final product. In addition, by using the same grading criteria sheet I use (Appendix B-5), students become more aware of my expectations for the project, as well as of their own strengths and weaknesses. Students reported that they felt less inhibited giving the critiques to peers without having me read them and that they received useful feedback from one another. Even informal verbal comments, particularly in a seminar setting, can promote a constructive team spirit. I believe that this open communication contributes to better oral and written products by all.

TEST REVIEW SESSIONS USING STUDENT-WRITTEN QUESTIONS

When a student comes to my office hours and asks questions that are nearly identical to those I have written for an upcoming test, I can predict that this student will do well on the exam. This is not because the student has some-how obtained a copy of the test, but because he or she has regularly partici-pated during class, has understood the concepts, and can anticipate impor-tant higher-order questions. Most students, however, need to be taught to formulate questions that require higher-level thinking.

Like other science educators, I believe that teaching students to become effective questioners is another way to encourage them to become more responsible for their own learning. I also agree that "good science begins with good questions," so spending time teaching students methods to formulate questions is another way to model how science is done (Marbach-Ad and Sokolove 2000a, 2000b).

From a large sample of student questions, Marbach-Ad and Sokolove (2000b) created a taxonomy to describe eight categories of questions, arranged in order from low level to high level. The questions requiring higher-level thinking skills connect information learned earlier in the semester to new material or contain thoughts that could be stated as a scientific research hypothesis. The taxonomy provides a rubric to evaluate students' questions and also illustrates what constitutes a high-level question. In another study the same authors compared two similar populations of undergraduate students in large introductory biology classes. One group was taught in a traditional lecture format, and a second group was taught in a cooperative/active learning style. Marbach-Ad and Sokolove presented the taxonomy for writing questions to both groups. After the active learning class learned the taxonomy, more students could pose written questions that were insightful, thoughtful, and content related but not easily answered by consulting the textbook or another readily available source. The best questions could be recast as scientific hypotheses. In contrast, when the same taxonomy was presented to students in the traditionally taught class, the quality of student-written questions remained unchanged (Marbach-Ad and Sokolove 2000a).

Throughout the semester my students practice both answering and creating questions that require higher-order thinking. As I describe in Chapter 6, I expect students to read and take notes on assigned reading before coming to class, and they have many opportunities to clarify content that they do not fully understand (Chapter 7). In addition, the questions I present for Peer Instruction (explained earlier in this chapter) model the type of question I pose on tests. More practice occurs when cooperative learning teams formulate hypotheses and conduct experiments during an inquiry-based lab exercise (Chapter 8). I encourage students to always think about what kind of question I might ask in the future.

In my introductory classes, I devote about an hour of class time to a test review session before each of the three tests, and students report that these sessions are beneficial. Cooperative learning teams compete for extra credit points by answering test review questions, but the questions are composed by the students themselves. To be eligible for extra credit points during an upcoming test review session, a student must submit an appropriate typewritten question, along with its answer, one class before the test review, to allow me time to organize questions for the session. Writing their own questions increases students' understanding and retention of content, and reading the questions they submit informs me of possible misconceptions. Test review sessions are effective formative assessments for all of us. To be counted toward eligibility for extra credit, a question must follow the guidelines in Appendix C-7.

After collecting students' questions, I edit and organize appropriate ones for a multiple-choice practice test. I return all submissions to their authors with written feedback for future improvements, especially for questions I cannot use. I type questions as a numbered practice test, adding the best student questions from previous years.

At the beginning of a test review session, each student receives a copy of the questions. Cooperative learning teams work together—without using their textbooks or other notes—to answer this set of multiple-choice questions using the Immediate Feedback Assessment Technique (IF-AT) (Epstein Educational Enterprises 2005; Epstein, Epstein, and Brosvic 2001). The IF-AT uses a multiple-choice answer sheet with a thin opaque film covering the answer options. Instead of using a pencil to fill in a circle, one member of each team scratches off the coating of the rectangle corresponding to the team's first-choice answer as if scratching a lottery ticket. If the answer is correct, a star symbol appears somewhere within the rectangle, the group's learning is immediately reinforced, and the team receives full credit for the answer. If incorrect, the group must reread and discuss the question and remaining answer options and scratch off a second or even third choice until the correct answer is identified. Students earn partial credit for multiple attempts and learn the correct response for each question as they take the test.

Using IF-AT forms is an efficient method for conducting a review session. But more important, students engage in animated discussions about why an answer is correct or incorrect, exposing misconceptions. At the end of the session, if there are four teams in the class, each eligible member of the team that earns the most points gets four extra credit points; the second-place winner gets three extra credit points; the third, two; and last place, one. But only students who have submitted appropriate questions in advance (by carefully following the guidelines) are eligible for extra credit points. This rule by and large prevents students from receiving points if they have not contributed to the team effort.

The exercise teaches students how to pose good questions; make thoughtful decisions when answering multiple-choice questions by weighing the pros and cons of an answer; learn content; work well with their team members; and, very important, review for a test before the last minute. Although the number of extra credit points for each of three sessions during the semester is minimal, I am surprised at how hard students work to earn these points. Even students who are not eligible to get the extra points get into the team spirit and obviously benefits from the exercise. They leave the session with accurate ideas about my expectations for higher-order thinking on the upcoming test.

As I discuss in the introductory paragraphs of this chapter, cooperative learning is an effective way to enhance student engagement and learning in small-, medium-, and large-enrollment classes. I present an assortment of methods for incorporating cooperative learning into science classes. I believe it is important to use several of these during a semester so that students experience teaching their peers, as well as learning from them in a variety of settings.

REFERENCES

Adams, J., and T. Slater. 2002. Learning through sharing: Supplementing the astronomy lecture with collaborative-learning group activities. *Journal of College Science Teaching* 31 (6): 384–387.

Bloom, B. S., ed. 1956. *Taxonomy of educational objectives: The classification of educational goals. Handbook 1: Cognitive domain.* New York: Longman.

Cooper, M. M. 1995. Cooperative learning: An approach for large enrollment courses. *Journal of Chemical Education* 72 (2): 162–164.

Crouch, C. H., and E. Mazur. 2001. Peer Instruction: Ten years of experience and results. *American Journal of Physics* 69 (9): 970–977.

Crowe, M., and C. Hill. 2006. Setting the stage for good group dynamics in semester-long projects in the sciences. *Journal of College Science Teaching* 35 (4): 32–35.

Dinan, F. J. 2006. Opening day: Getting started in a cooperative classroom. *Journal of College Science Teaching* 35 (4): 12–14.

Duch, B. J., S. E. Groh, and D. E. Allen, eds. 2001. *The power of Problem-Based Learning: A practical "how to" for teaching undergraduate courses in any discipline.* Sterling, VA: Stylus Publishing.

Epstein Educational Enterprises. 2005. IF-AT. Immediate Feedback Assessment Technique. *www.epsteineducation.com/index.php.*

Epstein, M. L., B. B. Epstein, and G. M. Brosvic. 2001. Immediate feedback during academic testing. *Psychological Reports* 88:889–894.

Freeman, S., E. O'Connor, J. W. Parks, M. Cunningham, D. Hurley, D. Haak, C. Dirks, and M. P. Wenderoth. 2007. Prescribed active learning increases performance in introductory biology. *CBE—Life Sciences Education* 6:132–139.

French, D. P. 2004. Tips for managing a large, active-learning class. In *Teaching tips: Innovations in undergraduate science instruction,* eds. M. Druger, E. D. Siebert, and L. W. Crow, 13–14. Arlington, VA: NSTA Press.

Goran, D., and S. Braude. 2007. Social and cooperative learning in the solving of case histories. *American Biology Teacher* 69 (2): 80–84.

Henderson, L., and C. Buising. 2000. A peer-reviewed research assignment for large classes: Honing students' writing skills in a collaborative endeavor. *Journal of College Science Teaching* 30 (2): 109–113.

Herreid, C. F. 1998. Why isn't cooperative learning used to teach science? *Bioscience* 48 (7): 553–559.

———. 2007a. The interrupted case method. In *Start with a story: The case study method of teaching college science,* ed. C. F. Herreid, 169–170. Arlington, VA: NSTA Press.

———. 2007b. Using case studies in science—and still "covering the content." In *Start with a story: The case study method of teaching college science,* ed. C. F. Herreid, 195–203. Arlington, VA: NSTA Press.

———. 2007c. When justice peeks: Evaluating students in case study teaching. In *Start with a story: The case study method of teaching college science,* ed. C. F. Herreid, 395–399. Arlington, VA: NSTA Press.

Hufford, T. L. 1991. Increasing academic performance in an introductory biology course. *BioScience* 41 (2): 107–108.

Jensen, M., R. Moore, and J. Hatch. 2002. Cooperative learning—Part II: Cooperative group activities for the first week of class; Setting the tone with group web pages. *American Biology Teacher* 64 (2): 118–120.

Johnson, D. W., and R. T. Johnson. 1989. *Cooperation and competition: Theory and research.* Edina, MN: Interaction Book Company.

Kaufman, D. B., R. M. Felder, and H. Fuller. 1999. Peer ratings in cooperative learning teams. Session 1430. Paper presented at the annual meeting of the American Society for Engineering Education, Charlotte, NC.

Klionsky, D. J. 2001/2002. Constructing knowledge in the lecture hall: A quiz-based, group-learning approach to introductory biology. *Journal of College Science Teaching* 31 (4): 246–251.

Knabb, M. T. 2000. Discovering teamwork: A novel cooperative learning activity to encourage group interdependence. *American Biology Teacher* 62 (3): 211–213.

Lasry, N. 2008. Clickers or flashcards: Is there really a difference? *Physics Teacher* 46:242–244.

Lasry, N., E. Mazur, and J. Watkins. 2008. Peer Instruction: From Harvard to the two-year college. *American Journal of Physics* 76 (11): 1066–1069.

Light, R. J. 2001. *Making the most of college: Students speak their minds*. Cambridge, MA: Harvard University Press.

Lord, T. R. 2001. 101 reasons for using cooperative learning in biology teaching. *American Biology Teacher* 63 (1): 30–38.

———. 2004. Increasing student accountability through collaborative work in the classroom. In *Teaching tips: Innovations in undergraduate science instruction*, eds. M. Druger, E. D. Siebert, and L. W. Crow, 26–27. Arlington, VA: NSTA Press.

Marbach-Ad, G., and P. G. Sokolove. 2000a. Can undergraduate biology students learn to ask higher level questions? *Journal of Research in Science Teaching* 37 (8): 854–870.

———. 2000b. Good science begins with good questions: Answering the need for high-level questions in science. *Journal of College Science Teaching* 30 (3): 192–195.

Mazur, E. 1997. *Peer Instruction. A user's manual*. Upper Saddle River, NJ: Prentice Hall.

Phillips, M., L. H. Gildensoph, M. J. Myers, C. G. Norton, A. M. Olson, K. A. Tweeten, and D. D. Wygal. 2007. Investigative labs in biology: The importance of attending to team dynamics. *Journal of College Science Teaching* 37 (2): 23–27.

Putnam, J. W. 1998. The process of collaborative learning. In *Cooperative learning and strategies for inclusion*, ed. J. W. Putnam, 17–47. Baltimore, MD: Paul H. Brookes Publishing Company.

Seymour, E., and N. M. Hewitt. 1997. *Talking about leaving: Why undergraduates leave the sciences*. Boulder, CO: Westview Press.

Smith, M. K., W. B. Wood, W. K. Adams, C. Wieman, J. K. Knight, N. Guild, and T. T. Su. 2009. Why peer discussion improves student performance on in-class concept questions. *Science* 323 (5910):122–124.

Treisman, U. 1992. Studying students studying calculus: A look at the lives of minority mathematics students in college. *College Mathematics Journal* 23 (5): 362–372.

Wood, B. S. 2007. Learning biology while constructing cooperative learning groups: The first 15 minutes. *American Biology Teacher* 69 (6): 330.

———. 2009. Learning science while constructing learning teams. *Journal of College Science Teaching* 38 (5): 28–32.

Chapter 13

Team-Based Learning (TBL)

Since launching my own pedagogical reform more than a decade ago, I have experimented with innumerable ideas gleaned from books and journals. Each of them, in one way or another, helped shape Lecture-Free Teaching. Interestingly, an instructional strategy that closely parallels what I do in my own classroom is one that I read about only recently. Although the creator and promoters of Team-Based Learning (TBL) do not teach in science classrooms (Michaelsen, Knight, and Fink 2004), science educators have demonstrated the effectiveness of this method in their own disciplines (Dinan 2004; Goodson 2004; Herreid 2004) and in large-enrollment classes (Carmichael 2009). Not only do the successes of Team-Based Learning affirm my own practices, but the book *Team-Based Learning: A Transformative Use of Small Groups in College Teaching* (Michaelsen, Knight, and Fink 2004) is an excellent guide for improving some of my group assignments.

As I described in Chapter 12, any educator using small-group learning faces similar challenges: shy students who remain silent; passive students who do not do their share of the work; domineering students who worry that the group grade will pull their own grade down unless they assume the bulk of the responsibility; peer evaluation procedures that permit students to inflate their own grade or deflate the grade of someone with whom they have not enjoyed working; and group assignments that neither promote participation by every member nor result in higher-level learning and retention of the content.

Team-Based Learning is a comprehensive instructional strategy for teaching almost any kind of course. Michaelsen, Knight, and Fink (2004) differentiate traditional teaching (lecture- and textbook-focused) from using small groups, and they describe small-group learning as having three distinct categories: casual use, cooperative learning, and Team-Based Learning. With TBL, permanent groups of students work together throughout the semester. At the beginning of each major unit of instruction, there is a preparation phase: Students read the content individually before coming to class, and at the beginning of class they engage in a Readiness Assurance Process during which they first take an individual quiz on the readings and then take the same quiz with their team. The preparation phase also includes a formal written appeal process by which teams can dispute an answer by providing the instructor with supporting material. Next comes an application phase: Students use the content to complete carefully designed in-class assignments that not only teach groups how to apply the terms and principles but also help the group members become more unified and committed to their team's success. In the final assessment phase, the instructor grades the students on a test they take individually or as a team project.

Lecture-Free Teaching combines characteristics of cooperative learning and Team-Based Learning. I refer to the small groups I build on the first day of class as "cooperative learning teams," a term that reflects this hybrid. A fundamental expectation I share with those who use TBL is that students will take responsibility for initial review of course content to prepare for in-class team work. As with Team-Based Learning, I form and manage permanent groups at the beginning of the semester, do not use assigned roles in the groups, do not analyze group process skills, and give prompt feedback on individual and group performance. But like cooperative learning, I use smaller groups of students (usually four), do not always grade the group work, and do not always include peer assessment.

An important component of Lecture-Free Teaching is the element of surprise provided by variety in the format of each class meeting and the different methods by which I present each content topic. Although a more consistent cadence can be advantageous and perhaps more comfortable for an anxious student, I find TBL in its purest form too structured with its predictable sequence of events for each major content topic. But with Team-Based Learning, as with my pedagogy, class attendance approaches 100%, students are less likely to withdraw at midterm, students learn more content and retain it better, coverage of the subject matter is at least as great as in a lecture course, and students prefer this format. Another finding that resonates with my own experience is that TBL not only "transforms the quality of student learning," but "for many teachers, transforms (or restores) the joy of teaching" (Michaelsen, Knight, and Fink 2004, p. 4).

An organic chemistry professor (Dinan 2004) countered concerns about how well students learn his content-driven subject with Team-Based Learning. He compared grades on common objective final examinations of students who were in Team-Based Learning versus those in traditional lecture classrooms. The TBL classes consistently earned statistically significant higher mean and average grades than the lecture classes. He also pointed out that because the TBL classes had higher student retention rates, students who would have long since withdrawn from a lecture class generally complete the term in the TBL class. This fact makes the TBL student performances on the final examinations even more impressive because many of the academically weaker students in the TBL groups remain in the course to take that examination, possibly lowering the class average.

Michaelsen and Knight (2004) argue that "almost all failed efforts to successfully use learning groups can be traced back to inappropriate group assignments" (p. 51) rather than bad groups. To remedy this, an instructor must eliminate those processes that detract from group cohesiveness and promote uneven member participation. The authors describe how to create an effective assignment, and they provide a checklist to help teachers assess the effectiveness of an assignment after it has been tried in the classroom. Five variables they believe build group cohesiveness share attributes, not surprisingly, with elements suggested for successful cooperative learning (Chapter 12): ensuring individual accountability, promoting close physical proximity, promoting discussion among team members, providing teams with meaningful feedback, and rewarding group success. I agree that one of the worst assignments is asking students to write a paper as a group. Because writing is an individual activity, students will divide the work among the members, so there is little discussion among them and limited learning about the other students' topics. Also, the feedback on a paper is, by necessity, delayed, so there is no opportunity to compare performance among different groups. To create effective group assignments, the promoters of TBL recommend that (1) the entire class should work on the same problem or assignment, (2) students should be required to make a specific choice and the group must reach a consensus about that choice, and (3) groups should simultaneously report their choices.

In my enthusiasm to try a new activity, I sometimes fail to give adequate attention to recommendations from the experts, such as those listed above. What follows are descriptions of two team activities that I have used regularly. The first is an example of an *effective* team activity that complies with the recommendations for a TBL assignment. The second is an example of an *ineffective* team activity and a description of how I plan to modify it according to the recommendations above.

AN EFFECTIVE GROUP ASSIGNMENT: TEAM QUIZZES USING THE IMMEDIATE FEEDBACK ASSESSMENT TECHNIQUE

As do the advocates of Team-Based Learning, I use Immediate Feedback Assessment Technique (IF-AT) forms (Epstein Educational Enterprises 2005; Epstein, Epstein, and Brosvic 2001) to provide instant feedback on answers to multiple-choice questions, as described in Chapter 12. Although some teachers use IF-AT forms for individual multiple-choice tests, I only use them for group pretests at the beginning of a class meeting and for test review competitions. Giving each team just one form to complete also reduces the expense of purchasing the forms. The team can continue using the same form for several group quizzes if I number the questions on consecutive quizzes sequentially and return the same form to the team for each subsequent quiz. In both cases, individuals answer the multiple-choice questions alone, and then the group uses one IF-AT form for a team effort to achieve the highest team score and earn extra credit points.

The team discusses the first question, reaches a consensus about the most likely correct answer, and then has one student scratch off the coating of the rectangle corresponding to their first-choice answer. If the answer is correct and the star symbol appears, the team's learning is immediately reinforced, and the team receives full credit for the answer. If the first choice answer is incorrect, the team must reread and discuss the remaining answer options, and then scratch off a second, third, or even fourth choice until they identify the correct answer. The team earns decreasing amounts of partial credit for multiple attempts.

I employ IF-AT forms for two types of group quizzes, with success for both. On the first day of my Human Nutrition class, the teams complete a short quiz called a Nutrition Aptitude Test (N.A.T.) (adapted from the University of California-Berkeley *Wellness Letter*) that gives members an initial experience working together and introduces them to IF-AT forms. Then, sprinkled throughout the semester, the forms are used for team pretests on homework reading about the content-heavy topics of lipids, fluids, and electrolytes; bone health; vitamins and minerals; and food safety. In each of my introductory courses, before each of three tests during the semester, teams complete a practice test, with student-written questions as described in Chapter 12. These activities meet all the criteria recommended by the proponents of TBL for effective group assignments:

(1) All of the teams work simultaneously on the quiz or set of test review questions.
(2) Students first try the quiz individually, and then the team must reach a consensus about a specific answer choice, continuing this process until they have discovered the correct answer.
(3) The teams report their scores simultaneously so students know how their team did in comparison with the other teams.

Significant benefits of this low-tech method are that IF-AT forms not only correct misconceptions immediately but also provide team members with opportunities to discuss why they misunderstood the material. The teams learn to work together because this method eliminates the tendency of more vocal students to overpower quiet but knowledgeable students. As I walk around the room, eavesdropping on animated conversations among the team members, I am amazed at how hard they work for a just a few extra credit points and how effectively this method encourages participation by even the most reluctant team member. Cotner, Baepler, and Kellerman (2008) describe several other uses, particularly in large lecture settings, for identifying problem areas and misconceptions during class and subsequently streamlining lectures or in-class discussions.

AN INEFFECTIVE GROUP ASSIGNMENT: SUPERMARKET BOTANY

Because I enjoy trying new teaching methods, I sometimes experiment with an assignment that has potential but does not achieve the learning goals I have determined for the course. A few years ago I read a journal article that described an appealing activity (Smith and Avery 1999) and subsequently asked an undergraduate student who was working with me to adapt it for a General Biology I learning team project (Hamlin 2004). For the assignment, students visited a grocery store and located examples that matched my descriptions of edible plants. The specific descriptions were categorized as stems, roots, leaves, flowers, and fruits so that students could learn about plant anatomy as they completed the activity. The groups were given one week to complete the task outside class and to submit one team answer sheet, for which they would receive a group grade. The project was a competition among the cooperative learning teams because members of the group who earned the highest number of points on the project would receive a few additional extra credit points. An anonymous peer grading form, described in Appendix C-6, ensured an equitable distribution of points among team members.

I believed this would be an engaging way to teach plant structure and introduce students to unfamiliar types of food. The teams generally did well answering the questions by locating appropriate examples of edible plants. But when I tested them individually on their understanding, application, and retention of the content covered in the activity, most students did poorly. By considering the principles of Team-Based Learning, I determined that a major flaw of this activity is requiring work outside of class: The "cost" of meeting outside class is so great that even if they go to the grocery store together, students divide up the work rather than working on each question individually before achieving a group consensus. In other words, individual accountability is missing, as are group discussions of members' individual choices. The activity also lacks immediate feedback and direct comparisons with the choices of other groups because the group decisions are not reported publicly but rather are graded privately by the instructor.

Because I believe there is value in retaining this activity, I decided to change it in the future in the following ways to increase its effectiveness:

- Reduce the number of questions, and be sure the remaining ones focus on key issues and require students to explain why they have chosen an answer.

- After the project, students take a graded quiz on the material individually and then as a group (using the IF-AT forms previously described) so that teams receive immediate feedback on their answers, share their individual knowledge with the group, correct misconceptions, and compare their team's performance with that of other teams.

Team-Based Learning can be used by a science educator as a comprehensive instructional strategy that incorporates each of the phases suggested by its creators (Michaelsen, Knight, and Fink 2004), or it can be hybridized with other cooperative learning techniques to produce an instructional strategy that best fits your course goals.

REFERENCES

Carmichael, J. 2009. Team-Based Learning enhances performance in introductory biology. *Journal of College Science Teaching* 37 (4): 54–61.

Cotner, S., P. Baepler, and A. Kellerman. 2008. Scratch this! The IF-AT as a technique for stimulating group discussion and exposing misconceptions. *Journal of College Science Teaching* 37 (4): 48–53.

Dinan, F. J. 2004. An alternative to lecturing in the sciences. In *Team-Based Learning: A transformative use of small groups in college teaching*, eds. L. K. Michaelsen, A. B. Knight, and L. D. Fink, 97–104. Sterling, VA: Stylus.

Epstein Educational Enterprises. 2005. IF-AT. Immediate Feedback Assessment Technique. *www.epsteineducation.com/index.php*.

Epstein, M. L., B. B. Epstein, and G. M. Brosvic. 2001. Immediate feedback during academic testing. *Psychological Reports* 88:889–894.

Goodson, P. 2004. Working with nontraditional and underprepared students in health education. In *Team-Based Learning: A transformative use of small groups in college teaching*, eds. L. K. Michaelsen, A. B. Knight, and L. D. Fink, 115–123. Sterling, VA: Stylus.

Hamlin, L. A. 2004. Supermarket botany. *General Biology I coursepack*. Presque Isle, ME: University of Maine at Presque Isle.

Herreid, C. F. 2004. Using case studies in science—and still "covering the content." In *Team-Based Learning: A transformative use of small groups in college teaching*, eds. L. K. Michaelsen, A. B. Knight, and L. D. Fink, 105–114. Sterling, VA: Stylus.

Michaelsen, L. K., and A. B. Knight. 2004. Creating effective assignments: A key component of Team-Based Learning. In *Team-Based Learning: A transformative use of small groups in college teaching*, eds. L. K. Michaelsen, A. B. Knight, and L. D. Fink, 51–72. Sterling, VA: Stylus.

Michaelsen, L. K., A. B. Knight, and L. D. Fink, eds. 2004. *Team-Based Learning: A transformative use of small groups in college teaching*. Sterling, VA: Stylus.

N.A.T.: Nutrition Aptitude Test. *Wellness Letter* 19 (9): 4.

Smith, D. G., and D. F. Avery. 1999. Supermarket botany. *American Biology Teacher* 61 (2): 128–131.

Chapter 14

Service-Learning

More than a decade ago a colleague—a health educator and also coordinator of the newly formed Campus Service-Learning Program at my school—encouraged me to incorporate service-learning into my Human Nutrition course. Before that I had barely heard of service-learning and could not imagine its possible function in a science course; now it is the foundation of at least one of my courses each academic year. This initial experience with service-learning led me to attend a weeklong Problem-Based Service-Learning Workshop sponsored by the Campus Compact (*www.compact.org*), which introduced me to a hybrid of Problem-Based Learning (discussed in Chapter 12) and service-learning. Clearly, not all Problem-Based Learning is service-learning, nor is all service-learning centered on problem solving. With Problem-Based Service-Learning (PBSL), students work in teams to find solutions to problems involving real needs in their communities. Ideally, as they do this, they acquire relevant knowledge, increase their understanding of academic concepts, and make important connections among ideas from their reading, teachers, and fellow students (Gordon 2000). Attending this workshop inspired me to design service-learning projects for my nonmajor science courses.

ACADEMIC SERVICE-LEARNING

The term *service-learning* has a variety of connotations. The traditional meaning implies providing charitable services, but situating the adjective *academic* ahead of this phrase emphasizes the application of classroom knowledge and skills in the community. In this academic form, service-learning encompasses more than teaching civic responsibility and shares attributes with what has been called *civic engagement* (Avard 2006; Rhoads and Howard 1998; Tai-Seale 2001). Service-learning can be a type of experiential education that is "a marriage between occupational and/or academic learning and service to the community" (Prentice and Garcia 2000, p. 9).

A growing number of college science courses incorporate service-learning. For an introductory environmental science course, students evaluate campus academic buildings and find ways to encourage and increase energy conservation (Bixby et al. 2003). Partnerships of college undergraduates with K–12 students include organizing an Earth science fair at a local elementary school, as well as long-term formal and short-term informal outreach (Francek 2002/2003; Rao, Shamath, and Collay 2007). In an informal educational setting designed for students pursuing science careers, participants learned about environmental education programs and applied their training at a local nature center (Haines 2003). Others engage in more traditional partnerships with external community organizations (Abrahams, Gillis, and Taylor 2000; Grossman and Cooper 2004; Phillips 1997).

I designed two examples of academic service-learning to enhance my Lecture-Free Teaching methods so that they follow three basic steps of preparation, participation, and reflection, which are considered essential for effective service-learning (Lott and Michelmore 1997). The examples I describe below, however, are quite different from each other in terms of how they support the learning goals of the courses.

ENVIRONMENTAL ACTION IN A NONMAJORS SCIENCE CLASS

This service-learning project takes place during the second semester of a two-semester course sequence that fulfills my university's general education curriculum science requirement for nonmajors. Sciences I introduces the scientific method and major unifying theories from physics and the Earth sciences, with applications to real-world problems; Sciences II takes the same approach but focuses on meteorology, chemistry, biology, and environmental sciences. I teach the course as a combined "lecture"-laboratory, as described in Chapter 8.

When I first began teaching these courses, one objective was to find ways to better engage these nonscience majors, many of whom professed minimal interest in science or had poor preparation in science and math. I also sought to connect the broad topics covered during the two semesters. Finally, I wanted to use writing as a tool for learning science as well as for improving communication skills. Because environmental sciences, the final content area in the two-course sequence, relates to all of the content topics and real-world problems, I decided to use this subject as the focus of my service-learning endeavor. The activity gradually evolved into what I call an Environmental Action Project, with considerable potential for further development.

My first attempt to lead an environmentally themed service-learning project exposed problems due to uneven effort among students. When cooperative learning teams visited different elementary school classrooms, some teams were well prepared, but others presented inaccurate information. When I was revising the assignment for the following year, my primary concern was ensuring that a potential lack of commitment affected no one but the individual students enrolled in my course.

I describe below a semester-long activity that proved more successful. While planning this project, I blended components of previously reported service-learning projects with validating written work (Bixby et al. 2003; Tessier 2006). This illustrates how I sometimes adapt and combine ideas of other educators. My nonmajor students successfully completed the three-part Environmental Action Project as we progressed through the semester's customary course content.

Preparation: The Book Review

Early in the semester each student reads and reviews a book of his or her choice about a current environmental issue. I supply a list of approximately 50 books appropriate for this project; all books are available in the campus library. Using the Sciences II Book Review Grading Criteria (Appendix B-6), students include in their reviews a discussion of how the book relates to the upcoming Environmental Action Project. A goal is to stimulate thinking in the first half of the semester about the Environmental Action Project that will be completed near the end of the semester. Another objective is to provide students with background information and ideas to support their project.

To ensure an early start on the preparation phase of the project, I follow a strict timeline explained in detail in the topic schedule (Appendix A-3) and syllabus for the course:

- By the end of the second week of classes, students submit the name of the author and the title of the book they plan to review. Each student must read a different book to avoid competition for single copies of books in the campus library and to increase the diversity of ideas that students will contribute to their learning team discussions. I also encourage them to choose a book about a topic in which they are already interested and that may relate to what they choose to do for subsequent steps of the Environmental Action Project. Also, the sooner they borrow their book from library, the more likely they are to get their first choice.

- By the end of the sixth week of the semester, students are required to take a draft of their review to the Writing Center for a consultation with a peer tutor, as described in Chapter 11.
- At the conclusion of the eighth week of the semester (just after midterm), students submit the final book review to me.

Participation: Estimating One's Ecological Footprint

This phase begins soon after the book review due date:

- During Week 9 of the semester, students enter data into the spreadsheet called "Assess Your Household's Ecological Footprint" to estimate their individual ecological footprints. A link to and explanation of this spreadsheet are in the case study "Watch Your Step: Understanding the Impact of Your Personal Consumption on the Environment" (Camill 2002). A variety of simpler ecological footprint calculators are easily located on the internet and could be substitutes (Best Foot Forward: Bringing Sustainability Down to Earth; Earth Day Network Footprint Calculator; World Wildlife Fund Footprint Calculator).
- Students use the spreadsheet to estimate their individual ecological footprints. Since they have only seven days to collect information, they extrapolate the data to estimate their annual footprints. Although this project occurs during the Northern Maine winter, a time of maximum energy consumption, the extrapolation cannot incorporate seasonal fluctuations and is considered a rough estimate.
- At the end of Week 10 of the semester, students submit printouts of their completed spreadsheets, as well their individual written answers to questions in the case study that ask them to examine the sustainability of their personal lifestyles and consider some more global issues.

Reflection: Environmental Action Project—Written Assignment and Oral Presentation

- During approximately Week 10, an elected government official (I invite a representative from the Maine State Legislature) speaks to the students about how to effect change by working through the government and answers questions about the pros and cons of methods used by citizens to change environmental laws. I also place on reserve in the campus library a large collection of relevant, timely articles describing ideas for environmental action.

- Also by Week 10, four-student cooperative learning teams begin planning team and individual contributions to the project. I reserve class time for these meetings so that I can facilitate the discussions.

- The team assignment is to determine possible ways to take environmental action at each of the following levels:

    1. Personal
    2. College campus
    3. City or town in which the students reside
    4. State or province in which the students reside
    5. Country in which the students reside

- The individual assignment is to review what the students learned in the participation phase about their personal consumption, choose one feasible lifestyle habit to modify, and then make that change for seven days. Each student writes a short paper that explains why he or she chose the individual action and describes the seven-day experience.

- The learning team also chooses four similarly achievable actions for each of the remaining levels (campus, city or town, state or province, and country).

- Group members divide these action levels among themselves, and each student writes a letter either to the appropriate editor of a newspaper or a government official in an attempt to achieve the desired result. Final copies of the letters must be ready to mail, with correct titles and complete addresses of newspapers or governmental officials.

- Although each learning team submits one written reflection for their Environmental Action Project, individual students must have drafts of their individual contributions reviewed during a consultation with a peer tutor in the Writing Center. Using the Environmental Action Project Reflection Phase Grading Criteria and Point Distribution (Appendix B-8), I evaluate both individual contributions and group participation.

- On my campus an event called University Day occurs near the end of the second semester; regular classes are canceled for a day of student presentations. Sciences II cooperative learning teams make presentations about their Environmental Action Projects.

- At the conclusion of the project, each student submits an Anonymous Peer Evaluation Form (Appendix C-6) so I can more accurately assess individual contributions to the group effort.

Evaluation of Environmental Action Project

- To modify their personal lifestyles for seven days, most students reported choosing to decrease their use of a personal vehicle by walking, bicycling, or carpooling. A similar number reported increasing their recycling efforts. A couple of students reported decreasing their water use, and one student reported decreasing the amount of wasted food in his household.

- Among those team members who wrote letters to relevant campus organizations, most advocated increasing recycling through better use of paper recycling receptacles or by establishing opportunities to recycle other materials on campus. One student wrote a letter to the editor of the student newspaper about students he observed driving between campus parking lots (only one-fifth of a mile!) rather than walking.

- For the city or town level, all letter writers asked the government to encourage or mandate more recycling. For the state or provincial level, the issues ranged from reducing pressure on the forest by increasing demand for paper made with postconsumer waste, to improving public transportation to the possible use of geothermal energy. For the national level, students articulated concern about the disproportionate consumption of natural resources by U.S. citizens and also suggested increased use of wind power.

- When describing what they learned from the Environmental Action Project, some students expressed a clear need for more public education at all levels, as well as surprise at how they could save money while helping protect the environment. Some student comments included:

    > Each and every one of us impacts the earth and leaves a 'footprint'... .

    > [I gained increased awareness of] "what I can do personally" ... .

    > [I learned] how we as Americans live, the amount of space we take up as individuals, and where we compare with the rest of the world ... .

    > Until this project, I never thought that something this small would help, but if it is done in the long run, it could make a large impact.

    > I have been more mindful of the resources available and the side effects of overusing them.

> Recycling is an inconvenience. Most people will not engage in it unless required to do so. As an individual who rarely recycles, this project helped me better understand [my] effect on my community.

> I believe this project has been the beginning of a new consciousness for my entire family. It has served as a lesson in ecological awareness and personal responsibility.

The generally good quality of the students' written work and oral presentations suggests that appropriate effort was invested in the Environmental Action Project. At the very least, students read a book about a timely topic, practiced writing skills, and increased their awareness of current environmental issues. Because it is impractical to measure the long-term effect of this project, my hope is that these students not only continued to be mindful of their personal lifestyle choices but also became comfortable with some legitimate methods that can be used by informed citizens to effect change in the world.

IMPROVING WELLNESS ON CAMPUS WITH A HUMAN NUTRITION CLASS PROJECT

Human Nutrition is an upper-level biology course required for athletic training majors, but it also serves as a nonlaboratory science course in the general education curriculum and as an elective for biology majors. One goal, listed in the box in Chapter 3, Step 2, is to actively engage students in learning about human nutrition so they can make effective dietary choices for themselves and others. As in all of my classes, I emphasize applying factual knowledge rather than memorizing it. For the service-learning portion of this one-semester course, I pair each of approximately 20 students with a different volunteer from the faculty or staff, for whom they will write a complete nutritional assessment.

As mentioned, an objective is to teach both students and volunteer service-learning partners about their own nutritional status and about how food consumption and physical activity contribute to their energy balance and overall health. A broader goal is to improve overall wellness among members of the University of Maine at Presque Isle campus community (Wood 2003). The project follows the three basic steps for academic service-learning, with instructions and deadlines detailed in the topic schedule (Appendix A-4) and syllabus, as well as in a section of the coursepack (Appendix C-8).

Preparation: Student Self-Assessment

Preparation occurs during the first half of the semester as students evaluate their own diet and physical activity. During homework and in-class activities students learn the components of a healthful diet, how to interpret food labels, and information about the major nutrients. As they acquire this knowledge, they progressively evaluate their own diets and energy balances using DINE Healthy, a computerized dietary analysis and scoring program available on all campus student computers (DINE Systems, Inc.).

Participation: Collecting Data From a Service-Learning Partner

Participation begins after midterm and continues through the end of the semester as students work outside class time to teach their service-learning partner how to keep an accurate seven-day record of his or her food consumption and physical activity and then collect and analyze the data. Before the semester begins, I obtain approval for this project from the Institutional Review Board for the Protection of Human Subjects (IRB) at the University of Maine at Presque Isle (*www.umpi.edu/faculty-staff/irb*). Then I solicit faculty and staff volunteers by sending an e-mail offering a "free nutritional assessment" and briefly explaining the service-learning project (Appendix C-9). Participants are accepted in the order in which they respond to the e-mail. A waiting list is generated, and these additional volunteers are included the next time I teach the course.

Around the middle of the semester, each student chooses a service-learning partner from my list of volunteers, and I spend an entire class meeting teaching them about IRB policies and guidelines, as well as procedures to follow during the project. I strongly emphasize the requirement of complete confidentiality regarding information about participants. Each service-learning partner is assigned a subject number that is used in place of his or her name on all written materials and in any conversations with me. All work with the volunteer partner is completed outside class time. Additional course content fills the remaining weeks of the semester.

Detailed instructions and a schedule for the participation phase of the service-learning project (Appendix C-8), as well as an informed consent form (Appendix C-10), are in each student's coursepack.

Reflection: Comprehensive Nutritional Assessment of a Service-Learning Partner

Reflection occurs when each student writes a complete nutritional assessment for his or her service-learning partner. One copy is given to the service-learning partner and one copy to me for grading. This assessment substitutes for a final exam.

A detailed outline for preparation of the written nutritional assessment and the grading criteria and point distribution are in each student's coursepack (Appendix B-9). Several days before the student meets with his or her partner to go over the completed assessment, I review a final draft with the student and

124

provide suggestions for improvements. I do not use the Writing Center for peer review of the draft to avoid a possible breach of confidentiality.

During the final week of the semester, the students and I prepare a healthful meal that we invite the volunteer service-learning partners to share. Each cooperative learning team plans a meal, and food from all of the teams is served on a buffet table. Each student prints a nutrition facts label (like those found on commercial food packages) by inputting their food recipe into the DINE Healthy software. As a thank-you gift, each participant is given a collection of these nutrition facts labels and recipes for food items served at the meal.

Evaluation by Students and Their Service-Learning Partners

Students commented both verbally and in written evaluations that they found this project valuable. One summer, two students subsequently volunteered to teach a four-week nutrition class to senior citizens, for whom they completed similar nutritional assessments.

At the conclusion of the project, an e-mail questionnaire is sent to volunteer participants to learn about the perceived success of the service-learning activity, gather suggestions for improvement, and assess individual students (Appendix C-11). Comments are generally positive and indicate that the project achieved its goals. After one of the first years for this project, a volunteer partner commented that his assigned student did not put much effort into the project (a fact reflected in the student's final grade). To minimize future disparity in the quality of the final nutritional assessments, I monitored each student's progress more carefully throughout the weeks of the project. Although variation among the final products is expected, my vigilance ensures that each volunteer reaps some benefit.

Adding a service-learning project to a course increases an instructor's preparation time, broadens his or her responsibility, and raises the probability of personal embarrassment if students do an inadequate job when working with people outside the classroom. But good planning, careful communication of expectations to students, and close monitoring of students' progress throughout the project can eliminate most negatives and provide an effective method to engage students in course content.

REFERENCES

Abrahams, M. V., D. M. Gillis, and K. L. Taylor. 2000. Applying ecological principles on the job: Engaging students in authentic environmental projects. *Journal of College Science Teaching* 30 (3): 166–171.

Avard, M. 2006. Civic engagement in the science classroom. *Journal of College Science Teaching* 36 (3): 12–13.

Best foot forward: Bringing sustainability down to Earth. *www.ecologicalfootprint.com.*

Bixby, J. A., J. R. Carpenter, P. L. Jerman, and B. C. Coull. 2003. Ecology on campus. Service-learning in introductory environmental courses. *Journal of College Science Teaching* 32 (5): 327–331.

Camill, P. 2002. Watch your step: Understanding the impact of your personal consumption on the environment. National Center for Case Study Teaching in Science Case Collection. *http://ublib.buffalo.edu/libraries/projects/cases/footprint/footprint.html.*

DINE Systems, Inc.. *www.dinesystems.com.*

Earth Day Network footprint calculator. *www.earthday.net/footprint/index.html.*

Francek, M. 2002/2003. Community service: Learning through an Earth science fair. *Journal of College Science Teaching* 32 (4): 246–251.

Gordon, R., ed. 2000. *Problem based service learning: A fieldguide for making a difference in higher education.* 2nd ed. Bedford, NH: Campus Compact for New Hampshire.

Grossman, J., and T. Cooper. 2004. Linking environmental science students to external community partners: A critical assessment of a service-learning course. *Journal of College Science Teaching* 33 (5): 32–35.

Haines, S. 2003. Informal life science: Incorporating service-learning components into biology education. *Journal of College Science Teaching* 32 (7): 440–442.

Lott, C., and C. W. Michelmore. 1997. Learning through service: A faculty perspective. *Liberal Education* 83 (1): 40–45.

Phillips, M. W. 1997. Teaching general biology for nonmajors through community service projects. *Journal of College Science Teaching* 26 (4): 253–257.

Prentice, M., and R. M. Garcia. 2000. Service-learning: The next generation in education. *Community College Journal of Research and Practice* 24 (1): 9–26.

Rao, S., D. Shamath, and R. Collay. 2007. Meaningful involvement of science undergraduates in K–12 outreach. *Journal of College Science Teaching* 36 (6): 54–58.

Rhoads, R. A., and J. P. F. Howard, eds. 1998. Academic service-learning: A pedagogy of action and reflection. In *New directions for teaching and learning, no. 73.* San Francisco: Jossey-Bass.

Tai-Seale, T. 2001. Liberating service-learning and applying the new practice. *College Teaching* 49 (1): 14–18.

Tessier, J. 2006. Writing assignments in a non-major introductory ecology class. *Journal of College Science Teaching* 35 (4): 25–29.

Wood, B. 2003. Improving wellness on campus: Service-learning in a human nutrition class. *Journal of College Science Teaching* 33 (2): 27–31.

World Wildlife Fund footprint calculator. *http://independent.footprint.wwf.org.uk.*

Chapter 15

Case Studies

Stories of medical mysteries and case studies of patients have always fascinated me. As a PhD candidate at a medical school, I found that scientific topics presented in the context of a disease or syndrome, sometimes with actual patients brought into the lecture hall, were the concepts that I most fully understood. Decades later I can recall some of these cases and what I learned from them. Today my favorite columns in the periodicals I read are those that tell the story of how an unusual medical diagnosis was made or an epidemiological puzzle was solved: "Annals of Medicine" in the *New Yorker*, "Diagnosis" in the *New York Times Magazine*, "Vital Signs" in *Discover Magazine*, and even "Clinical Problem Solving" in the *New England Journal of Medicine*. And, of course, most of us love an interesting story, and if we have a tale of our own, we enjoying sharing it with others.

Years ago I would remove pages of magazines that related those interesting true stories, apply a three-hole punch, and insert them in the middle of the appropriate section of my lecture notes. When I got to those lectures, I shared with my students what I had read. I observed that when I removed those tattered articles from my three-ring binder and began to tell a story, students paused their furious note-taking, turned their faces toward me, and listened intently. They were actually absorbing information during the class meeting rather than writing something for future "learning" the night before the next test. Although I was delighted that I had grabbed their attention, this passive listening still failed to involve them in practicing their own problem-solving skills as they considered the case.

For a time I used prepared cases from a couple of published workbooks of case studies (Allen 1993; Lewis 1994) sold as supplements to textbooks.

Although these workbooks were well designed for demonstrating the scientific process, many of the topics and difficulty levels were inappropriate for my classes, so I could only draw on a fraction of the case studies in each workbook. Also, abruptly inserting the cases into a lecture sometimes resulted in a disjointed presentation.

A significant side trip in my journey to pedagogical reform was my participation in a five-day summer workshop at the State University of New York at Buffalo. This workshop expanded my use of case studies beyond medical topics, stimulated my creativity about ways to teach with cases, and forever changed my use of cases in every course I teach. Over the years, with grants from the U.S. Department of Education Fund for the Improvement of Postsecondary Education, the Pew Charitable Trusts, and the National Science Foundation, Clyde (Kipp) Herreid and his colleague Nancy Schiller built the National Center for Case Study Teaching in Science at the State University of New York at Buffalo. Since 1993 thousands of science teachers—including high school, undergraduate, graduate, and professional school faculty—have been introduced to case study teaching by attending center-sponsored workshops and conferences. The center's website is a comprehensive resource that not only publishes hundreds of peer-reviewed cases and teaching notes in the National Center for Case Study Teaching in Science Case Collection but also lists videotapes, articles, books, bibliographies, and web links to the case study literature; possible sources of case study ideas; other case websites for both science and nonscience disciplines; resources and references for assessing case-based teaching and learning; reports, studies, and other innovative projects related to science pedagogy; a directory of teachers who use case studies; and titles of science education journals for 19 different science, engineering, and mathematics disciplines. Monthly columns in the *Journal of College Science Teaching*, plus an annual edition of this periodical, are devoted to case studies from this collection that put science and mathematics into context.

As explained by Gallucci (2006), employing the case study method can help solve some major problems in science education today as identified by the National Research Council (2005): addressing students' prior knowledge and misconceptions about concepts they bring to our courses; providing a conceptual framework in which to organize the large volume of factual knowledge; and teaching students to take responsibility for their learning by defining their learning goals and assessing their own progress. The case study method of instruction tackles all three of these challenges.

DIVERSIFYING YOUR PEDAGOGY

In the words of Herreid, whose work has made the case study method both attractive and accessible to science educators, "Case studies are stories with an educational message" (Herreid 2007c, p. xiv). This adaptable definition invites an instructor to use case studies either to support a variety of teaching strategies or as a primary instructional strategy around which an entire course is designed. Teaching with case studies embodies the flexibility I encourage in my final step to Lecture-Free Teaching in Chapter 3. But incorporating case studies into one's course requires thoughtful planning. I strongly agree with Gallucci's (2006) contention that if cases are not congruent with an instructor's learning goals and teaching strategies, students may enjoy the experience but the case study exercise may fail to promote the intended learning goals.

Case studies work in classes of all sizes. I have used case studies in classes or workshops ranging from 20 to 50 people. Peer Instruction (described in Chapter 12) works well with case studies, and both Brickman (2007) and Herreid (2007a) report successful use of case studies in large lecture halls with as many as 450 students by using clickers or personal response systems to facilitate discussion. Many instructors (Field 2003, 2005), including myself, have designed an entire seminar around experiencing, presenting, and writing case studies, as I describe in Chapter 5.

My favorite way to present cases is with role-playing (Cherif and Somervill 1995; Cherif, Verma, and Somervill 1998), for which students read the parts of various characters in the case narrative. Depending on the size of the class and the self-consciousness of the students, I have them stand in front of the classroom or simply read from their seats. Most students are quite willing to participate in this thespian exercise, which engages and is enjoyed by the entire class.

I use case studies in virtually every course I teach and every workshop I lead, because they serve as a way to involve those with different learning styles and to diversify my teaching portfolio (Camill 2006). But more important, case studies model the scientific process effectively and make inquiry-based learning possible in educational contexts in which it is impractical to have a laboratory experience. Neither traditional lectures nor cookbook-style laboratory exercises give students the opportunity to think like scientists struggling with real-world problems. With good planning, case studies can be incorporated easily into a course taught primarily by lecture.

I have also used case studies in the laboratory as the structure around which an investigatory activity is built. An example of this is in my Sciences II class, for which I use a case called Avogadro Goes to Court (Bieron and Dinan 1999). This case study was inspired by a lawsuit brought by students against a computer sciences professor at Pace University who assigned them the task of calculating the cost of a single aluminum atom in a roll of aluminum foil. The content explores the concepts of Avogadro's number and the mole, so it would be relevant to nearly any introductory-level science course. After role-playing the case study and reading the original *Wall Street Journal* article in which the lawsuit was reported (Felsenthal 1995), students work in their cooperative learning teams to complete the assignment originally given by the ill-fated professor. I give each team a piece of aluminum foil similar to that described in the case study. Using a meterstick and a simple balance scale, groups design and execute the solution. By thinking through the problem of how to complete the calculation, students learn that they must read the information on the aluminum foil box to determine an unused roll's area and cost; then measure the mass and area of the piece they were given; and, finally, apply concepts of Avogadro's number, the mole, significant figures, unit conversions, scientific notation, and mass units of atoms of elements.

Other cases introduce problems that encourage higher-order thinking without the goal of a "correct" answer. Two categories of case studies published in the National Center for Case Study Teaching in Science Case Collection are Medical Ethics and Ecology/Environment. Both of these, almost by definition, expose conflicts between science and society. Cases listed in other categories may also deal with timely societal dilemmas. A brief scan of abstracts in the collection provided me with the following examples:

- A case designed for physics or environmental geology students teaches the physics of hurricane formation by applying the principles of fluid dynamics and thermodynamics to Hurricane Katrina, along with consideration of the conflict between politics and science (Lancor 2008).
- A chemistry case explores the current debate over the use of DDT to control malaria in poor, developing countries (Dinan and Bieron 2001).
- For a computer science course, students consider the consequences of inadequate testing of new software (Zubairi 2002).
- Preservice teachers would benefit by debating whether intelligent design should be taught in a science classroom (Herreid 2007b).

PROMOTING COOPERATIVE LEARNING

As I explain in Chapter 10, I organize students into permanent cooperative learning teams within the first 15 minutes of the first class meeting of the semester. Collaborative learning, described in detail in Chapter 12, is an integral part of lecture-free pedagogy, and teaching students from the beginning how to work in a supportive rather than competitive fashion is vital to the success of this strategy. To facilitate bonding of group members, soon after building cooperative learning teams I lead an activity that requires members to work together to solve a problem. A glance at my sample topic schedules in Appendix A shows that in five out of six courses, the initial activity is a case study. This also provides an early introduction to a teaching method I use frequently throughout the semester in every course I teach.

For my introductory courses I choose a case that teaches students to apply the scientific process and that is often the title of the coursepack's content topic outline for the first week of the semester. The General Cases category in the collection contains a variety of cases that not only cover themes engaging to high school and college students, but also expect them to practice the scientific method. I also choose a first case that assumes minimal previous knowledge of a topic and works well for a group of students contributing diverse life experiences and representing a variety of college majors. Numerous appropriate first-day cases are sprinkled throughout the other categories in the collection. Appendix C-12 lists courses for which I adapt a case study for the initial cooperative learning team activity, along with titles and abstracts of the cases from the online collection. New cases are published each year, constantly expanding my choices.

Science educators use case studies to promote cooperative learning in a variety of ways. Sample topic schedules in Appendix A demonstrate how I weave case studies into course content. Gallucci (2006) published a table showing her connections among content topics, questions, concepts, and cases. Ribbens's (2006) table identifies cases in the order in which they were used in biology courses and provides comments as to the effectiveness of the case in the course.

As mentioned earlier, science educators report the effective use of case studies in large lecture classes to promote cooperative learning. Brickman (2007) gives one personal response system clicker to each team or group rather than to each individual. Chapter 5 describes my Science Seminar for junior and senior college science majors. Each week students give one another feedback on their written and oral presentations of case studies, thereby nurturing a supportive rather than competitive classroom ethos.

ENCOURAGING HIGHER-ORDER THINKING

The hierarchical learning levels within the cognitive domain, as defined by Bloom's taxonomy (1956), include knowledge, comprehension, application, analysis, synthesis, and evaluation. Each element of a lower level provides the foundation for an element in the next level. For knowledge, students acquire factual information; for comprehension, they demonstrate their understanding of terms and concepts by explaining them in their own words; for application, they use a concept in a new situation; for analysis, they must explain the facts presented and determine how constituent parts of the material being considered relate to one another; for synthesis, they make connections among the elements of the lower-level skills (knowledge, comprehension, and application) and the higher-level skills (analysis, synthesis, and evaluation); and for evaluation, students use elements of all of the underlying levels to construct an argument for or against an opinion or to determine the quality of information or value of ideas.

A survey of 101 science faculty at universities and colleges in the United States and Canada provides evidence that case-based instruction encourages higher-order thinking among participating students. Faculty report that cases have a positive effect on student learning, critical thinking, and participation. They believe that as a result of using cases, students gained critical thinking skills, made better connections across multiple content areas, had a better grasp of the practical applications of core concepts, and were better able to view an issue from multiple perspectives (Yadav et al. 2007).

Students understand more clearly how scientists make discoveries if they learn about concrete examples from current scientific research, as in Guilfoile's (1999) scientific method case studies on antisense technology and on HIV vaccines. Similarly, the case study method can be used as an alternative (Smith and Murphy 1998) or in addition to the investigative laboratory as I describe in a previous section of this chapter ("Diversifying Your Pedagogy"). Chamany (2006) reported that using case studies to bring discussions of social justice into science curricula can attract and maintain the interest of students who ordinarily avoid science because they believe it has no immediate relevance to them. The cases allow them to make connections between what they learn in the classroom and what is meaningful in their everyday lives. As explained earlier, case studies offer numerous opportunities to connect what are considered nonscientific areas with the content of science. When students participate in these exercises, they cannot help but employ their higher-level thinking skills.

Contentious topics abound in science, but it is important to introduce students to a controversial science case in a way that motivates them to discuss, debate, and learn from these issues (Brickman, Glynn, and Graybeal 2008). I have learned the importance of preventing discussions from ballooning into emotional expressions of opinions that are not based on scientific content. If an instructor launches an activity by posing questions whose answers depend on knowledge, comprehension, and application (the lower levels of Bloom's taxonomy), and gradually adds questions requiring analysis, synthesis, and evaluation (the higher thinking levels), the exercise will more likely prove fruitful.

ORGANIZING A SEMINAR AROUND CASE STUDIES

I considered offering a case studies seminar for science majors for several years before I got around to submitting a course proposal. The initial inspiration was Field's descriptions of incorporating a case study format into a senior seminar course (2003, 2005). My course proposal was also a response to years of observing less-than-satisfactory oral and written products at the conclusion of an environmental studies senior capstone course.

The fortuitous publication of the book *Start With a Story: The Case Study Method of Teaching College Science* (Herreid 2007c) supplied me with an unconventional but effective textbook. Although this book was written for college science educators, it proved appropriate for seminar participants, who expressed how much they enjoyed the author's colorful narrative style.

As Field (2003) explains, the typical senior seminar course strives to have students use the same higher-order thinking skills as those demonstrated by an effective case study presentation. He reports that the case study method is at least as effective as the traditional lecture for presenting and teaching current scientific discoveries (2005). The case study method is an excellent fit for a seminar format because it eliminates the content-heavy lecture but remains factually informative.

In this chapter I briefly summarize my design for Science Seminar. Details of this course are in Chapter 5. Science Seminar is open to any student pursuing a science major or minor, as well as to elementary and secondary education majors with a concentration in science. Class members are juniors or seniors who have successfully completed both English courses required by the general education curriculum. The seminar also fulfills the general education curriculum requirement for a three-credit-hour writing-intensive course.

During this semester-long course, students learn how to choose an appropriate scientific topic for a case study, complete weekly written or oral assignments designed to improve science writing and presentation skills, submit a final manuscript in a form suitable for publication in a peer-reviewed journal, and present their original case study in a public forum. Each week's homework readings, class discussions, oral presentations, and peer critiques are designed to progressively teach students to use the case study method so they can create a clear and comprehensive written manuscript and oral presentation on a topic of their choice. They work on their projects outside the scheduled class meetings.

The seminar meets during weekly three-hour sessions for a total of approximately 45 hours of class time, during which students participate in discussions of their written and oral assignments and critique each other's presentations using the same criteria I use for graded assessments. Students report that ungraded peer critiques are one of the most useful aspects of the seminar. Because I do not read the written peer evaluations, student evaluators are less inhibited about helping their peers improve because negative comments cannot influence my grading. Candid feedback promotes camaraderie among students and strengthens cooperative learning.

The seminar emphasizes scientific inquiry. Each student finds, reads, and interprets relevant scientific data while investigating a current topic in depth. Students already involved in original laboratory or field research can choose to write data-intensive cases that guide readers through their projects.

Using criteria I have organized, each student chooses a topic about which she or he will write an original case study in one of several case study styles demonstrated throughout the semester. Students use factual information from the primary scientific literature to write the case story as well as thought-provoking discussion questions and teaching notes that describe how the case should be presented to a participating audience. In the written manuscript the student logically defends or counters a position proposed during discussion of the topic. During an oral presentation, he or she familiarizes the audience with relevant background information, presents the case, and facilitates a discussion of the case's research questions. As illustrated by Appendix B-5, the final product is graded on story structure, oral presentation, and written teaching notes.

Each week I assign appropriate chapters from Herreid's book (see Appendix A-6, Science Seminar Topic Schedule), starting with those describing the nature of case studies and the characteristics of a good case. The class spends several weeks reading about and experiencing various styles of case studies, all while students consider ideas for their final project by completing short assignments that are shared during class (Appendixes B-2 and B-3). During the first half of the semester, I model methods of presenting case studies by leading them through examples from the National Center for Case Study Teaching in Science Case Collection and having the students participate just as they would in a nonseminar class. During the second half of the semester, the students complete readings on how to teach with case studies, and then each student presents to the class a case chosen from the collection. The class and I critique each student's presentation with a set of grading criteria (Appendix B-4). During the final weeks of the semester, students read extensively from textbook chapters about how to write case studies and case study teaching notes. The student's final presentation to the class is of his or her original case study, which is again critiqued by the class and by me (Appendix B-5) before being presented in a public forum.

OBTAINING COPYRIGHT PERMISSION

I include a copy of each case study I plan to use during the semester in the coursepacks sold to students. Case studies are readily available online in the National Center for Case Study Teaching in Science Case Collection, and each can be easily converted via a link to Adobe Portable Document Format (PDF) to print.

The guidelines for using the cases are available through a link at the end of each case study. Copyright for most of the cases on the website is held by the National Center for Case Study Teaching in Science. Educational, not-for-profit use of these cases in the classroom by individual instructors does not require permission, but reproduction of a case in a printed work (such as my coursepacks) as well as reproduction on a website does require permission. For years I have easily requested and promptly been granted copyright permission to include specific case studies via this e-mail address: *permissions@sciencecases.org*. I place a copy of the permission letter in the front of each coursepack.

TEACHING WITH SPONTANEITY

I met Eric Ribbens in 2000 when we were both participants in the annual Case Studies in Science Workshop presented by the National Center for Case Study Teaching in Science at the State University of New York at Buffalo. He subsequently became a regular and frequent user of case studies in his courses, as well as a prolific contributor of original case studies to the Case Collection. He describes teaching introductory courses with case studies in a way that rings true to me—perhaps because as a result of latent genes I produced two sons who are professional jazz musicians. Ribbens wrote, "Just as jazz is a combination of preparation overlaid with improvisation, case teaching for me has been a combination of preparation, improvisation, and chaos" (2006, p. 10). The spontaneity of using case studies is analogous to performing jazz. In teaching, the spontaneity consists of letting go of control—leaving your teacher-centered style at the podium and moving into the classroom using a student-centered style, modifying cases to better fit a topic in your course, and using unanticipated discussions as opportunities for creativity. This extemporaneous style still requires good preparation, just as my sons' performances require much prior practice alone and with other musicians. Improvisation in the classroom, as on the concert stage, is successful only after thoughtful planning. Case studies embody the flexibility I advocate in my 13 steps to Lecture-Free Teaching.

REFERENCES

Allen, R. 1993. *Critical thinking case study workbook: Biology.* 4th ed. Dubuque, IA: W. C. Brown.

Bieron, J. F., and F. J. Dinan. 1999. Avogadro goes to court. National Center for Case Study Teaching in Science Case Collection. *www.sciencecases. org/avogadro/avogadro.asp.*

Bloom, B. S., ed. 1956. *Taxonomy of educational objectives: The classification of educational goals. Handbook 1: Cognitive domain.* New York: Longman.

Brickman, P. 2007. The case of the druid Dracula: A directed "clicker" case study on DNA fingerprinting. In *Start with a story: The case study method of teaching college science,* ed. C. F. Herreid, 227–235. Arlington, VA: NSTA Press.

Brickman, P., S. Glynn, and G. Graybeal. 2008. Introducing students to cases. *Journal of College Science Teaching* 37 (3): 12–16.

Camill, P. 2006. Case studies add value to a diverse teaching portfolio in science courses. *Journal of College Science Teaching* 36 (2): 31–37.

Case Studies in Science, State University of New York at Buffalo. National Center for Case Study Teaching in Science. *http://ublib.buffalo.edu/ libraries/projects/cases/case.html.*

Chamany, K. 2006. Science and social justice: Making the case for case studies. *Journal of College Science Teaching* 36 (2): 54–59.

Cherif, A. H., and C. H. Somervill. 1995. Maximizing learning: Using role playing in the classroom. *American Biology Teacher* 57 (1): 28–33.

Cherif, A. H., S. Verma and C. Somervill. 1998. From the Los Angeles zoo to the classroom: Transforming real cases via role-play into productive learning activities. *American Biology Teacher* 60 (8): 613–617.

Dinan, F. J., and J. F. Bieron. 2001. To spray or not to spray: A debate over malaria and DDT. National Center for Case Study Teaching in Science Case Collection. *http://ublib.buffalo.edu/libraries/projects/cases/ddt/ddt.html.*

Felsenthal, E. 1995. Avogadro's number, you say, Professor? I don't think so. *Wall Street Journal Eastern Edition,* May 9. A1.

Field, P. R. 2003. Senior seminar: Using case studies to teach the components of a successful seminar. *Journal of College Science Teaching* 32 (5): 298–301.

———. 2005. Creating case study presentations: A survey of senior seminar students. *Journal of College Science Teaching* 35 (1): 56–59.

Gallucci, K. 2006. Learning concepts with cases. *Journal of College Science Teaching* 36 (2):16–20.

Guilfoile, P. 1999. Two case studies in the scientific method: Antisense experiments and HIV vaccination studies. *American Biology Teacher* 61 (4): 259–263.

Herreid, C. F. 2007a. "Clicker" cases: Introducing case study teaching into large classrooms. In *Start with a story: The case study method of teaching college science,* ed. C. F. Herreid, 221–226. Arlington, VA: NSTA Press.

———. 2007b. Equal time for intelligent design? An intimate debate case. National Center for Case Study Teaching in Science Case Collection. *www.sciencecases.org/id_debate/id_debate.asp.*

———, ed. 2007c. *Start with a story: The case study method of teaching college science.* Arlington, VA: NSTA Press.

Lancor, R. A. 2008. In the eye of the storm: A case study in natural disasters. National Center for Case Study Teaching in Science Case Collection. *www.sciencecases.org/hurricane/hurricane.asp.*

Lewis, R. 1994. *Case workbook in human genetics.* Dubuque, IA: W. C. Brown.

National Research Council (NRC). 2005. *How students learn: Science in the classroom.* Washington, DC: National Academies Press.

Ribbens, E. 2006. Teaching with jazz: Using multiple cases to teach introductory biology. *Journal of College Science Teaching* 36 (2): 10–15.

Smith, R. A., and S. K. Murphy. 1998. Using case studies to increase learning and interest in biology. *American Biology Teacher* 60 (4): 265–268.

Yadav, A., M. Lundeberg, M. DeSchryver, K. Dirkin, N. A. Schiller, K. Maier, and C. F. Herreid. 2007. Teaching science with case studies: A national survey of faculty perceptions of the benefits and challenges of using cases. *Journal of College Science Teaching* 37 (1): 34–38.

Zubairi, J. A. 2002. To test or not to test the software: A case study on ethics in computing. National Center for Case Study Teaching in Science Case Collection. *http://ublib.buffalo.edu/libraries/projects/cases/computing/computing_ethics.html.*

Chapter 16

Student-Led Teaching Models

When I began to fundamentally reform my methods for teaching introductory science courses, the first step was to assemble a large collection of student-centered active learning exercises. My idea was to use the activities, gleaned from books and journal articles, to gradually replace my instructor-centered lectures. I determined which ones would teach students the factual course content I would have ordinarily presented in a lecture. Then I collected the supplies necessary to lead these activities during class, purchasing most at local stores. Although I saved my department money by using inexpensive household items rather than kits from scientific supply companies, the process was expensive in terms of my own time and effort. Nevertheless, after a summer of preparation I was equipped with many new activities and looking forward to teaching my introductory biology course.

Another course I taught that fall was Biology 350, Genetics. As I discovered while reviewing ideas for active learning, genetics lends itself particularly well to simulations using models constructed from household supplies. Having students manipulate objects representing molecules or cell structures helps them comprehend abstract molecular biological processes and step-by-step procedures for genetic analysis. When the semester began, I had a stack of articles describing imaginative ways to model genetic processes, but no time remaining to purchase and organize the necessary supplies. Reluctant to let these promising teaching opportunities slip by, I tried something new: I assigned each of my Genetics students one teaching model to assemble and lead, hoping that later in the semester I would have time to take over. I gave each student a copy of a different article (mostly from *The American Biology Teacher*) that described how to build and teach with an easily manipulated model. I asked the students to collect all of the supplies listed in the Materials and Methods sections of their assigned article—and bring me receipts so that I could reimburse them with department funds—and to carefully follow the instructions for leading the activity. On a scheduled date the student taught the appropriate concept to the rest of the class.

Students took this assignment seriously, and most of them did a terrific job. When we completed the first set of models a few weeks into the term, they asked, "Can we do more of these?" By serendipity I had stumbled on what would become the foundation of my upper-level genetics course (Wood 2009). The students' discovery is what we educators have always known: Explaining a concept to someone else is the best way to learn and understand it yourself. Tessier (2004) assessed the effectiveness of peer teaching in biology and reported that, not surprisingly, students performed best on exam questions covering material they themselves had taught. Test averages increased significantly after student teaching experience, with improvement most pronounced for struggling students. Another advantage is that a student sometimes provides more effective explanations than a teacher because the student has only recently grasped the concept and is therefore more aware of possible misconceptions (Mazur 1997; McManus 2005).

Open any journal written for science educators and you will find an abundance of innovative methods for teaching difficult concepts. Although I faithfully save and file articles describing potentially useful ideas, I cannot cram more into the scheduled class meeting hours for a semester. For example, I currently have more than 80 articles in my folder of genetics activities alone. So every year I substitute some new activities for old ones, gather feedback from my students, and either return to the old ones or keep the new ones until a possibly more effective suggestion comes my way. Some articles I keep were written for middle- or high-school teachers, and these often explain which National Science Education Standards (National Research Council 1996) are addressed, facilitating incorporation of the activity into a required K–12 curriculum. I find that nearly all can be adapted to appropriately model concepts for college students.

For example, one activity I modified for classroom presentations to middle school, high school, and college students—as well as to secondary and postsecondary science teachers during hands-on workshops—is a DNA profiling simulation (Reed 2001). Participants become suspects in a school robbery, create their own DNA paper molecules, cut their molecules with scissors acting as restriction enzymes, create their own banding patterns on a chalkboard electrophoresis gel, and compare them to the mock-up crime scene sample. Although the term *DNA fingerprinting* is familiar to most, misconceptions abound. A model like this is both simple and effective as a teaching tool, and my upper-level students find the preparation and presentation of similar activities to be challenging but valuable educational experiences.

In my introductory courses I maintain responsibility for leading in-class activities. In Genetics, however, each student prepares and demonstrates a hands-on interactive model as one of his or her graded assessments. During the first week of the semester students choose, from my list of articles, the teaching model they will present. The dates for each presentation are listed on the Genetics Topic Schedule (see Appendix A-5). I explain that it may be more beneficial to select a topic that is less familiar or appears more complicated because at the end of the presentation, the student will understand the concept better than anyone else in the class. Appendix C-13 lists content topics and teaching models assigned to students for a typical semester.

In the Genetics Coursepack is a copy of the Student-Led Teaching Model Grading Rubric (Appendix B-10). To familiarize students with these criteria, I ask them to evaluate me, using the grading sheet, as I lead the first teaching model of the semester. This helps them consider the qualities of an effective presentation, as well as understand my expectations for this assignment. This initial exercise establishes an openness between my students and me, promoting the learning partnership to which I refer in the subtitle of this book. As with other learner-centered teaching methods, this one introduces a change in the distribution of power in the classroom (Weimer 2002), benefiting both students and me by encouraging them to take more responsibility for their own learning and creating a classroom environment more conducive to both teaching and learning.

Also, during student-led teaching models I take the classroom seat of the presenter, temporarily joining that student's learning team. This gives me the opportunity to closely observe and facilitate each team's cooperative work a few times each semester.

Student-led teaching models begin in Week 2 of the semester. On the assigned date the presenter explains appropriate background information and then guides classmates through a cellular process or laboratory procedure by having them manipulate the components of the model. The articles I give them are written so that the teaching activity can be easily repeated by another educator, in the same way a publication in a scientific research journal describes materials and methods for precise replication by another laboratory. The authors frequently include templates of figures to duplicate and distribute to student participants.

Many models use manipulatives, a set of objects that students maneuver with their hands to simulate or represent a biological topic under study. Using both their visual and tactile senses facilitates students' comprehension of abstract terms, structures, and processes. The materials my students and I use to create most of the manipulatives include food items such as candy, cookies, and uncooked linguine noodles; common household items such as paper, index cards, paper bags, scissors, glue, tape, pushpins, paper clips, coins, and socks; toys or games such as Legos, Pop-It Beads, playing cards, or dice; and sewing or craft items such as velcro, ribbon, thread, yarn, small beads, plastic tubing, Styrofoam balls, Popsicle sticks, and pipe cleaners. I encourage students to be creative and substitute materials when they cannot find what the article suggests or when they think a modification would improve the accuracy or effectiveness of the model. To discourage wasting time or money, if a model has been presented in previous years I keep materials that can be reused with the warning to avoid copying what another student has done in the past without contributing new ideas and improvements. Points are awarded on the grading rubric for such improvements (Appendix B-10). Students also need to prepare enough kits so that everyone can participate fully and the activity is more than simply a demonstration with most classmates as passive observers.

Some students practice their models ahead of time on their own children or other family members or friends. Others later ask to borrow the materials to use for presentations in their teacher education classes. Although none of my classes is for a teacher education department, I believe that student-led teaching models would be a valuable assignment, particularly for a class on science teaching methods.

In a traditional instructor-centered classroom, student presentations are often scheduled at the end of the semester, serving as a capstone to the course. Other students are generally not responsible for learning the information presented by their peers. By contrast, in the course design I describe here, student-led teaching models are the opportunity for classmates to understand and learn about a topic. I must therefore do all I can to ensure that presentations are of consistent, good quality. Over the years my grading criteria have evolved into an extremely specific rubric. Although more rare now, I still encounter an unevenness of effort and must be prepared to jump in and help with the teaching model when the presentation is of low quality or contains factual errors or when the presenter is absent from class on the scheduled date.

REFERENCES

Mazur, E. 1997. *Peer Instruction: A user's manual.* Upper Saddle River, NJ: Prentice-Hall.

McManus, D. A. 2005. *Leaving the lectern: Cooperative learning and the critical first days of students working in groups.* Bolton, MA: Anker Publishing Company.

National Research Council (NRC). 1996. *National science education standards.* Washington, DC: National Academy Press.

Reed, E. 2001. A DNA fingerprint simulation: Different, simple, effective. *American Biology Teacher* 63 (6): 437–441.

Tessier, J. 2004. Using peer teaching to promote learning in biology. *Journal of College Science Teaching* 33 (6): 16–19.

Weimer, M. 2002. *Learner-centered teaching: Five key changes to practice.* San Francisco: Jossey-Bass.

Wood, B. S. 2009. Student-led teaching models. In *College science teachers guide to assessment,* eds. T. R. Lord, D. P. French, and L. W. Crow, 117–120. Arlington, VA: NSTA Press.

PART IV

The Process and Progress of Change in Science Education

Chapter 17

The Continuing Need for Science Education Reform

WHAT CHANGED AFTER WORLD WAR II?

When World War II began in 1939, economic, industrial, and scientific capabilities were committed to the war effort, effectively alleviating the hardships of the Great Depression. With the war's conclusion in 1945, federal support for research continued and scientific progress became a priority. A change in academic life occurred: New young scholars joined college and university faculties, and although hired to teach, their evaluations were based primarily on research productivity. Simultaneously, the 1944 GI Bill of Rights dramatically shifted the demography of college student populations. Nearly eight million former service people went to college, and higher education was considered a right of every American. So at the same time that colleges and universities were growing more open and inclusive, the standards for tenure and promotion were becoming more restrictive. With professors experiencing increasing pressure to conduct research and publish results, their pedagogy inevitably suffered (Boyer 1990). Students entering college in 2001 encountered faculty who spent only 57% of their time on teaching-related activities. Time devoted to teaching was even lower at research or doctoral institutions and among full professors (National Research Council 2003).

Something that Tagg (2003) calls the "instruction paradigm" has been part of higher education since World War II. Responding to the dramatic growth in college enrollment after the war, combined with an increasingly mobile population, institutions in the United States developed standards that allow for an easy transfer of college credits. This resulted in similar course requirements and nearly identical course designs among colleges and universities, despite their very different missions. The definition of a successful college became one that filled its classes and had a growing student body. The emphasis on transferability of credits and enrollment numbers continues today, particularly in the current economic climate.

Science also gained a presence in K–12 education that did not exist before the war. I was 11 years old in October 1957 when the Soviet Union launched Sputnik, the world's first satellite, initiating a frenzy of activity to improve science teaching in the United States. I became a beneficiary of this new emphasis on science education and remember my public high school offering "experimental" Biological Science Curriculum Study (BSCS) and Physical Science Study Committee (PSSC) courses in the 1960s. We students felt special using the plain-looking, softbound textbooks and watching demonstrations by actual M.I.T. physicists on 16 millimeter films produced with no more polish than today's home video and screened with reel-to-reel movie projectors. Perhaps because my teachers were enthusiastic about trying something new or because the pedagogy was, in fact, more engaging, I majored in biology in college and went on to earn my doctorate in medical sciences.

More recent decades brought concern about science literacy and produced reports such as *Benchmarks for Science Literacy* (American Association for the Advancement of Science 1993), *National Science Education Standards* (National Research Council 1996), and *The Liberal Art of Science: Agenda for Action* (American Association for the Advancement of Science 1990) to guide K–16 science curriculum design. Calls to use learning research results to pilot development and implementation of courses and curricula also emerged (National Research Council 2000). Nor can we ignore what students of all ages bring to the classroom in the form of preconceptions. The Harvard-Smithsonian video *A Private Universe* dramatized how misconceptions can thwart the acquisition of new and accurate knowledge (Sadler 1989).

WHAT NEEDS TO CHANGE TODAY?

Although we witnessed enormous changes in society, technology, and student demographics in the past seven decades, how we teach remains relatively the same. The traditional student of yesterday is now an exception. F. James Rutherford, the retired chief education officer of the American Association for the Advancement of Science, expressed disappointment with the absence of significant and sustained improvements in the quality of K–12 science teaching during the past half century. He does not blame this failure on lack of human effort or financial investment, but rather on the fact that "schools *accommodated* the post-war changes when they might very well have taken advantage of them to radically *transform* the K–12 education system, creating a system for the 21st century rather than sprucing up the early 20th century system that still mostly prevails" (2005, p. 376). He observes that science, technology, engineering, and mathematics are still taught as separate disciplines, ignoring the fact that they are increasingly intertwined.

Graduate programs do not teach how to work at the junctions of these disciplines, collaborate with others, or move easily from one topic to another (Monastersky 2007). Much undergraduate teaching, especially in the early years, is done by graduate assistants with little, if any, experience whose primary concerns are, by necessity, completing their own graduate programs. PhD programs provide expertise in ever-narrowing subject areas and highly developed research skills but rarely any preparation for teaching (Scarlett 2004). In the meantime, courses remain dependent on textbooks that become bulkier with content but do not improve in quality (Rutherford 2005).

Another change in student demographics is the influx of post–9/11 war veterans recently returned from the Afghan and Iraqi conflicts. Many of these new students chose military service immediately after high school because they found school boring or frustrating. Now, with their new maturity and motivation, they are anxious to continue their education. But stepping from a highly structured military life into the looseness of an American college campus is a major hurdle. Classes structured around cooperative learning (as discussed in Chapter 12) with the resulting camaraderie provide an environment in which the veterans function well, and such courses can do much to keep these students in college (Alvarez 2008). A new GI Bill (officially the Post–9/11 Veterans Educational Assistance Act of 2008) will undoubtedly increase the numbers of these promising students in higher education. Pedagogical changes we make in response to their presence in our classrooms will benefit all students.

Similarly, preparation of science teachers has not responded appropriately to changes in the composition of K–12 student bodies. Although Rutherford applauds the reports cited in the previous section of this chapter, I fear that the state and local learning standards that grew from these publications stifle creative and flexible classroom pedagogy and require teachers and their administrators to focus on content coverage rather than application and understanding of concepts that lead to long-term retention of knowledge. Many teachers are worn out by the effort to implement each iteration of standards; they have neither the time nor the energy to incorporate new methods for presenting content. Even Advanced Placement courses, thought by many to represent the pinnacle of secondary school education, require exams that are standardized in a way that does not assess basic understanding of fundamental principles and concepts, but favors rote learning of terminology (Klymkowsky, Garvin-Doxas, and Zeilik 2003).

In higher education, even without the rigid imposition of learning standards, increasing pressure toward the easily transferable student credit hour encourages cookie-cutter courses among community colleges, four-year colleges, and universities, despite widely divergent missions and student bodies. Another result of the nearly universal use of student credit hours is that degree levels are defined by the hours of classroom time required to complete them. This implies a direct correlation between classroom time and educational value, an untested hypothesis. Some educators recommend less emphasis on the accumulation of student credit hours based on time in classrooms with more emphasis on assessment through competency-based broad examinations (Scarlett 2004).

Tagg (2003) recommends that colleges change from the currently dominant *instruction paradigm* to what he calls a *learning paradigm*. He criticizes the instruction paradigm in which the educational mission of colleges is defined by offering courses and putting more students in more classes. A learning paradigm, on the other hand, provides a long-term goal of learning itself, in which students derive meaning from encountering new problems.

Tagg cites as an example how, in an instruction paradigm, students separate classroom learning from their fundamental long-term beliefs and concerns. When physics professor Eric Mazur (whose methods are described in Chapter 12) was administering the Force Concept Inventory (Hestenes, Wells, and Swackhamer 1992), a student asked, "Professor Mazur, how should I answer these questions? According to what you taught us, or by the way I think about these things?" Mazur observed that about 40% of the students did better on the difficult quantitative problems than on the simple conceptual ones; he gradually realized that many students concentrate on learning specific problem-solving strategies without attention to the underlying concepts. In Tagg's learning paradigm, these emphases would be reversed.

Lack of formal learning standards does not liberate science professors from the pressure to cover content at the expense of concept comprehension and retention of knowledge. Sometimes pressure is self-imposed by teaching scientists who are acutely aware of their discipline's rapidly expanding body of knowledge; other times senior faculty enforce content-driven syllabi in an effort to ensure appropriate preparation for upper-level courses. Unfortunately, postsecondary science educators are often quick to blame the K–12 system for the shortfall in science professionals, rather than institute their own reforms at the college level, where many students who are capable of remaining in science instead choose other careers (Tobias 1990).

Grants that support individual educators for short-term instructional-improvement projects seem at first glance to be a good idea. Unfortunately, innovations tend to vanish from the public eye once the funding cycle ends or when the originator moves on to new endeavors. These projects often must result in some sort of tangible product, such as instructional material or teaching enhancements that, although useful, do not initiate true pedagogical reform. We continue to spend money in this way not because we truly believe that someone will devise the perfect pedagogy, but simply because we are used to attempting reform in this manner (Tobias 1992).

Although some effective instructional strategies persist (such as the ones I describe in Part III of this book), they are not widely used in science education. The lecture remains dominant, and we have yet to experience real pedagogical transformation in science. We need to move from the instructor-centered delivery of knowledge to the student-centered participation in the learning process.

WHY DO WE NEED REFORM?

We need science education reform because of the decreasing numbers of young Americans who wish to become scientists, shortages of science and math teachers, and declining science literacy among ordinary American citizens. The recently released Trends in International Mathematics and Science Study (TIMSS) reports that although average math scores for U.S. fourth- and eighth-graders increased, the science scores were statistically unchanged compared to 1995, whereas other countries improved in science (Martin, Mullis, and Foy 2008). At the same time, the corporate world (future employers of our students) demands a highly trained workforce that can put knowledge to work by analyzing and solving problems, working in groups, and applying quantitative methods (American Association of State Colleges and Universities 2005; Brainard 2007; DeHaan 2005; National Science Board 2008).

Identification of these issues is not new, but attempted solutions are often flawed. For example, when faculty and administrators recognize the need to improve science learning for all students, the reaction is usually to change curriculum content and structure. Such modifications are unlikely to improve comprehension of content and ability to apply science knowledge, nor are they likely to enhance recruitment and retention of science majors.

Because women and certain minorities are traditionally underrepresented among scientists, some believed that Caucasian males were the most interested in and able to do science. We now know that a much larger and more diverse group of high school graduates enrolls in introductory college science courses, many with the intention of majoring in these disciplines. As I discuss in Chapter 2, at each educational stage science loses students to other majors. Some leave even after they have earned a science degree. Not only are the numbers of women and minorities fewer to begin with, but these groups abandon science majors more frequently, reducing their proportional representation even further (Seymour and Hewitt 1997).

When recruitment and retention programs for women and minorities first gathered strength in the 1980s, existing practices of science teaching were considered satisfactory. The focus was on aggressive recruitment of underrepresented groups to increase their numbers in science. But as we gained more understanding of how students learn, we discovered that reformed pedagogy enhances retention not only of women and other underrepresented groups but also of many Caucasian males whose talent and potential contributions were overlooked in the past. All students benefit from reformed teaching methods, potentially adding citizens to the science workforce and improving the science literacy of anyone enrolled in a science course.

The recently released *Bayer Facts of Science Education Survey XIII* (Bayer Corporation 2008) reports that although women and underrepresented minorities account for roughly two-thirds of today's U.S. workforce, women compose only 25% of the science, technology, engineering, and mathematics (STEM) workforce, and minorities much less than that. The poll of senior executives leading America's Fortune 1000 STEM companies reveals concern about the country's ability to attract and retain STEM workers to maintain America's global leadership in innovation. Eighty-seven percent of executives surveyed recommended teaching science with a hands-on, inquiry-based approach as a method to encourage more students to pursue these careers.

A curious discrepancy exists when comparing science majors graduating from research universities with those from four-year colleges. For some years now liberal arts colleges have produced a larger share of physical science majors than have research universities. According to Kim Bottomly, former Yale immunologist and the current president of Wellesley College: "A disproportionate number of science professors at top research institutions graduated from liberal-arts colleges. In 1998 Thomas Cech, president of the Howard Hughes Medical Institute, stated that liberal arts colleges produce about twice as many students who go on to science PhDs per graduate as other schools" (2008, p. 4). Historical data from both all-women colleges and certain all-black institutions demonstrate similar trends (Tobias 1990).

Despite this information, high school students considering future STEM careers often favor research universities for their undergraduate work. They learn about the strength of research being done there and logically choose those schools. As a professor at a small four-year public university, I sometimes meet with high school students and their parents while they are in the process of selecting a college. A student with a goal of future graduate work worries about gaining admission to a medical, dental, or veterinary school without an undergraduate degree from a university offering these programs. But the data support the contrary view that students are more likely to achieve their career goals by attending small liberal arts colleges. These perhaps counterintuitive success rates point to the need for science education reform at research universities.

A big obstacle for many students at different types of schools is the introductory science course. First-year experiences often make the difference in a student's choice of major. As educators we must view introductory science courses as opportunities to both recruit and retain science majors; additionally, as I emphasize in Chapter 19, one of the most important things we can do is improve our teaching of introductory courses. The class size of an introductory science course at a liberal arts college may be smaller than at a research university, but the smaller colleges also lose their share of majors, so simply limiting class size cannot reverse the pattern. Dudley Herschbach, winner of the 1986 Nobel Prize in chemistry and now emeritus professor at Harvard University, believes there are at least two kinds of science students: those he calls "sprinters," who are quick to grasp new material and do very well at whatever is demanded of them in introductory science, and those he calls "long-distance runners," who may appear to move more slowly and with greater difficulty, but whose grasp of concepts over time is profound. Science as it is currently taught and evaluated in college favors sprinters, but the long-distance runners, if they persist, often make the most important contributions in the long term (Tobias 1990). Although some science professors pride themselves on using introductory courses to weed out inappropriate students, Herschbach put considerable effort into significant and successful revisions of his introductory course in chemistry—a course he describes as his most challenging assignment (Harvard Department of Chemistry and Chemical Biology). Many of our students who typically leave science are the very ones we should have encouraged.

Improving introductory science courses can do more than increase the numbers of practicing scientists and science teachers. Both potential science majors and nonmajors fulfilling their general education requirements take these classes. Sometimes the two groups learn together in the same classroom. If we transform our teaching, we may not only bring more talented scientists into the workforce but also send nonmajors into society knowing how to address issues that require analytical and scientific thinking. The attrition in STEM majors cannot be attributed simply to different levels of ability and motivation; we must accept that classroom climate and activities play an important role in determining which students, and how many, persist.

Although several research institutions have undertaken initiatives to promote better teaching of undergraduate science courses, their efforts have focused more on changing the content of courses and seeking improvements in instructional technology than on modifying faculty pedagogical methods (Kardash and Wallace 2001). A student may actually have more opportunities for independent research, enhanced by close interaction with a professor, at a liberal arts college—and that experience can inspire a future scientist.

Clearly, there will always be some proportion of students who enter science lacking insufficient interest or preparation or who later discover that their passion and talent lie elsewhere. But there is evidence that the proportion of appropriate switchers is far smaller than is popularly believed. Seymour and Hewitt's three-year study (1997) concluded that no set of problems among STEM disciplines needed more improvement than faculty pedagogy. They found no evidence to support contentions of significant contributions to attrition by class size *per se*; the poor abilities of teaching assistants; the inadequacy of laboratory or computer facilities; or flaws in the linguistic, pedagogical, or social skills of foreign faculty or teaching assistants. When these authors visited departments that had initiated reforms, they learned that STEM faculty invariably had changed curriculum structure, rather than their teaching methods.

We are currently stalled in post–World War II teaching methods and have not appropriately responded to the exponential growth of scientific factual information and the readily accessible nature of that content. In more than six decades we have effectively changed what we teach and whom we teach, but have not adequately altered *how* we teach. As a result, we bypass an untapped resource of individuals who could contribute their talents and creativity to STEM disciplines. Recognition of the need for science teaching reform has moved from the purview of those who classify themselves as educational researchers to include those with credible careers as research scientists. Among the most outspoken are some who have spent more of their professional lives focusing on laboratory research while teaching university students in traditional ways. They now call for and model in their own classrooms more effective ways to engage students in science.

REFERENCES

Alvarez, L. 2008. Combat to college. *New York Times Education Life*, November 2, 24–29.

American Association for the Advancement of Science (AAAS). 1990. *The liberal art of science: Agenda for action: The report of the project on liberal education and the sciences.* Washington, DC: American Association for the Advancement of Science.

————. 1993. *Benchmarks for science literacy: Project 2061.* New York: Oxford University Press.

American Association of State Colleges and Universities. 2005. Strengthening the science and mathematics pipeline for a better America. *Policy Matters* 2 (11). *www.aascu.org/policy_matters/pdf/v2n11.pdf.*

Bayer Corporation. 2008. Bayer facts of science education survey XIII: Fortune 1000 STEM executives on STEM education, STEM diversity and U.S. competitiveness. *www.bayerus.com/msms/Survey/summary_13. aspx.*

Bottomly, H. K. 2008. From the president: The value of liberal arts. *Wellesley* 92 (3): 4.

Boyer, E. L. 1990. *Scholarship reconsidered: Priorities of the professoriate.* Princeton, NJ: Carnegie Foundation for the Advancement of Teaching.

Brainard, J. 2007. Board offers plan for science education. *Chronicle of Higher Education* 53 (50): 22.

DeHaan, R. L. 2005. The impending revolution in undergraduate science education. *Journal of Science Education and Technology* 14 (2): 253–269.

Harvard Department of Chemistry and Chemical Biology. Dudley R. Herschbach faculty page. *www.chem.harvard.edu/herschbach/dudley.php.*

Hestenes, D., M. Wells, and G. Swackhamer. 1992. Force Concept Inventory. *Physics Teacher* 30:141–158.

Kardash, C. M., and M. L. Wallace. 2001. The perceptions of science classes survey: What undergraduate science reform efforts really need to address. *Journal of Educational Psychology* 93 (1): 199–210.

Klymkowsky, M. W., K. Garvin-Doxas, and M. Zeilik. 2003. Bioliteracy and teaching efficacy: What biologists can learn from physicists. *Cell Biology Education* 2:155–161.

Martin, M. O., I. V. S. Mullis, and P. Foy. 2008. Trends in international mathematics and science study (TIMSS) 2007 international science report. *http://timssandpirls.bc.edu/TIMSS2007/release.html.*

Monastersky, R. 2007. The real science crisis: Bleak prospects for young researchers. *Chronicle of Higher Education* 54 (4): A1.

National Research Council (NRC). 1996. *National science education standards.* Washington, DC: National Academy Press.

———. 2000. *How people learn: Brain, mind experience and school.* Expanded ed. Washington, DC: National Academy Press.

———. 2003. BIO 2010: Transforming undergraduate education for future research biologists. Washington, DC: National Academies Press. *www. nap.edu/catalog.php?record_id=10497#toc.*

National Science Board. 2008. Science and engineering indicators 2008. *www. spaceref.com/news/viewsr.html?pid=26695.*

Rutherford, F. J. 2005. The 2005 Paul F. Brandwein lecture: Is our past our future? Thoughts on the next 50 years of science education reform in the light of judgments on the past 50 years. *Journal of Science Education and Technology* 14 (4): 367–386.

Sadler, P. M. 1989. *A private universe: Misconceptions that block learning.* VHS. Santa Monica, CA: Pyramid Film & Video.

Scarlett, M. 2004. *The great rip-off in American education: Undergrads underserved.* Amherst, NY: Prometheus Books.

Seymour, E., and N. M. Hewitt. 1997. *Talking about leaving: Why undergraduates leave the sciences.* Boulder, CO: Westview Press.

Tagg, J. 2003. *The learning paradigm college.* Bolton, MA: Anker Publishing Company.

Tobias, S. 1990. *They're not dumb, they're different: Stalking the second tier.* Tucson, AZ: Research Corporation.

———. 1992. *Revitalizing undergraduate science: Why some things work and most don't.* Tucson, AZ: Research Corporation.

Chapter 18

Resistance to Science Education Reform

WHY DO MANY SCIENCE EDUCATORS RESIST REFORM?

Most of us who are currently science educators survived or even flourished in traditional lecture-based science courses. Among us are Herschbach's "sprinters" (Chapter 17), for whom the old methods worked well. Some faculty resist incorporating new teaching methods because of a perceived lack of evidence for their efficacy. Many are unaware of the rigorous research findings that favor pedagogical reform because reports of these studies are rarely read by academic scientists. Postsecondary faculty continue to blame student attrition in the sciences on students' poor K–12 academic preparation and their inability to cope with these difficult disciplines. Of great concern is that faculty also fail to see the decrease in the number of science majors as a problem, and thus maintain the tradition of using introductory science courses as a means of weeding out students who can't "make it."

The scientists who have become vocal advocates of teaching reform are astonished by how the same educators who demand rigorous proof of research conclusions do not apply the same standards to their teaching methods. They continue teaching the way they were taught and are unaware of, or ignore, current evidence from research on how people learn (DeHaan 2005; Handelsman et al. 2004).

The typical college educator (and I belong to this group) has never taken a teacher education course. In fact, many of us are intimidated by the unfamiliar methods and language of educational research. Without this background we are reluctant to take on the challenge of learning new teaching methods. But unless an effort is made to discard lecturing habits and instruct new graduate students on how to teach, ineffective methods will continue to be passed on to future generations of science educators. We must abandon the erroneous assumption that anyone who has mastered the content is prepared to teach it.

A typical concern is the possible loss of content "coverage" in an interactive classroom setting. In Chapter 3, Step 8, of my chronology of course design, I explain how my use of content outlines substitutes for giving lectures. Other educators describe their methods for ensuring that students grasp essential content (Klionsky 2004; Knight and Wood 2005; Mazur 1997; Novak et al. 1999; Walker et al. 2008). A common element is giving students more responsibility for learning content outside class time. Educators should keep in mind that factual knowledge may not be the most important benefit of an effective course. Nearly two decades of research on both secondary and postsecondary science teaching have established that active learning methods increase students' problem-solving abilities, conceptual understanding, success in subsequent science courses, and student satisfaction. Most high school and college instructors, however, still primarily lecture.

When I demonstrate Lecture-Free Teaching during workshops, some skeptical participants point out that although my methods may work well for a seasoned educator such as myself, it would be difficult for a new instructor to teach this way. I disagree. If more high school and college faculty use participative methods, then newly minted educators will comfortably teach as they have been taught—which is, after all, what we have always done. Others agree that for a beginning instructor, creating an interactive course may not require any more effort than creating a semester's worth of lectures (Knight and Wood 2005).

Some factors that contribute to resistance to pedagogical reform are, in fact, beyond the control of individual educators. Many who teach science at colleges and universities do have valid reasons for not investing the same time, creativity, and energy in their teaching as they do in their research. Although mission statements of higher education institutions in the United States commonly emphasize high-quality instruction, the reality is that tenure, promotion, salaries, and prestige depend on success in publishing and acquiring grant funds. Most postsecondary institutions use three criteria for awarding tenure and promotion: teaching, research, and service. The criteria are generally not given equal weight. Research—with its quantifiable, peer-reviewed publications—dominates. Although good teaching and service are appreciated and respected, evaluating accomplishments in these areas is complicated, so they receive less consideration in the reward process (Cech 2003; National Research Council 2003).

Universities legitimately fear that if they encourage all faculty to devote a greater proportion of their time to teaching reform, they will fall behind other institutions in research productivity and prestige. Individual faculty embrace new methods when they become frustrated by the ineffectiveness and limitations of traditional lecturing, but few institutions or departments as a whole adopt new approaches to teaching science. Among the prominent scientists actively promoting reform are Nobel laureates Thomas Cech, Dudley Herschbach, and Carl Wieman, as well as Harvard University's Eric Mazur. They all gained tenure, promotions, and international prominence by working within the research-based model, but they now devote considerable effort to improving science education. Many others with active research labs also instituted successful teaching reforms, but it may be significant that many of the most vocal proponents of transforming pedagogy are at the top of the promotion hierarchy and secure in their careers, their reputations as researchers firmly established. These scientists lend credibility to the effort, but they are beyond the personal concern that their identification as teachers will reduce their status as researchers. Even people such as myself who teach at institutions with heavy teaching loads—and, by necessity, face less pressure to do research and publish—feel more comfortable about "rocking the boat" once we have achieved our final promotions.

For some junior faculty, not only is there a reluctance to take the time to incorporate active learning methods or transform an introductory course, but there are clear disincentives. Although the following story was recounted in the *Chronicle of Higher Education* in 1989, similar scenarios undoubtedly occur today.

> A young woman I know described what happened as she conducted an introductory biology class by having the students work in small groups. The class was prepared for the lesson and was comfortable with that strategy. A senior faculty member who was observing the junior faculty member stood up shortly after the students assembled themselves in groups and said, loudly enough for all to hear, "I'll come back when you're teaching."
>
> The young woman was astounded and quite unnerved by this statement, and when she later tried to explain what she had been doing, the older professor was unable or unwilling to understand. The evaluation she received after this visit was negative and discouraging, saying there was too much interaction in class and that she didn't use the blackboard enough. (Berry 1989, p. A36)

I accepted my first tenure-track faculty position 15 years after earning my PhD. Although I was neither particularly young nor green, having engaged in relevant employment before returning to full-time academia, when I began to stray from the traditional lecture methods that prevailed at my institution, I experienced similar disapproval. Luckily, my stubborn streak and strong belief that I was doing the right thing kept me on the right track. But it wasn't until I became a full professor that I felt truly liberated to develop Lecture-Free Teaching.

Despite the obstacles summarized above, a scholarship of teaching is emerging that I hope will become more credible in the promotion and tenure process. Indeed, articles comparing the effectiveness of teaching methods are published with increasing frequency in the scientific research journals (Crouch and Mazur 2001; Handelsman et al. 2004; Pukkila 2004). The constraint remains, however, that if one engages in this type of research, one has to produce something original. Even though restructuring one's own courses by applying someone else's proven methods is a rigorous and time-consuming exercise, our postsecondary system does not generally reward this.

A more practical reason to abandon lecturing as the dominant form of instruction was stated by Robert J. Beichner, a physics professor at North Carolina State University: "If all that a university can do is offer a large lecture hall with somebody talking at students, you can easily do better than that with the University of Phoenix or Western Governors University" with their online lectures. He warns that we need to give students a reason to attend live classes, or we may be out of work (Brainard 2007, p. 16).

WHAT DO OUR STUDENT-PARTNERS SAY ABOUT REFORM?

Ken Bain, author of the book *What the Best College Teachers Do* (a 15-year study of 63 teachers at 24 institutions), "found no great teachers who relied solely on lectures, not even the highly gifted ones" (2004, p. 107). That said, many students strongly resist new teaching strategies. Student opposition is certainly something I—and others—sometimes experience when we diverge from the traditional lecture as a primary instructional approach. The hostility stems from expectations associated with previously experienced teacher-centered learning. With learner-centered approaches, students must do more firsthand learning, be more collaborative, and take more responsibility (Doyle 2008). This does not mean that we should avoid reform any more than we should make our tests easy so that all students get As. Instead, we need to anticipate student discomfort and provide careful explanations of the benefits of changes.

In her book *Learner-Centered Teaching*, Weimer (2002) devotes an entire chapter to responding to opposition from both faculty and students. She believes that students resist learner-centered approaches because they require more work by the student, are more threatening, involve a loss of certainty, and may be beyond their abilities. She emphasizes the importance of understanding potential resistance and recognizing it in its early stages, and she shares strategies for helping students accept the challenge.

My experiences are similar to those reported by faculty studying the effectiveness of active learning at the University of Oregon's Workshop Biology classes: Students both value their learning experiences and are more critical of them (Udovic et al. 2002). Because students and teachers forge a partnership, students understand that their feedback is respected, and they learn to share their opinions freely, both positive and negative. With my daily "murkies" (described in Chapter 3) I receive immediate feedback on the success or failure of a particular technique or the day's activity.

Barnes (2008) reports mixed opinions about his lecture-free high school biology course, for which he used a personal response system (clickers). Students answered questions comparing his lecture-free methods with his traditional lecturing method for different units of the course. About half of the students preferred the lecture-free approach, but their comments reveal that they were frustrated by not immediately knowing if their initial response was correct and by having to reconsider questions they had already answered. On the other hand, many recognized the value of having to actually comprehend the concepts and reported that their learning had improved.

Students who previously experienced success in traditional teacher-centered courses may object to the demands of student-centered courses that require them to take more responsibility for their own learning. For some it is more difficult to understand concepts than it is to memorize and regurgitate information. I have learned the value of expending effort on the first day of class to explain that research has demonstrated that these methods are a more effective way to learn and to reassure students that they are not test subjects. Students who develop negative reactions during the first few classes sometimes dig in their heels and waste their energy orchestrating a semester of complaints. One researcher reported student complaints that included annoyance at being "forced" to attend class (Knight and Wood 2005)! I and others (Walker et al. 2008) observe less resistance from first-year students who are more open to trying new ways of learning in college. Some of the most vocal complainers are seniors who know how to successfully memorize information for tests and do not want to risk change at the end of their college careers.

Both instructors and students need to put aside misconceptions about the most effective ways to teach and learn. As teachers we expect our students to correct mistakes based on prior knowledge; we need to do the same and open our minds to growing evidence that pedagogical reform can result in significant student learning gains.

REFERENCES

Bain, K. 2004. *What the best college teachers do.* Cambridge, MA: Harvard University Press.

Barnes, L. J. 2008. Lecture-free high school biology using an audience response system. *American Biology Teacher* 70 (9): 531–536.

Berry, E. 1989. Newly hired young scholars should be nurtured, not resented. *Chronicle of Higher Education,* June 21: A36.

Brainard, J. 2007. The tough road to better science teaching. *Chronicle of Higher Education* 53 (48): 16.

Cech, T. R. 2003. Rebalancing teaching and research. *Science* 299 (5604): 165.

Crouch, C. H., and E. Mazur. 2001. Peer Instruction: Ten years of experience and results. *American Journal of Physics* 69 (9): 970–977.

DeHaan, R. L. 2005. The impending revolution in undergraduate science education. *Journal of Science Education and Technology* 14 (2): 253–269.

Doyle, T. 2008. The learner-centered classroom. *National Education Association Higher Education Advocate: Thriving in Academe* 26 (1): 5–8.

Handelsman, J., D. Ebert-May, R. Beichner, P. Bruns, A. Chang, R. DeHaan, J. Gentile et al. 2004. Scientific teaching. *Science* 304 (5670): 521–522.

Klionsky, D. J. 2004. Talking biology: Learning outside the book—and the lecture. *Cell Biology Education* 3:204–211.

Knight, J. K., and W. B. Wood. 2005. Teaching more by lecturing less. *Cell Biology Education* 4:298-310.

Mazur, E. 1997. *Peer Instruction: A user's manual.* Upper Saddle River, NJ: Prentice-Hall.

National Research Council (NRC). 2003. *Evaluating and improving undergraduate teaching in science, technology, engineering, and mathematics.* Washington, DC: National Academies Press.

Novak, G. M., A. Gavrin, W. Christian, and E. Patterson. 1999. *Just-in-time teaching: Blending active learning with web technology.* Upper Saddle River, NJ: Prentice Hall.

Pukkila, P. J. 2004. Introducing student inquiry in large introductory genetics classes. *Genetics* 166:11–18.

Udovic, D., D. Morris, A. Dickman, J. Postlethwait, and P. Wetherwax. 2002. Workshop Biology: Demonstrating the effectiveness of active learning in an introductory biology course. *BioScience* 52 (3): 272–281.

Walker, J. D., S. H. Cotner, P. M. Baepler, and M. D. Decker. 2008. A delicate balance: Integrating active learning into a large lecture course. *CBE—Life Sciences Education* 7:361–367.

Weimer, M. 2002. *Learner-centered teaching: Five key changes to practice.* San Francisco: Jossey-Bass.

Chapter 19

How to Achieve Science Education Reform

WHAT ARE SOME RECENT INITIATIVES TO REFORM SCIENCE EDUCATION?

Funding agencies, both government and private, play an important role in improving science education. The reform movement that calls for a shift from traditional lecture-based courses with cookbook-style labs is now supported by organizations such as the National Science Foundation, the National Science Resources Center, the National Science Teachers Association, the National Institutes of Health, and discipline-specific professional societies. In this chapter I discuss examples of current initiatives, both large and small scale, that promote reform of science education. I make no attempt to compile a comprehensive list but instead provide a sample of the variety of programs that may be helpful to readers of this book.

Efforts like those of the Carl Wieman Science Education Initiative (CWSEI) (University of British Columbia) work to link research on science, technology, engineering, and mathematics (STEM) learning to teaching methods using a scientific approach to transform pedagogy. The National Science Foundation (NSF) has long been a leader by combining research and education in its programs and grant offers. Every proposal for scientific research must be reviewed not only for intellectual merit but also for how the project will improve science education. A more focused effort of the NSF is the Course, Curriculum, and Laboratory Improvement program (CCLI), which seeks to improve the quality of STEM education for all undergraduate students by supporting, among other endeavors, research on teaching and learning.

In 1988 the Howard Hughes Medical Institute (HHMI) decided that its grants program would focus on science education, and it initially concentrated on attracting women and minority students to the biomedical sciences. In 2002, HHMI began a huge initiative to reward teaching innovations. This private organization empowers "million dollar professors" to have an effect on university education by giving outstanding teacher-scholars one million dollars over four years to develop and test new models of science teaching (Cech 2003).

To encourage skilled teaching among graduate students, the Association of American Colleges and Universities (AAC&U) supports the K. Patricia Cross Future Leaders Award, which "recognizes graduate students who show exemplary promise as future leaders of higher education; who demonstrate a commitment to developing academic and civic responsibility in themselves and others; and whose work reflects a strong emphasis on teaching and learning" (Association of American Colleges and Universities). A more formal effort to emphasize teaching in the preparation of graduate students is the Preparing Future Faculty program (PFF), a joint effort of the Council of Graduate Schools (CGS) and the AAC&U.

Some disciplines have made more progress than others. Physics educators have been ahead of the curve since 1956, when they formed the Physical Science Study Committee (PSSC) to consider ways to improve the teaching of introductory physics. Physicists continue to lead the march away from traditional lecture methods of science instruction in both high school and postsecondary classes, and it was physicists who designed the Force Concept Inventory (FCI), an accurate and reliable instrument for comparing the effectiveness of teaching methods. The FCI demonstrated that active learning, when compared to didactic lectures, leads to better student conceptual learning in physics (Hestenes, Wells, and Swackhamer 1992). Additional concept inventories, modeled after the FCI, for other physical science disciplines are being developed to assess student understanding of fundamental concepts and to identify commonly held misconceptions of students. These instruments can measure conceptual learning following the traditional lecture mode compared with various interactive engagement modes (Evans et al. 2003).

Because biology illiteracy may have an even more direct and personal effect on daily life than poor comprehension of physics concepts, an effort is in progress to develop, validate, and disseminate a Biology Concept Inventory (BCI) (Bioliteracy). This inventory has two goals: to define what a bioliterate person should know to make informed decisions and to measure the degree to which a course innovation improves student comprehension of—and ability to correctly apply—biological concepts (Klymkowsky, Garvin-Doxas, and Zeilik 2003). A Genetics Concept Assessment (GCA) is intended as a pre- and posttest measurement of student learning gains and as a way to identify strengths and weaknesses in teaching approaches for specific concepts (Smith, Wood, and Knight 2008). The ability to assess learning outcomes objectively may encourage science educators to reconsider how they have been teaching. The concept inventories could also provide equitable ways to evaluate teachers, something sorely lacking at all levels of the education hierarchy.

Improved high school science teaching is supported by programs such as Project-Based Science (University of Michigan School of Education) and Physics First (Physics First). Focused more on postsecondary education are BioQUEST Curriculum Consortium (Beloit College), SENCER (Science Education for New Civic Engagements and Responsibilities), and PKAL (Project Kaleidoscope). Examples of disciplinary societies that address K–16 teaching are the American Society for Microbiology, the Association of College & University Biology Educators, and the National Association of Biology Teachers. The American Society for Cell Biology now publishes a peer-reviewed, web-based journal, *CBE—Life Science Education*.

Reports and funding agencies advocate improvement of undergraduate education at research universities through large-scale participation of undergraduates in a university's research mission (Boyer Commission on Educating Undergraduates in the Research University 1998). Because an independent research experience for every undergraduate may not be feasible or even desirable, transformation of lecture courses to more inquiry-based, interactive formats can achieve similar results. Examples of established programs that promote such pedagogies are the Case Study Method (Herreid 2007), Just-in-Time Teaching (Novak et al. 1999), Peer Instruction (Mazur 1997), Problem-Based Learning (Duch, Groh, and Allen 2001), and studio teaching (Carleton College). The Student-Centered Active Learning Environment for Undergraduate Programs, or SCALE-UP (North Carolina State University), works to establish a highly collaborative, hands-on, computer-rich, interactive learning environment for large-enrollment courses.

One cannot just assume that any graduating PhD knows how to teach. A number of universities have created centers to prepare faculty to branch out from the traditional lecture. These centers work toward having doctoral programs prepare graduate students to teach, develop curricula, and advise undergraduates. They include, but are not limited to, the University of Delaware's Institute for Transforming Undergraduate Education; the University of Wisconsin-Madison's Center for the Integration of Research, Teaching, and Learning; the University of British Columbia's Carl Wieman Science Education Initiative; the University of Calgary's Learning Commons; Harvard University's Derek Bok Center for Teaching and Learning; and the University of Miami's Reinvention Center.

Increasingly, universities encourage faculty to try alternative teaching methods and conduct research on how to put them into practice. Stanford University, for example, recently reallocated funds previously awarded to a single faculty member in recognition of outstanding teaching: The Hoagland Award Fund for Innovations in Undergraduate Teaching now "seeks to support faculty in the creation of new learning materials and pedagogical approaches, and/or the implementation or adaptation of established educational innovations that—in either case—promise to contribute both to improved student learning and faculty's enjoyment of teaching" (Stanford University). An Earth science course was the recent beneficiary of this award (*Stanford Magazine* 2007). Harvard University initiated an effort to improve teaching and make it a more significant factor in whether professors get tenure or raises. The hope is that Harvard will offer tenure to more professors who are outstanding teachers, even if their research achievements are not necessarily as prestigious as those teachers who have received tenure in the past (Bombardieri 2006).

Accreditation agencies can also influence how STEM courses are taught. The Accreditation Board for Engineering and Technology (the recognized credentialing body for college and university programs in applied science, computing, engineering, and technology) specifically required student-centered teaching in its 1996 standards. Students who are taught this way improved their scores in math and science, as well as on tests of written communication (Brainard 2007).

Once a department has incorporated more effective teaching methods, the issue of improving inflexible classroom and laboratory spaces—ill suited to new pedagogical approaches because they inhibit interactions among students—is addressed in publications such as those by Project Kaleidoscope (1995, 2006). Such resources are useful to schools that plan to update science teaching spaces in buildings designed in the immediate post-Sputnik era.

WHAT SHOULD WE AS INDIVIDUAL EDUCATORS AND ADMINISTRATORS DO?

"Teaching by lecture rather than interactive engagement may be among the significant factors limiting the quality of science education in this nation" (Wyckoff 2001, p. 307). Evidence in report after report supports the view that we must transform our educational system at all levels to insist on active student participation in the learning process. Our institutions of higher education are particularly slow to change, despite mounting evidence that the lecture is an ineffective way to teach undergraduates (Scarlett 2004).

Clearly, the dominant science pedagogy in the United States needs to change. The question is, can individual science educators and administrators—including those of you reading this and other books—promote science education reforms that will effectively improve the number of scientists, increase the population of science educators, and raise the science literacy of U.S. citizens?

Science content in every discipline is increasing at a rate impossible to cover in a one- or two-semester introductory course or even in a four-year major. We must halt the emphasis on the memorization of facts and replace it with engaging activities that invite students to experience the excitement of real science. Rather than using our classroom teaching time for the transfer of scientific facts, we must offer students the knowledge and skills to glean information from reliable sources, recognize good science, and apply scientific information to the challenges of everyday life.

At the same time that educators are overwhelmed by the exponential growth of information in our disciplines, we are also inundated by reports of commissions, committees, and panels telling us that we need to improve the standing of science in the United States. The alarms sounded are not that different from those in 1957, except this time the threat is not the Soviet Union's Sputnik, but rather low science literacy, not enough science and math teachers, and the fact that we are falling behind other countries in technology. K–12 teachers are weary of the sets of recommendations in the form of standards that may or may not change the learning outcomes of their students. Postsecondary teachers are barely beginning to realize that the pedagogy of science education should not remain static, but must be treated like scientific research itself.

What follow are my suggestions for how we, as individual science educators and administrators, can begin to effect change.

Advocate for Higher Value for Our Teaching

Like most college and university professors, I have never taken an education course. So a decade ago, when I delved into the literature of education research, I was curious about the repeated references to "Bloom's taxonomy." Finally reading the book from which this terminology originated (Bloom 1956) clarified for me why it has retained its relevance for more than five decades. Two more recent publications in which the thoughts of Ernest L. Boyer play a central role will, I believe, demonstrate a similar persistence (Boyer 1990; Boyer Commission on Educating Undergraduates in the Research University 1998).

Although high-quality teaching is ostensibly the mission of our education institutions, we are distracted too often by revising curricula or publishing research results. Even our students raise concerns about the low priority assigned to teaching, particularly on college and university campuses. We need to change the reward systems so that rewards reflect the importance of time spent both with our students and on improving our teaching methods. We also need to set an example by becoming learners ourselves and devoting more of our time throughout our careers to becoming better informed about pedagogical methods proven effective in science. Faculty interested in working on course reconstruction should be able to do so as part of their professional work. Through our grassroots efforts, we should insist that our colleagues, administrators, accrediting bodies, and granting agencies applaud the scholarship of teaching.

We must welcome and nurture new educators in our departments and appreciate their novel teaching methods and ideas for curricular reform. As individuals, we should work within our own institutions to create a climate of mutual respect among faculty members and administrators and encourage a tangible demonstration of greater value for the teaching part of our jobs.

Establish Reliable Instruments to Evaluate Our Teaching

To accomplish my first suggestion, our institutions must develop tools to evaluate our instruction equitably. The tools should include more than the usual end-of-semester student evaluations that are common in higher education or scrutiny of student performances on the standardized assessments used in most school districts. Those instruments are both inadequate and flawed because they address neither student comprehension and long-term retention of concepts nor students' ability to apply what they have learned. Examples of improved end-of-course student questionnaires as well as questions for conducting peer evaluations of teaching are available in the appendixes of *Evaluating and Improving Undergraduate Teaching in Science, Technology, Engineering, and Mathematics* (National Research Council 2003).

Because schools vary broadly in their missions, sizes, the communities in which they are located, and characteristics of students, the criteria used to evaluate teaching should reflect these differences. Teaching should be considered a scholarly activity, and an instructor should be able to articulate and provide evidence for why he or she teaches in a particular way, incorporating what is currently known about teaching and learning in his or her discipline (French 2006).

Most STEM faculty at postsecondary institutions have little or no formal training in teaching techniques, assessing student learning, or evaluating their own teaching effectiveness. In the long term this could be remedied by mandating courses about pedagogy in graduate school programs. An Australian university requires that new members of the academic staff gain formal qualifications in university teaching during their probationary period by obtaining a Graduate Certificate in Higher Education (Monash University). In the short term the research literature suggests that some combination of formative and summative evidence about student learning can be used to evaluate and improve a faculty member's teaching. Institutionalizing effective evaluation practices can build an appropriate reward system for teaching scholarship, equivalent to the one used to scrutinize research productivity. The evaluative process should also reflect the unique balance among teaching, research, and service that is appropriate for a particular institution or even for a specific discipline.

As individual educators, we must work within our institutions to establish objective, comprehensive, quantitative, and qualitative methods to evaluate and improve teaching and learning. This should be done without imposing additional burdens on the faculty being evaluated.

Begin With Reforms of Secondary and Postsecondary Education

When lamenting the lack of science literacy among our citizenry and the fact that our educational systems do not produce enough scientists and science educators to meet the needs of our country, a lot of finger-pointing occurs. A common hierarchy of blame is that the teachers of lower grades are accused of preparing students inadequately for upcoming STEM courses. Conversely, K–12 teachers may blame professors at colleges and universities for failing to model effective science pedagogy for future teachers or for contributing to science phobia among their students' parents.

I suggest simultaneous science education reform in high schools, colleges, and universities that can encourage future teachers and also parents of our students to be more inquisitive about and comfortable with science. Reform in high schools will not only persuade more students to choose college science majors but also will prepare them for success in inquiry-based college courses for which they must take more responsibility for their own learning and focus on comprehension and ability to apply knowledge to novel situations. If college educators improve their teaching, more students will remain in science majors, and those who stay will represent more diverse backgrounds; we can no longer afford to ignore the potential contributions of women and underrepresented minorities. But, perhaps most important, when college science educators employ more engaging ways of teaching, the next generation of K–16 educators will feel comfortable with these methods and will use them effortlessly in their own classrooms in the future. Teaching the way we were taught is, after all, what we have been doing all along.

As individual educators, we can work to effect changes in our own districts and on our own campuses by setting an example. We can use innovative teaching methods, share them with others, and work to obtain more support for ourselves and our colleagues to experiment with new techniques. Support does not have to come in the form of funding; one can request time for professional development and can prepare a product as a result of this continuing education. A good place to start is to identify common misconceptions among our science students and then develop concept inventories and other tools to assess whether a different teaching technique will effectively change the preconceptions that students bring to the classroom based on their prior knowledge.

Transform the Most Basic Courses We Teach

The initial semester is in many ways the most important and formative of a student's college years, but introductory courses, taken primarily by first-year students, are often the most poorly taught (Boyer Commission 1998). One suggestion is that the institution's best professors be assigned to teach these courses, and to require these professors to use a student-centered teaching approach. This is, unfortunately, the opposite of standard practice.

If we adopt the attitude that the purpose of an introductory science course is to provide all students with a learning experience that will excite them and encourage them to consider a science career, they will be better-informed citizens, even if they ultimately decide their passions lie elsewhere. The introductory course should never be designed to weed out students by demonstrating their inadequacies; classroom methods should be respectful and inclusive of all types of learners. If you focus your time and energy on reforming the most basic courses you teach, your newly acquired pedagogical skills will naturally spill over into your upper-level courses.

Switching to Lecture-Free Teaching need not be an all-or-nothing prospect. A multitude of recent publications describe alternating short lectures with activities designed to make students think, especially in large-enrollment classes (Allen and Tanner 2005; Bland, Saunders, and Frisch 2007; Jones 2003; Klionsky 2004; Knight and Wood 2005; Lodish and Rodriguez 2004; Walker et al. 2008). If it is not financially feasible for your school to reduce class size, most of the lecture-free methods I discuss can also be accomplished with large classes.

Course transformation can occur incrementally by focusing on one thing at a time. I suggest starting with a problematic area for which you have a predetermined goal: a topic about which students chronically demonstrate misconceptions, an issue about which you scribbled in the margin of your lecture notes because you were dissatisfied with the way you taught it, or a criticism from students in an end-of-semester course evaluation. Once you have chosen a problem area, do some research along with creative thinking about improving your assessments and teaching. Talk to others who teach the same course. Once you make changes in that area, the methods will generalize and the reforms you make in other problem areas or even in other courses will be faster and easier. If your ultimate goal is lecture-free, you will notice that gradually, as your skills and comfort level increase, lecturing vanishes from your repertoire.

Look for ways to incorporate inquiry into every topic you teach. Inquiry is not synonymous with research. Instead of telling students the answer, let them investigate a problem on their own and come up with the answer individually or in a cooperative learning team. This may take more class time, but students learn and remember far more than just an answer to a question.

Share Our Enthusiasm for Reform With Colleagues, Administrators, and Students

Over the years I have facilitated two different series of discussions and demonstrations of teaching methods for faculty and staff on my campus. I organized these in large part for my own benefit because I believe much can be learned by observing the techniques of educators in different disciplines. In both cases I was surprised and encouraged by the consistent participation of colleagues who voluntarily participated in these gatherings.

The first series, one I called the Active Learning Discussion Group, took place during six two-hour sessions. I asked each participant to prepare a topic from an introductory class in her or his own discipline and teach it to the rest of us using an active learning method. A topic from a class typically taken by first-year students ensured that our diverse group would have appropriate background knowledge (or lack thereof). My colleagues signed up in advance to give 30-minute demonstrations. I gave the first presentation to model what I expected and to create a nonjudgmental atmosphere. On reserve in the campus library I placed a resource book, *Active Learning: 101 Strategies to Teach Any Subject* (Silberman 1996). I encouraged participants to try a method they had not previously used to receive feedback on something new for the future. During each presentation, the rest of us assumed the role of students, which gave us a feel for what it is like for students in our own classes. We experienced similar anxieties—specifically not wanting to appear stupid in front of our peers!

At the conclusion of each teaching demonstration, members of the audience provided verbal critiques and completed written feedback forms they shared with the presenter. In this open forum we gave honest comments and suggestions to one another without concern about possible repercussions—modeling how we should work with our students in the classroom. I believe we were all surprised at the ways ideas from someone teaching a subject such as poetry could be adapted to a field such as chemistry.

A couple of years later, as I was working on improving my classroom assessment methods, I recalled the success of the active learning demonstrations and invited faculty and staff to participate in similar discussions and demonstrations of formative assessments. I used the book *Classroom Assessment Techniques: A Handbook for College Teachers* (Angelo and Cross 1993) as the foundation of our sessions.

At the first session I distributed copies of the Teaching Goals Inventory and Self-Scorable Worksheet from the Angelo and Cross book and asked participants to complete the worksheet based on one specific course they teach that was going fairly well. I then distributed lists of the book's Classroom Assessment Techniques (CATs) and explained that each participant would choose a different CAT to demonstrate to the group at one of the future meetings. I placed a copy of *Classroom Assessment Techniques: A Handbook for College Teachers* on reserve in the campus library.

As before, I gave the first demonstration to model what I had in mind. At each of the subsequent five sessions, the other participants demonstrated a CAT as the rest of us assumed the role of students. Lively discussion followed each presentation, with many ideas about how the CAT could be improved or used by teachers in various disciplines.

As part of my participative workshops on Lecture-Free Teaching for middle and high school science teachers, I follow a similar format. I bring to the workshops copies of a series of books with detailed instructions for using simple formative assessment probes (Keeley 2008; Keeley, Eberle, and Dorsey 2008; Keeley, Eberle, and Farrin 2005; Keeley, Eberle, and Tugel 2007; Keeley and Tugel 2009). Each participant chooses a formative assessment probe appropriate for one of his or her classes and presents it to the rest of us. Afterward we critique each presentation and discuss how the probe could be adapted to other subjects and age groups.

To change teaching methods requires significant effort. But as you accomplish step-by-step reforms, the drudgery of predictable lecture preparation recedes and you anticipate—not without some apprehension—a lively interaction with your students during each class meeting. Although you lose the control you had as an information-delivering lecturer, you gain enhanced enjoyment of your teaching responsibilities along with the pleasure of a partnership with your students. The exchange of ideas among students and instructor reveals unexpected avenues of learning for everyone.

As an individual educator, you can be among the trailblazers in your science teaching community. You can experience the satisfaction of preparing for and teaching an interactive, inquiry-based class, and you can share your enthusiasm in ways that encourage the development of a culture of change to learner-centered instruction.

REFERENCES

Allen, D., and K. Tanner. 2005. Infusing active learning into the large-enrollment biology class: Seven strategies, from the simple to complex. *Cell Biology Education* 4:262–268.

American Society for Cell Biology. *CBE—Life Science Education. www.life-scied.org.*

American Society for Microbiology. *www.asm.org.*

Angelo, T. A., and K. P. Cross. 1993. *Classroom assessment techniques: A handbook for college teachers.* 2nd ed. San Francisco: Jossey-Bass.

Association of American Colleges and Universities (AAC&U). The 2009 K. Patricia Cross Future Leaders Award. *www.aacu.org/CrossAward/index.cfm.*

Association of College & University Biology Educators (ACUBE). *www.acube.org.*

Beloit College. BioQUEST Curriculum Consortium. *www.bioquest.org/index.php.*

Bioliteracy. Biological Concept Inventory Projects. *http://bioliteracy.net.*

Bland, M., G. Saunders, and J. K. Frisch. 2007. In defense of the lecture. *Journal of College Science Teaching* 37 (2): 10–13.

Bloom, B. S., ed. 1956. *Taxonomy of educational objectives: The classification of educational goals. Handbook 1: Cognitive domain.* New York: Longman.

Bombardieri, M. 2006. Harvard studies ways to promote teaching. *Boston Globe,* September 5.

Boyer Commission on Educating Undergraduates in the Research University. 1998. Reinventing undergraduate education: A blueprint for America's research universities. *http://naples.cc.sunysb.edu/Pres/boyer.nsf.*

Boyer, E. L. 1990. *Scholarship reconsidered: Priorities of the professoriate.* Princeton, NJ: Carnegie Foundation for the Advancement of Teaching.

Brainard, J. 2007. The tough road to better science teaching. *Chronicle of Higher Education* 53 (48): 16.

Carleton College. What is studio teaching? *http://serc.carleton.edu/introgeo/ studio/what.html.*

Cech, T. R. 2003. Rebalancing teaching and research. *Science* 299 (5604): 165.

Duch, B. J., S. E. Groh, and D. E. Allen, eds. 2001. *The power of Problem-Based Learning: A practical "how to" for teaching undergraduate courses in any discipline.* Sterling, VA: Stylus.

Evans, D. L., G. L. Gray, S. Krause, J. Martin, C. Midkiff, B. M. Notaros, M. Pavelich et al. 2003. Progress on concept inventory assessment tools. Panel at 33rd ASEE/IEEE Frontiers in Education Conference. Boulder, CO. *http://fie.engrng.pitt.edu/fie2003/papers/1346.pdf.*

French, D. P. 2006. Society for College Science Teachers: What currency should we use? *Journal of College Science Teaching* 35 (4): 60–61.

Herreid, C. F., ed. 2007. *Start with a story: The case study method of teaching college science.* Arlington, VA: NSTA Press.

Hestenes, D., M. Wells, and G. Swackhamer. 1992. Force concept inventory. *Physics Teacher* 30:141–158.

Jones, L. L. C. 2003. Are lectures a thing of the past? *Journal of College Science Teaching* 32 (7): 453–457.

Keeley, P. 2008. *Science formative assessments: 75 practical strategies for linking assessment, instruction, and learning.* Arlington, VA: NSTA Press.

Keeley, P., F. Eberle, and C. Dorsey. 2008. *Uncovering student ideas in science, vol. 3: Another 25 formative assessment probes.* Arlington, VA: NSTA Press.

Keeley, P., F. Eberle, and L. Farrin. 2005. *Uncovering student ideas in science, vol. 1: 25 formative assessment probes.* Arlington, VA: NSTA Press.

Keeley, P., F. Eberle, and J. Tugel. 2007. *Uncovering student ideas in science, vol. 2: 25 more formative assessment probes.* Arlington, VA: NSTA Press.

Keeley, P., and J. Tugel. 2009. *Uncovering student ideas in science, vol. 4: 25 new formative assessment probes.* Arlington, VA: NSTA Press.

Klionsky, D. J. 2004. Talking biology: Learning outside the book—and the lecture. *Cell Biology Education* 3:204–211.

Klymkowsky, M. W., K. Garvin-Doxas, and M. Zeilik. 2003. Bioliteracy and teaching efficacy: What biologists can learn from physicists. *Cell Biology Education* 2:155–161.

Knight, J. K., and W. B. Wood. 2005. Teaching more by lecturing less. *Cell Biology Education* 4: 298–310.

Lodish, H. F., and R. K. Rodriguez. 2004. A combination of lectures, problem sets, and recitation sections is an excellent way to teach undergraduate cell biology at a high level. *Cell Biology Education* 3:202–204.

Mazur, E. 1997. *Peer Instruction: A user's manual.* Upper Saddle River, NJ: Prentice Hall.

Monash University. Graduate Certificate in Higher Education. *www.calt. monash.edu.au/staff-teaching/gche.html.*

National Association of Biology Teachers (NABT). *www.nabt.org.*

National Research Council (NRC). 2003. *Evaluating and improving undergraduate teaching in science, technology, engineering, and mathematics.* Washington, DC: National Academies Press.

North Carolina State University. About the SCALE-UP project. *www.ncsu. edu/PER/scaleup.html.*

Novak, G. M., A. Gavrin, W. Christian, and E. Patterson. 1999. *Just-in-time teaching: Blending active learning with web technology.* Upper Saddle River, NJ: Prentice Hall.

Physics First. *http://physicsfirst.net.*

Preparing Future Faculty. The Preparing Future Faculty Program. *www.preparing-faculty.org.*

Project Kaleidoscope (PKAL). About Project Kaleidoscope. *www.pkal.org/ collections/About.cfm.*

———. 1995. *Volume III: Structures for science; A handbook on planning facilities for undergraduate natural science communities.* Washington, DC: Project Kaleidoscope.

———. 2006. *Volume III supplement: Handbook on facilities; A companion to structures for science.* Washington, DC: Project Kaleidoscope.

Scarlett, M. 2004. *The great rip-off in American education: Undergrads underserved.* Amherst, NY: Prometheus Books.

Science Education for New Civic Engagements and Responsibilities (SENCER). *http://sencer.net.*

Silberman, M. 1996. *Active learning: 101 strategies to teach any subject.* Boston: Allyn and Bacon.

Smith, M. K., W. B. Wood, and J. K. Knight. 2008. The genetics concept assessment: A new concept inventory for gauging student understanding of genetics. *CBE—Life Sciences Education* 7:422–430.

Stanford Magazine. 2007. Wanted: Bright, new teaching ideas. Fund supports innovative pedagogy. Farm Report. 38–39.

Stanford University. Hoagland Award Fund for Innovations in Undergraduate Teaching: Request for proposals. *http://ual.stanford.edu/pdf/ctl_hoagland_08.pdf.*

University of British Columbia. Carl Wieman Science Education Initiative. *www.cwsei.ubc.ca.*

University of Michigan School of Education. Project-Based Science. *www. umich.edu/~pbsgroup.*

Walker, J. D., S. H. Cotner, P. M. Baepler, and M. D. Decker. 2008. A delicate balance: Integrating active learning into a large lecture course. *CBE—Life Sciences Education* 7:361–367.

Wyckoff, S. 2001. Changing the culture of undergraduate science teaching: Shifting from lecture to interactive engagement and scientific reasoning. *Journal of College Science Teaching* 30 (5): 306–312.

Examples of Course Information Documents

A-1. EXAMPLE OF A TOPIC SCHEDULE

GENERAL BIOLOGY I TOPIC SCHEDULE
FALL 2007
Mondays and Wednesdays, 11:00 a.m.–1:45 p.m.

Key to Fonts:
Outline Titles and Numbers
In-class and laboratory activities
STUDENT PRESENTATIONS, OTHER ASSIGNMENTS, TESTS
Textbook chapters and other homework

WEEK	HOMEWORK	MONDAY	WEDNESDAY
1	Ch. 1, 18 **Read syllabus**	8/27: The Scientific Process (Outline 1) • *Find your learning group/ Introductions* • *Case study: Cell Phone Use and Cancer*	8/29: Characteristics of Living Organisms (Outline 2) • *Lab etiquette and safety* • *The Compound and Dissecting Microscopes* • *Word Roots*
2	Chs. 3, 4 **Due 9/5: Visit the model of a DNA double helix/Submit lab report choices**	9/3: HOLIDAY—NO CLASSES	9/5: Chemistry of Living Things (Outline 3) • *Properties of Water* • *Case study: Sweet Indigestion* • *Where Do You Find Organic Molecules?*
3	Ch. 5 **Due 9/10: Conceptualizing metric units/Making measurements, questions 1–8.** **Due 9/12: Cell structure crossword**	9/10: Cells (Outline 4) • *Conceptualizing Metric Units* • *Making Measurements* • *Making Measurements With the Compound Microscope* • *Diffusion and Osmosis, Class 1*	9/12: Cells (Outline 4) **Bring drawing paper and hard lead , blue, green, and red pencils** • *Size and Shapes of Cells. Surface Area: Volume Ratios* • *Making a Drawing From a Prepared Slide* • *Equilibrium: Throwing Paper Wads* • *Diffusion and Osmosis, Class 2*
4	**Due 9/17: Test review questions**	9/17: Cells (Outline 4) • *Plant and Animal Cells*	9/19: Cells (Outline 4) • *Diffusion and Osmosis in Plant and Animal Cells* • *Test review activity*

5	Ch. 6 **Due 9/26:** Enzyme dietary supplements	9/24: **TEST (Outlines 1–4)**	9/26: Cellular Energy and Enzymes (Outline 5) • *Discussion of information on enzyme dietary supplements* • *Simulation of the Nature of Enzymes* • *In Vitro Gas Suppression: Beano* • *Begin germinating seeds for Cellular Respiration in Plants*
6	Chs. 7, 8 **Due 10/3:** Test review questions	10/1: Photosynthesis (Outline 6) • *Photosynthesis vs. Respiration* • *Cellular Respiration in Plants*	10/3: Cellular Respiration (Outline 7) • *Effects of Experimental Variables on Fermentation Ability of Yeast* • *Sex Differences in Athletic Performance*
	UMPI FALL BREAK: NO CLASSES 10/8–10/12		
7	Ch. 12 **Due 10/15:** Cut out pink and blue chromosomes and bring to class with 6 paperclips	10/15: DNA Replication (Outline 8) • *Extraction and Spooling of DNA* • *DNA Replication Outside the (Cereal) Box* • *Test review activity*	10/17: **TEST (Outlines 5–8)** • *Begin sprouting onion bulbets* [10/19: Midterm grades submitted]
8	Chs. 9, 10 **Due 10/22: Your Body Is Younger Than You Think** **Due 10/24:** Book review title	10/22: Cell Reproduction (Outline 9) • *Sock Chromosomes—Mitosis* • *Paper Chromosomes—Mitosis* • *Mitosis in Allium cepa*	10/24: Cell Reproduction (Outline 9) • *Sock Chromosomes—Meiosis* • *Paper Chromosomes—Meiosis* • *Clarifying Misconceptions About Meiosis With Pipe Cleaners* • *Karyotyping*
9	Chs. 11, 33 (p. 640 only) **Due 10/30:** DNA Fingerprinting, Coursepack, pp. 87–88.	10/29: Genetics (Outline 10) • *Inheritance of ABO Blood Types in Humans* • *Relating Enzyme Function to Phenotype* • *Case study: Sometimes It Is All in the Genes*	10/31: Genetics (Outline 10) • *The Pedigree Chart* • *Coin Toss Pedigrees* • *Restriction Enzyme/DNA Fingerprinting Simulation* • *Case study: Two Peas in a Pod?* **DISTRIBUTION OF SUPERMARKET BOTANY LEARNING GROUP PROJECT**
10	Chs. 23, 24 **Due 11/7:** Supermarket Botany and Thermoregulation	11/5: Plant Structure (Outline 11) • *The Organs of the Vascular Plant*	11/7: Plant Growth and Development (Outline 12) **WEAR OUTDOOR CLOTHING!** • *Thermoregulation: How Do Plants Deal With the Cold?*

11	Chs. 29, 30, 33 **Due 11/14**: Test review questions	11/12: HOLIDAY. NO CLASSES	11/14: Animal Circulatory, Respiratory, and Immune Systems (Outline 13) • *Case study: Anyone Who Had a Heart* • *Circulation Challenge Questions* • *Sickle Cell Anemia*
12		11/19: Animal Circulatory, Respiratory, and Immune Systems (Outline 13) • *ABO/Rh Blood-Typing Model* • *Blood Typing for Organ Donations* • *ABO-Rh Blood Typing With Synthetic Blood* • *Test review activity* **DIVIDE TAKE-HOME CASE STUDIES AMONG GROUP MEMBERS**	11/21: HOLIDAY. NO CLASSES.
13	**By 11/29**: Book review: Writing Center consultation	11/26: **TEST (Outlines 9–13) SIGN UP FOR MICROSCOPE SKILLS ASSESSMENT APPOINTMENT**	11/28: **MICROSCOPE SKILLS ASSESSMENT (individual 10-minute appointments) COMPLETE TAKE-HOME CASE STUDIES**
14	Ch. 2, 17 **Due 12/3**: Take-home case studies, answers to questions **Due 12/5**: Final book review (include signed grading criteria sheet and draft)	12/3: Animal Dissection **PRESENTATIONS OF CASE STUDIES** • *Frog dissection and sheep brain lab*	• *12/5: Evolution (Outline 14)* • *Natural Selection of Jelly Beans* • *Sickle Cell Trait* • *Embryos as Evidence for Evolution*
15		12/10: Evolution (Outline 14) • *Case study: I'm Looking Over a White-Striped Clover* • *Review of all old tests*	**WEDNESDAY, DECEMBER 12, 2007 10:15 a.m. TO 12:15 p.m. COMPREHENSIVE FINAL EXAM**

SCIENCES I TOPIC SCHEDULE
SPRING 2004
Mondays and Wednesdays, 11:00 a.m.-1:15 p.m.

Key to Fonts:
Outline Titles and Numbers
In-class and laboratory activities
STUDENT PRESENTATIONS, OTHER ASSIGNMENTS, TESTS
Textbook chapters and other homework

WEEK	HOMEWORK	MONDAY	WEDNESDAY
1		1/19: HOLIDAY—NO CLASS	*1/21:* • *Find your learning group/ Introductions* • *Case study: Love Potion #10*
2	Ch. 1 Outline 1	1/26: Scientific Measurement and the Scientific Method (Outline 1) • *Grouping Geometric Figures* • *The Nature of Science* • *Lab safety* • *Lab Exercise 1A—Measurement*	1/28: Scientific Measurement and the Scientific Method (Outline 1) • *Lab Exercise 1A—Measurement*
3	Ch. 2 Outline 2 Homeworks: A, B, C (D)	2/2: Motion (Outline 2) • *Lab Exercise 2A—Motion* • *Life in a Vacuum*	2/4: Motion (Outline 2) • *How Fast Do You Walk?* • *Exercise 3A—Mechanics* TEST REVIEW QUESTIONS DUE
4		2/9: MECHANICAL ENERGY GROUP: "ASK THE EXPERTS" PRESENTATIONS • *Case study: The Cheerleader and the Football Player: Physics and Physical Exertion* • *Test review activity*	2/11: TEST (Outlines 1 and 2 and Labs 1A, 2A, and 3A)
	WINTER BREAK—NO CLASSES		
5	Ch. 3 Outline 3 Homeworks: A, B, C/D	2/23: Energy (Outline 3) • *Lab Exercise 3A—Mechanics*	2/25: Energy (Outline 3) • *What Is Your Horsepower Rating?*

6	Ch. 4 Outline 4 Homeworks: A, B, C	3/1: Heat and Temperature (Outline 4) • *Lab Exercise 4A—Heat and Temperature*	3/3: Heat and Temperature (Outline 4) • *Drinking Bird* • *Radiometer* **TEST REVIEW QUESTIONS DUE**
7		3/8: **RADIANT ENERGY GROUP: "ASK THE EXPERTS" PRESENTATIONS** • *Case study: A Case in Point: From Active Learning to the Job Market* • *Test review activity*	3/10: **TEST (Outlines 3 and 4 and Labs 3A and 4A)** **(Midterm grades are submitted on 3/12/04)**
8	Ch. 5 Outline 5 Homeworks: A, B www.fearofphysics.com Ch. 6 Outline 6 Homeworks: A, B, C, D Begin celestial observations	3/15: Wave Motions and Sound (Outline 5) • *Doppler Effect* • *Lab Exercise 7A—Particle Waves* **BOOK REVIEW TITLE DUE**	3/17: Electricity (Outline 6) • *Organize learning group activity, Celestial Observations (Outline 9—Learning Group Homework Activities)* • *Lab Exercise 5A—Electricity*
9	Read case study: *The Day They Turned the Falls on: The Invention of the Universal Electrical Power System* Ch. 7 Outline 7 Homework: A (all parts) Continue celestial observations	3/22: Electricity (Outline 6) **ELECTRICAL ENERGY GROUP: "ASK THE EXPERTS" PRESENTATIONS** • *Lab Exercise 6A—Magnetism*	3/24: Light (Outline 7) • *Lab Exercise 8A—Visible Light* • *Case study: As Light Meets Matter—Art Under Scrutiny*
10	Chs. 8, 11 **Homeworks Outline 8: A,B,C** **Continue celestial observations**	3/29: Light (Outline 7) • *Playing Around With Lenses; Interference Colors With Polaroids* • *Case study: A Light on Physics: F-Number and Exposure Time: A Case Study in Optics* • **BOOK REVIEW WRITING CENTER CONSULTATION DUE**	3/31: Atomic Structure/Radioactivity (Outline 8) • *Case study: The Benign Hamburger* **TEST REVIEW QUESTIONS DUE** **SUBMIT PEER-GRADED BOOK REVIEWS**
	SPRING BREAK—NO CLASSES		

11	**Complete celestial observations and Maine solar system model critique (Outline 9, Learning Group Homework Activities)**	4/12: Atomic Structure/Radioactivity (Outline 8) **NUCLEAR ENERGY GROUP: "ASK THE EXPERTS" PRESENTATIONS** • *Case study: Irradiation: Is It Consumer-Friendly?* • *Test review activity*	4/14: UNIVERSITY DAY
12	**Ch. 13 Outline 9**	4/19: **TEST (Outlines 6, 7, 8 and Labs 5A, 6A, 7A, 8A)**	4/21: The Solar System (Outline 9) **LEARNING GROUP PRESENTATIONS, CELESTIAL OBSERVATIONS AND MAINE SOLAR SYSTEM MODEL CRITIQUE** • *Video:* A Private Universe • *Modeling the Interaction of Sun, Earth, and Moon*
13	**Ch. 14 Outline 10**	4/26: The Solar System (Outline 9) • *Case study: Life on Mars: A Dilemma Case Study in Planetary Geology* • *Case study: Is a Mars Sample Return Mission Too Risky?* • *Modeling the Rotation of the Earth With a Foucault Pendulum*	4/28: The Earth (Outline 10) *Lab Exercise 10A—Rocks*
14		5/3: The Earth (Outline 10) • *Lab Exercise 11A—Map Coordinates* **FINAL BOOK REVIEW DUE**	5/5: • *Lab Exercise 12A—Topographic Maps* • *Final exam review*
COMPREHENSIVE FINAL EXAM (OUTLINES 1–10 and LABS 10A, 11A, 12A) WEDNESDAY, MAY 12, 2004 12:45 p.m.–2:45 p.m.			

SCIENCES II TOPIC SCHEDULE
SPRING 2004
Mondays and Wednesdays, 11:00 a.m.–1:15 p.m.

Key to Fonts:
Outline Titles and Numbers
In-class and laboratory activities
STUDENT PRESENTATIONS, OTHER ASSIGNMENTS, TESTS
Textbook chapters and other homework

WEEK	HOMEWORK	MONDAY	WEDNESDAY
1		1/16: HOLIDAY—NO CLASSES	1/18: • *Find your learning group/ Introductions* • *Case study: Thinking Inside the Box* • *Lab safety*
2	**Read syllabus** **Ch. 17, Outline 1** <u>1/25:</u> **Book review title due**	1/23: Earth's Weather (Outline 1) • *Weather Maps and Measurements* • *Cartesian Diver* • *Organize "Graphing 7 Days of Presque Isle Weather" data collection*	1/25: Earth's Weather (Outline 1) guest speaker, Mark Turner, hydrologist, National Weather Service, Caribou • *Work on "Graphing 7 Days of Presque Isle Weather"*
3	**Chs. 8 and 9, Outline 2** <u>1/30:</u> **Graphing 7 Days of Weather due** <u>2/1:</u> **Test review questions due** <u>By 3/1:</u> **Book review draft consultation at Writing Center**	1/30: Earth's Weather (Outline 1) **PRESENTATIONS: GRAPHING 7 DAYS OF WEATHER** • *Case study: Cancel the Cardinals Home Opener?* • *The Petition: A Global Warming Case Study*	2/1: Atoms and Periodic Properties (Outline 2) • *Classification of Matter* • *Demonstration: Suspension vs. Solution* • *Density Columns* • *The Relationship Between Mass and Volume*
4	<u>2/6:</u> **Postlab questions due (Mass and Volume)**	2/6: Atoms and Periodic Properties (Outline 2) • *Diet or Regular?* • *Test review activity*	2/8: **TEST (Outlines 1, 2)**

5	Ch. 9, Outline 3 **2/13:** Homework on household chemicals due **By 3/1:** Book review draft consultation at Writing Center	2/13: Chemical Reactions (Outline 3) • *Atoms Represented by Bolts, Screws, Nuts, and Washers* • *Types of Compounds*	2/15: Chemical Reactions (Outline 3) • *Atoms Represented by Bolts, Screws, Nuts, and Washers* • *Equilibrium: Throwing Paper Wads in the Classroom*
	WINTER BREAK—NO CLASSES		
6	Ch. 10, Outline 4 **3/1:** Test review questions due **By 3/1:** Book review draft consultation at Writing Center	2/27: Water and Solutions (Outline 4) • *Like Dissolves Like* • *How Many Molecules of Sucrose in a Sugar Granule?* • *"Mole"asses Cookies Recipe (Learning group members divide responsibilities)*	3/1: Water and Solutions (Outline 4) • *Case study: Avogadro Goes to Court*
7	**3/6:** Bring a household product to test pH. "Mole"asses cookie recipe translation due. **3/10:** Midterm grades submitted	3/6: Water and Solutions (Outline 4) • *Cabbage Chemistry* • *Awards: "Mole"asses Cookies Competition* • *Test review activity*	3/8: **TEST (Outlines 3,4)** • *Diffusion and Osmosis in a Chicken Egg, Class 1 (see Outline 5): Start eggs*
8	Ch. 20, Outline 5. **3/15:** Final book review due	3/13: Cells (Outline 5) • *Diffusion and Osmosis in a Chicken Egg, Class 2* • *Size and Shape of Cells. Surface Area: Volume*	3/15: Cells (Outline 5) • *Diffusion and Osmosis in a Chicken Egg, Class 3* • *The Compound Microscope*
9	Ch. 23, Outline 6 **3/22:** Read Green Manhattan and Watch Your Step <u>before</u> class. Homework on Trophic Levels, Energy, and Price due	3/20: Cells (Outline 5) • *Diffusion and Osmosis in a Chicken Egg, Class 4* • *Plant and Animal Cells*	3/22: Ecology and Environment (Outline 6) **MEET IN COMPUTER LAB FOLSOM 101A** • *Case study: Watch Your Step: Understanding the Impact of Your Personal Consumption on the Environment*
10	**3/29:** Ecological Footprint Spreadsheet and written answers to Questions 1–5, Part V, Watch Your Step due **3/29:** Test review questions due	3/27: Cells (Outline 5) • *A Problem About Osmosis* • *Diffusion and Osmosis in Plant and Animal Cells*	3/29: Ecology and Environment (Outline 6) guest speaker, State Representative Jeremy Fischer, "How to Effect Change" • *Plan Environmental Action Projects*
	SPRING BREAK—NO CLASSES		

11	**Ch. 20, Outline 7. See www.cellsalive.com (Cell Biology: Mitosis; The Cell Cycle)** **By 4/14: Environmental Action Project draft consultation at Writing Center**	4/10: Cell Reproduction (Outline 7) • *DNA Replication Outside the (Cereal) Box* • *Paper Chromosomes—Mitosis Mitosis in Allium cepa* • *Test review activity*	4/12: **UNIVERSITY DAY**
12	**4/19: Written Environmental Action Projects due**	4/17: **TEST (Outlines 5, 6, 7)**	4/19: Ecology and Environment (Outline 6) • **ORAL PRESENTATIONS ON ENVIRONMENTAL ACTION PROJECTS**
13	**Chs. 25 and 26, Outline 8** **4/26: Karyotype due**	4/24: Human Biology: Genetics (Outline 8) • *Sweat Sock Chromosomes—Meiosis* • *Paper Chromosomes—Meiosis* • *Karyotyping* • *Extraction and Spooling of DNA*	4/26: Human Biology: Genetics (Outline 8) • *Inheritance of ABO Blood Types Taste Test* • *Coin Toss Pedigrees* • *Case study: Sometimes It Is All in the Genes*
14		5/1: Human Biology: Genetics (Outline 8) • *DNA Fingerprinting* • *Restriction Enzyme/DNA Fingerprinting Simulation* • *Case study: Two Peas in a Pod?*	5/3: Final exam review
15	**COMPREHENSIVE FINAL EXAM (OUTLINES 1–8): WEDNESDAY, MAY 10, 2006** **12:45 p.m.–2:45 p.m.**		

HUMAN NUTRITION TOPIC SCHEDULE
SPRING 2008
Tuesdays and Thursdays, 10:50 a.m.–12:05 p.m.

Key to Fonts:
Outline Titles and Numbers
In-class and laboratory activities
STUDENT PRESENTATIONS, ASSIGNMENTS, TESTS
Textbook chapters and other homework

WEEK	HOMEWORK	TUESDAY	THURSDAY
1	Read syllabus Ch. 1, Outline 1 Due 1/17: Homeworks A, B, C	1/15: • *Find your learning group/ Introductions* • *N.A.T.: Nutrition Aptitude Test*	1/17: What You Eat and Why (Outline 1)
2	Ch. 2, Outline 2 Due 1/22: Homeworks A, B Dine Healthy 6 Due 1/29: Homework A Begin Homework B Due 1/31: Homework C	1/22: Planning a Healthful Diet (Outline 2) • *Estimating Serving Size* • *Comparing Nutrient Density*	1/24: Dine Healthy 6—The Computer Lab MEET IN FOLSOM 101B COMPUTER LAB BE SURE YOU HAVE AN ACTIVE UMPI NDS COMPUTER LAB ACCOUNT • *Entering Your One-Day Food and Activity Record Into Dine Healthy 6*
3	Ch. 2, Outline 3 Due 1/29: Homeworks A, B, C; Week 2 homework Ch. 3, Outline 4, Due 1/31: Homeworks A–G; Week 2 homework	1/29: Food Labels (Outline 3) • *Personalizing the Daily Values* • *Computation of Your Personal Daily Values Using Food Cards*	1/31: Digestive System and Related Functions (Outline 4) guest speaker, Kim-Anne Perkins, professor of social work, director of social work program • *Jigsaw Activity Using Homework A–G* • *Journey of Food*
4	Ch. 4, Outline 5 Due 2/5: Homework A, B, C; Submit book review title Due 2/7: Homework D	2/5: Carbohydrates (Outline 5) • *Case study: Sweet Indigestion* • *Case study: Morgan: A Case of Diabetes* • *Lactaid and Beano* • *Guessing How Much Sugar*	2/7: Carbohydrates (Outline 5) guest speaker, Dr. Deborah Hodgkins, associate professor of English • *Carbohydrate Counting* • *Case study: Morgan: A Case of Diabetes*

5	Ch. 5, Outline 6 <u>Due 2/14:</u> Homeworks A, B, C	2/12: **TEST (Outlines 1–5)**	2/14: Lipids (Outline 6) • *P/S Ratios* • *Sources of Fat* • *Trans-Fats* • *Lipid Transport Jigsaw Activity*
	**WINTER BREAK—NO CLASSES: 2/18 to 2/22**		
6	Ch. 6, Outline 7 <u>Due 2/28:</u> Homeworks A, B	2/26: Lipids (Outline 6) • *Analysis of Lipid Profiles From Actual Patients* • *Case study: Wake-up Call*	2/28: Proteins (Outline 7) • *Taste Test: Soy Products* • *Revise a Recipe*
7	IRB policies and guidelines. IRB application Parts I and II 3/7: Midterm grades submitted	3/4: **TEST (Outlines 6–7)**	3/6: *IRB policies and procedures guest speaker, member of UMPI Institutional Review Board for Research on Human Subjects* • *Preparation for Service-Learning Project* • *Pairing of Students and Participants*
8	Ch. 11, Outline 8 <u>Due 3/11:</u> Homeworks A, B Make appt. w/ service-learning partner to meet at UMPI Health Center Ch. 12, Outline 9 <u>Due 3/13:</u> Homework A	3/11: Energy Balance (Outline 8) • *Calculating Energy Use* • *Calculating Your Waist-to-Hip Ratio* • *Estimating Your Frame Size* • *Your Healthful Weight According to Height-Weight Tables*	3/13: Nutrition and Physical Activity (Outline 9) • *Case study: A Can of Bull?*
9	Ch. 7, Outline 10 <u>Due 3/18:</u> Homeworks A, B Ch. 8, Outline 11 <u>Due 3/20:</u> **Read Nutrition Debate, pp. 302–307; Homework A. First and second meetings with service-learning partner**	3/18: Nutrients Involved in Fluid/Electrolyte Balance (Outline 10) • *Case study: Lost in the Desert* • *Make Your Own Sports Drink* • *Researching the Supplements: Divide homework for Outlines 11, 12, 13 among learning group members*	3/20: Nutrients Involved in Antioxidant Function (Outline 11) **REPORTS ON SUPPLEMENTS** • *Case study: All That Glitters May Not Be Gold: A Troublesome Case of Transgenic Rice*
10	Ch. 9, Outline 12 <u>Due 3/25:</u> Homework A <u>By 3/28:</u> **Book review draft consultation at Writing Center**	3/25: Nutrients Involved in Bone Health (Outline 12) guest speaker, Krista Delahunty, researcher at the Jackson Laboratory, "Using Mice to Investigate the Genetics of Osteoporosis" **REPORTS ON SUPPLEMENTS** • *Case study: Osteoporosis: Marissa, Jeremy, and Eleanor*	3/27: Guest instructor, Dr. Sue Beaudet, professor of physical education, "Body Composition Assessment: Underwater Weighing" **MEET AT POOL AT GENTILE HALL**

	**SPRING BREAK—NO CLASSES 3/31 to 4/4**		
11	**Ch. 10, Outline 13** **Due 4/8:** Homework A **Ch. 13, Outline 14** **Due 4/10:** Homework A, **Submit final book review**	4/8: Nutrients Involved in Energy Metabolism and Blood Health (Outline 13) **REPORTS ON SUPPLEMENTS** • *Case study: Thiamin Deficiency: A Directed Case Study* • *Case study: The Chemistry of Cooley's Anemia*	4/10: Disordered Eating (Outline 14) guest speaker, Kim McCrea, lecturer/clinical ed. coordinator athletic training, "Female Athlete Triad" **REPORTS ON SUPPLEMENTS** • *Discussion* • *Design an Invitation* • *Plan Menu for May 1 Luncheon*
12	**Chs. 15–16, Outline 15** **Ch. 14, Outline 16** **Due 4/17:** Homework A **Third meeting with service-learning partner**	4/15: Nutrition Through the Lifecycle (Outline 15) guest speaker, Colette Thompson, public health nutrition educator **DISCUSSION OF RESULTS OF HOMEWORK ACTIVITIES**	4/17: Food Safety (Outline 16) • *Case study: The Benign Hamburger* • *Case study: Irradiation: Is It Consumer-Friendly?*
13	**Due 4/24:** Draft of nutritional assessment. Make appt. for fourth meeting with service-learning partner	4/22: **TEST (OUTLINES 8–16)** • *Sign up for individual appointment with Dr. Wood*	4/24: *Individual meetings with Dr. Wood to review your nutritional assessment draft.* *10:00 a.m. to 1:00 p.m., 316 South Hall.*
14	**Due 5/1:** Bring food item with its nutrition facts label to the luncheon	4/29: **Meet with your service-learning partner to explain nutritional assessment and present him/her with a written copy**	5/1: (10:45–1:30) 11:30 **LUNCHEON FOR SERVICE-LEARNING PARTNERS, ALLAGASH ROOM, CAMPUS CENTER** SIT WITH YOUR PARTNER!!
15		**FINAL COPY OF NUTRITIONAL ASSESSMENT OF YOUR SERVICE-LEARNING PARTNER IS DUE IN MY OFFICE BY 5:00 p.m.** **TUESDAY, MAY 6, 2008** **NO FINAL EXAM.**	

National Science Teachers Association

A-5. GENETICS TOPIC SCHEDULE

GENETICS TOPIC SCHEDULE
FALL 2007
Tuesdays and Thursdays, 11:00 a.m.–1:45 p.m.

Key to Fonts:
Outline Titles and Numbers
In-class and laboratory activities led by Dr. Wood
Teaching models led by students
Textbook chapters and other homework/TESTS

WEEK	HOMEWORK	TUESDAY	THURSDAY
1	**Chs. 1, 10, 11 (p. 298) Read syllabus/Visit the DNA model, Northern Maine Museum of Science**	8/28: Three Areas of Genetics • *Find your learning group/ Introductions* • *Laboratory use agreement* • *How to Extract and Spool DNA in Your Kitchen* • *Case study: A Sickeningly Sweet Baby Boy: A Case Study on Recessive Inheritance in Inbred Populations* **Student-led teaching model signups**	8/30: DNA Structure (Outline 1) • *Teaching Outside the (Cereal) Box: DNA Structure (Grade the Professor! Demonstration of a Teaching Model)* • *Polarity and Antiparallel Structure* • *Properties of DNA* • *Video: Photo 51*
2	**Chs. 11, 12**	9/4: Chromosome Structure (Outline 2) • *Chromatin to Chromosome Model* • *The Size of the E. Coli Genome* • *Giant (Polytene) Chromosomes*	9/6: DNA Replication (Outline 3) • *Teaching Outside the (Cereal) Box: DNA Replication* • **Modeling the Classic Meselson and Stahl Experiment + Meselson-Stahl Experimental Simulation Using Lego Building Blocks** • **Modeling DNA Replication**
3	**Chs. 13, 14, 15**	9/11: Transcription and RNA (Outline 4) • *Prep for Week 5: Pour LB agar plates and streak and restreak Serratia during the week to achieve all white/yellow cultures. Incubate at 37°C* • *Teaching Outside the (Cereal) Box: Transcription* • **DNA Puzzle Kit: Student Worksheets—DNA: The Genetic Code, RNA: The Code Transcribed, and Protein Synthesis**	9/13: Genetic Code and Translation (Outline 5) • *Teaching Outside the (Cereal) Box: Translation* • **Modeling Protein Folding** • **Demonstrating Translation With a Student-Centered Activity** • **A Working Model of Protein Synthesis Using Lego Building Blocks** • *Restreak Serratia during the week to achieve all white/yellow cultures. Incubate at 37°C.*

4		9/18: Genetic Code and Translation (Outline 5) • *Restreak and incubate the white/ yellow <u>Serratia</u> at two different temperatures* • *Case study: Tazswana's Story: How Alternative mRNA Splicing Leads to Genetic Disease and Cure* • *Guest speaker, Donald Sawyer, M.D., "Beta-Thalassemia in Afghanistan"*	9/20: **TEST (Outlines 1–5)** • *Prepare plates A and B of <u>Serratia</u> according to Outline 6 instructions* • *Prepare tobacco solution*
5	**Ch. 17**	9/25: Gene Mutations and DNA Repair (Outline 6) • *Regulation of Gene Expression using <u>S. marcescens</u>* • *Tobacco-Induced Mutations— Class 1* • *Mutations and Expression of the Beta-Globin Gene* • *Video:* Accidents of Creation	9/27: Gene Mutations and DNA Repair (Outline 6) • *Tobacco-Induced Mutations— Class 2* • *For Colony Transformation: Use previously poured agar to streak <u>E. coli</u> and incubate* • *Video:* Bacterial Transformation • *Case study: A Right to Her Genes*
6	**Ch. 8, 18** <u>**Due 10/2:**</u> **Read case study: Niños Desaparecidos, and be prepared to discuss/ Submit book review title**	10/2: Bacterial and Viral Genetics (Outline 7) • *Colony Transformation* • *Pour electrophoresis gels for 10/16 laboratory* • *Case study:* Niños Desaparecidos • *Video:* The Dirty War	10/4: Recombinant DNA Technology (Outline 8) • ***Linguini Models of Molecular Genetic Mapping and Fingerprinting*** • ***Teaching DNA Fingerprinting Using a Hands-On Simulation*** • ***Recombinant DNA Paper Model Simulation*** • ***PCR Tutorial*** • *Case study: The Case of the Druid Dracula*
		UMPI FALL BREAK: NO CLASSES 10/8–10/12	
7	**Take-home portion of test: FrankenFoods OR Taco Shells Case Study**	10/16: Recombinant DNA Technology (Outline 8) • *Teaching Outside the (Cereal) Box: Restriction Digestion and Polymerase Chain Reaction* • *Guest speaker, Jason Johnson, Ph.D., assistant professor of wildlife ecology, " Using PCR to Determine Sex of Wood Thrush Nestlings"*	10/18: **TEST (Outlines 6–8)** [10/19: Midterm grades submitted]

8	**Ch. 19** **Due 10/23:** **Human Genome Project homework**	10/23: Genomics (Outline 9) **Meet in Computer Lab, Folsom 101B** • *Case study: Genetic Testing and Breast Cancer: Is a Little Knowledge a Dangerous Thing?* • *Guest speaker, Kim Borges-Therien, Ph.D., associate professor of environmental studies, UMFK, "BLASTing Can be a Blast!"*	10/25: Genomics (Outline 9) • *Teaching Outside the (Cereal) Box (Sequencing, Hybridization, and Probing)* • ***A Demonstration of Automated DNA Sequencing*** • ***Microarrays Made Simple: "DNA Chips" Paper Activity*** • ***Understanding the Human Genome Project*** • *Prepare onion bulbets for sprouting*
9	**Ch. 2** **Due 10/30:** **Cut out pink and blue chromosomes and bring to class with 6 paperclips/Submit book review title**	10/30: Eukaryotic Cell Reproduction (Outline 10) ***Mitosis Sections of:*** • *Chromosome Socks* • ***Hands-on Activities That Relate Mendelian Genetics to Cell Division*** • ***Students as Human Chromosomes*** • *Mitosis in Plants and Animals*	11/1: Eukaryotic Cell Reproduction (Outline 10) ***Meiosis Sections of:*** • *Chromosome Socks* • ***Hands-on Activities That Relate Mendelian Genetics to Cell Division*** • ***Students as Human Chromosomes*** • *Meiosis and Fertilization* • *Gamete Problem Sets* • *Case study: Bringing Back Baby Jason*
10	**Chs. 3, 5**	11/6: Principles of Heredity (Outline 11) • **Cookie-Ases: Interactive Models for Teaching Genotype-Phenotype Relationships** • **Using Manipulatives to Teach Basic Mendelian Genetics Concepts** • *Case study: Woe to That Child: A Case of CF*	11/8: Principles of Heredity (Outline 11) • *ABO/Rh Blood-Typing Model* • *Simulated Blood Typing: Whodunit* • *Epistasis in Labrador Retrievers*
11	**Ch. 4, 5** **By 11/13:** **Visit color-blindness exhibit, Northern Maine Museum of Science**	11/13: **Second Biennial Genetics Consortium: UMPI/UMFK at Eureka Hall, Stockholm 11:00 a.m.–4:00 p.m.** • Sex-Related Inheritance (Outline 12) • *Case study: In the Genes or in the Jeans?* • *Video:* Birth, Sex, and Death	11/15: Use of Probability Formulations and the Chi-Square Test (Outline 13) • *Taste Test* • *Predicting Probabilities in Dihybrid and Multifactorial Crosses* • *Case study: Hemophilia: The Royal Disease*
12		11/20: **TEST (Outlines 9–13)**	11/22: THANKSGIVING HOLIDAY

13	Ch. 22 __By 11/30:__ **Writing Center consultation for book review draft**	11/27: Quantitative Genetics (Outline 14) • *Tests returned* • *Pour all Sordaria agar plates* • *Make Sordaria stock cultures* • *(Follow instructions on page 115 of Coursepack)*	11/29: No class today. **Work independently on projects described below.**
		Read "The Case of Desiree's Baby: The Genetics and Evolution of Human Skin Color" and write answers to Part I and Part II questions. Appointment at the Writing Center for consultation on your book review draft.	
14	Chs. 6, 9 __Due 12/4:__ **"The Case of Desiree's Baby," typed answers to Part I, Questions 1–4, and Part II, Questions 1–5.**	12/4: Human Pedigrees (Outline 15) • *The Allium Test: Make solutions and begin sprouting onion bulbets in chemicals* • *Cross wildtype and mutant Sordaria* • *Coin Toss Pedigrees (in outline)* • *Case study: In Sickness and in Health: A Trip to the Genetic Counselor*	12/6: Chromosome Variation (Outline 16) • ***Modeling Mitosis/Meiosis*** • ***Using Ribbon Models of Chromosome Modifications to Explore the Process of Meiosis*** • *Human Chromosome Analysis* • *The Allium Test—A Simple Eukaryote Genotoxicity Assay* • *Check Sordaria Cultures*
15	Ch. 7 __Due 12/11:__ **Final book review (include signed grading criteria sheet and draft)**	12/11: Eukaryotic Chromosome Linkage and Mapping (Outline 17) *guest speaker, Krista Delahunty, the Jackson Lab, "Using Mice as a Tool to Investigate the Genetics of Osteoporosis"* • *Mapping in Sordaria fimicola* • ***FISH-ing for Genes: Modeling Fluorescence in situ Hybridization***	**THURSDAY, DECEMBER 13, 2007 10:30 a.m. TO 12:30 p.m. COMPREHENSIVE FINAL EXAM**

A-6. SCIENCE SEMINAR TOPIC SCHEDULE

SCIENCE SEMINAR TOPIC SCHEDULE
SPRING 2008
Tuesdays, 3:00 p.m.–6:00 p.m.

Key to Fonts: Reading Assignment, page numbers; ○ **Written assignment**; • *In-class activities*; **CLASS TOPIC**

WEEK	READING, WRITING, AND OTHER <u>BEFORE</u>-CLASS RESPONSIBILITIES	IN-CLASS ACTIVITIES
1 1/15		• *Introductions* • *Thinking Inside the Box* • *A Cool Glass of Water*
2 1/22	Read the syllabus Section II: What Are Case Studies? 27 Ch. 5. Case Studies in Science, 29–39 Ch. 7. What Makes a Good Case? 45–48 Section III: Types of Case Studies, 53 Ch. 9. Sorting Potatoes for Miss Bonner, 55–59 Section V: Whole Class Discussion: The Classical Method, 83–84 Ch. 14. Using Novels as Bases of Case Studies, 85–87 (Analysis case-contemporary)	**WHOLE CLASS DISCUSSION** • *Ch. 15. Journal Articles as Case Studies, 91–98 (Dilemma case)* • *Ch. 16. Bad Blood, 99–110 (Analysis case-historical)* • *Ch. 38. What to Do About Mother? 265–270 (Discussion with group role)*
3 1/29	Introduction to Ch. 15, 89–91 ○ **Write topic idea and outline for a possible case study using the whole class discussion format**	• *Ch. 17. Case Study Teaching in Science: A Dilemma Case on "Animal Rights," 111–117 (Dilemma case)* • *Ch. 18. Is There Life on Mars? 119–123 (Dilemma case)*
4 2/5	Section VI: Small-Group Methods, 125 Ch. 22. The Pima Experience, 147–150 Section VII: Problem-Based Learning, 151 Ch. 23. The Death of Problem-Based Learning? 153–156	**SMALL GROUP METHODS** • *Ch. 24. AIDS and the Duesberg Phenomenon, 157–160* • *Ch. 25. The Petition, 161–166*
5 2/12	○ **Write topic and outline for a possible case study using a small group format** Section VIII: Interrupted Case Method, 167 Ch. 26. The Interrupted Case Method, 169–170 ○ **Write tentative topic for your original case study and answers to questions at top of handout "How to Choose a Topic for Your Original Case Study," 9** ○ **Make Writing Center appointment for before 2/29 for consultation on original dialogue**	**INTERRUPTED CASE METHOD** • *Ch. 27. Mom Always Liked You Best, 171–177* • *Each student presents to the class his or her tentative topic for an original case study*

6 2/19	Section XII: Individual Case Study Methods, 237 Ch. 35. Dialogues as Case Studies—A Discussion on Human Cloning, 239–245 Ch. 36 Student Paper on the Atlantic Salmon Controversy, 247–250 ○ **Write an original dialogue**	**WINTER BREAK—NO CLASS**
7 2/26	○ **Write topic and outline for a possible case study using Interrupted Case Format** Section IX: Intimate Debate Method, 179 Ch. 28. Should Marijuana Be Legalized for Medicinal Purposes? 181–186 Section X: Team-Based Learning, 187 ○ **By Friday 2/29: Complete Writing Center consultation on original dialogue**	• *Ch. 32 Of Mammoths and Men, 211–218 (Team-Based Learning)* • *Students practice using the "Evaluation Criteria for Oral Presentation of Case Study" to evaluate Dr. Wood's presentation* • *Critique and possible revision of evaluation criteria*
8 3/4	○ **Complete final copy of original dialogue** Section XIII: Hybrid Case Methods, 251 Section XIV: The Directed Case Method, 299 ○ **Choose a case study from the National Center for Case Study Teaching in Science Case Collection** (Each student must choose a different case and one in which seminar students have never participated.) ○ **Submit title of this case study and date you prefer to present it** (choose among Weeks 9, 10, 11)	• *Each student presents to the class his or her original dialogue.* • *Hybrid or directed case study from Chs. 37–45* • *Practice using revised "Evaluation Criteria for Oral Presentation of Case Study"*
9 3/11	Section XV: How Not to Teach With Case Studies, 331 Ch. 46. Return to Mars, 333–337 Ch. 47. Why a "Case-Based Course Failed," 339–341 Ch. 48. DON'T! What Not to Do When Teaching Case Studies, 343–347	• *3 student presentations from National Center for Case Study Teaching in Science Case Collection* • *Students use "Evaluation Criteria for Oral Presentation of Case Study" to critique each other* • *Discussion and critique of each presentation*
10 3/18	Section XVI: How to Write Case Studies, 349 Ch. 49. Case Studies and the Media, 351–353 Ch. 50. Cooking With Betty Crocker, 355–359 Ch. 51 Too Much, Too Little, or Just Right? 361–364 ○ **Write a narrative and detailed outline of your original case study, including a description of the appropriate audience and the case study format you will use**	• *3 student presentations from National Center for Case Study Teaching in Science Case Collection* • *Students use "Evaluation Criteria for Oral Presentation of Case Study" to critique each other* • *Discussion and critique of each presentation*

11 3/25	Ch. 52. The Way of Flesch, 365–369 Ch. 53. Twixt Fact and Fiction, 371–374 Ch. 54. An Open or Shut Case? 375–379 Ch. 55 Racism and All Sorts of Politically Correct *Isms* in Case Studies, 381–383 ○ **Make Writing Center appointment for before 4/18 for consultation on original case study and teaching notes** ○ **Bring ideas for class presentation on 2008 University Day**	• *3 student presentations from National Center for Case Study Teaching in Science Case Collection* • *Students use "Evaluation Criteria for Oral Presentation of Case Study" to critique each other* • *Discussion and critique of each presentation* • *Class chooses a case study to present on University Day*
12 4/1	**Write your original case study and teaching notes**	**SPRING BREAK—NO CLASS**
13 4/8	Section XVI: How to Write Case Study Teaching Notes, 385 Ch. 56. And All That Jazz, 387–391	• *Determine dates for each student's presentation of original case study* • *Dress rehearsal for University Day Presentation*
14 4/15	○ **By Friday 4/18: Complete Writing Center consultation on draft of original case study and teaching notes** ○ **University Day presentation. April 16, 2008**	*Wednesday, April 16* *Case Study Presentation at 2008 University Day* *(Time and room to be announced)* — • *3 student presentations of original case studies* • *Discussion and critique of each presentation*
15 4/22	○ **Rewrite your original case study and teaching notes**	• *3 student presentations or original case studies* • *Discussion and critique of each presentation*
16 4/29	○ **Rewrite your original case study and teaching notes**	• *3 student presentations of original case studies* • *Discussion and critique of each presentation*
17 5/6	**FINAL COPY OF CASE STUDY AND TEACHING NOTES DUE IN ROOM 316, SOUTH HALL BY 5:00 p.m., TUESDAY, MAY 6, 2008**	

A-7. EXAMPLE OF A CONTENT OUTLINE IN A GENERAL BIOLOGY I COURSEPACK

OUTLINE 10
GENETICS

I. Relating meiosis to genetics
  A. Chromosomes
    1. Timing of DNA replication (production of chromatids)
    2. Chromosomal separation during meiosis
    3. Chromosomal movement during meiosis affects inherited trait transmission

  B. Genes
    1. Gene locus
    2. Allele
      a. Allelic pairs and chromosomal movement during meiosis
      b. Allelic pairs and expression of inherited traits
      c. Multiple alleles
        (1) Mutations (not necessarily harmful)
  C. Genotype and phenotype
    1. Homozygous and heterozygous genotypes
    2. "Dominant" and "recessive" phenotypes (traits)
      a. Why the terms *dominant* and *recessive* are misleading
        (1) A diploid organism's phenotype is based on two alleles (yielding two traits)
        (2) Absence of dominance is the norm
          (a) Inheritance of ABO blood types in humans
        (3) Homozygous alleles produce "dominant" phenotype
        (4) Homozygous alleles produce "recessive" phenotype
        (5) Heterozygous alleles produce "dominant" phenotype (one trait may mask other)

II. Predicting the results of crosses
  A. Symbols used in genetics
  B. Monohybrid cross
    1. Test cross
  C. Punnett square
    1. F_1 generation
    2. F_2 generation
    3. Further generations

III. From gene to protein
    A.   Transcription
    B.   The genetic code
    C.   Translation
    D.   Mutation

IV. Recombinant DNA technology
    A.   Genetically engineered organisms
    B.   GM (genetically modified) food—pros and cons
    C.   Drugs produced by recombinant DNA technology
    D.   Gene therapy
    E.   The human genome project

V. DNA fingerprinting

A-8. EXAMPLE OF A COURSE SYLLABUS

GENERAL BIOLOGY I SYLLABUS
FALL 2007
Mondays and Wednesdays, 11:00 a.m. to 1:45 p.m.

HOW TO FIND ME

Office hours, 316 South Hall: Monday and Wednesday, 2:00–3:30 p.m.
768-9446 (you may leave a voice mail message)

Use Blackboard (*www.courses.maine.edu*), my e-mail address (*bonnie.s. wood@umpi.edu*), or my web page (*www.umpi.maine.edu/~wood*).

If you need to see me but cannot come during regular office hours, you may make an appointment for a more convenient time. If you do not understand some of the course material, please ask questions before it is too late!

WHAT'S DIFFERENT ABOUT THIS COURSE?

In this section of General Biology, the arbitrary distinction between "lecture" and "laboratory" is eliminated. Instead, both parts of the course are interwoven during two longer class meetings each week, held in the laboratory. Take a look at the topic schedule to see what we will cover this semester.

Biology 112 is the first course of a two-semester sequence. Although some of you are science majors, many are not and may consider the science course graduation requirement a major obstacle. My goal is to engage you in learning biology so this course becomes a positive component of your undergraduate experience—a part that not only is a stepping stone to a degree but also enriches your life. Because I emphasize using facts about biology rather than memorizing information, I hope the teaching methods I use will significantly change the way you view the world. Sometimes you will practice applying material alone, and sometimes you will do so with members of your learning team.

I want to foster an interest in biology that continues beyond the date of the final exam, prepare you to make effective choices in the voting booth, enable you to be a citizen of the world, and help you acquire thinking you can use in other endeavors.

To accomplish my goals, I use Lecture-Free Teaching. You participate in inquiry-based exercises that require you to think about real-world problems. Active learning does not make the course easier and does not take less of your time. However, if you follow my guidelines, you will not only enjoy the course more but also increase your likelihood of success in the class. To be successful, you must take responsibility for your own learning. This syllabus describes how to do this and is a resource for the entire semester.

HOW TO SUCCEED IN BIOLOGY 112
All class meetings require active involvement. To participate, you must prepare before each class.

The General Biology I coursepack (which you must buy at the campus bookstore) contains content outlines informing you of what you are expected to know about each subject listed on your topic schedule. Before each scheduled class, read the appropriate parts of the suggested textbook chapters (indicated in the left-hand column of the topic schedule) and take notes—in your own words—on the outlines. The outlines and sections within an outline are not necessarily in the same order as the chapters in your text, and you may need to use the textbook index or glossary to learn about them. If an outline is scheduled for several class meetings, complete the outline before the first date for which it is relevant. After taking notes on the outline, complete Homework Activities described at the end of the outline and be prepared to discuss your results on the topic schedule date.

Homework is done before class meetings—a change from what you may have experienced in previous classes.

E-mail me before 7:00 a.m. on the day of each class if you have specific questions or topics you want me to clarify that day, and I will respond at the beginning of class. If I receive no questions or requests, I will assume everyone in the class understands the reading on the topic, and I will not spend time explaining information. You are responsible for any concept listed in the outlines, even if I do not discuss it in class. Your responsibility is to let me know about anything you want me to explain further, and you cannot do this without first reading the chapter and taking notes on the content outline.

Periodically I collect (without prior notification!) a content outline to grade and to give you feedback on your note-taking. No late submissions are accepted because the outlines are most useful to you if completed before class.

Class time is for in-class and laboratory exercises that assume prior knowledge from reading the chapters. You work with your learning team for many of these activities. Some will be fun, and all will help you apply your knowledge and prepare you for upcoming tests. If you fail to read the chapter or take notes on the outline before each class, you will let your learning team down, and you will not acquire comprehension and expertise during the activities.

During the last two minutes of each class meeting, you will describe in writing the Murkiest Point—something from that class you still do not fully understand. If you understand everything, instead describe the Most Interesting Point. You will sign this paper and hand it in as you leave. To be marked as attending the class, you must write something other than your name! I will begin the next class with an explanation of "murkies," so this is an important opportunity for additional clarification.

ACADEMIC HONESTY
In cases of violation of academic honesty, I will discuss the matter with you and assign you a grade of F (zero points) for the violated work or require that you withdraw from the course with a grade of F, depending on the gravity of the offense.

ATTENDANCE

Attendance at all scheduled class meetings is very important. Each class includes activities that you complete alone or with your learning team. You are responsible for all material covered during class, whether you were present or not. If you are absent, look at what you missed on the topic schedule and discuss what we did with a learning team member or me. A record of the Murkiest Point papers will assess your attendance.

RESOURCES: THESE MUST BE PURCHASED AT THE BOOKSTORE AND BROUGHT TO ALL CLASSES.

The Living World, Fifth Edition, by George B. Johnson and Jonathan B. Losos. This text is used for both General Biology I and II and was chosen because it is easy to read and does not contain excessive detail. The chapters of this book that correspond to each week's classes are indicated on the Topic Schedule.

The General Biology I coursepack is a three-ring binder containing content outlines you must complete before class, as well as detailed instructions for homework and in-class and laboratory activities. Handouts (like this syllabus and the topic schedule) that you will receive throughout the semester should be added to the coursepack.

BLACKBOARD

Blackboard is an online course-management system that we will use in Biology 112 that is accessible with any UMPI computer and with most home and public computers. Through Blackboard, you will receive important announcements from me, communicate with me, access course materials, and participate in other activities I explain during the semester.

To log on to Blackboard, go to *www.courses.maine.edu*, click the Login button, and enter your username and password. All your UMS courses that use Blackboard will be listed under "My Courses," and you can access each one by clicking on its link.

COMPUTER LABS

You may learn about locations and hours of Houlton and Presque Isle computer labs from the UMPI homepage (*www.umpi.maine.edu*) by going to Information For→Current Students→Computer Services→Fishing Hole (on left of screen)→ Lab Hours.

TUTORING AND OTHER ASSISTANCE

If you are in any way concerned about your ability to succeed in this course, you should sign up for tutoring immediately. Do not wait until you have done poorly on the first test because that may be too late! To sign up, see the Tutor Coordinator, 120 South Hall, 768-9614. If you have a disability and need accommodation or assistance in this course, contact the Director of Student Support Services, 123 South Hall, 768-9613, or e-mail *mary.barbosa@umpi.edu*.

ASSIGNMENTS
LEARNING TEAMS

As part of an activity on the first day of class about the classification of organisms, you are randomly assigned to a learning team. You work with these students in and out of class for the entire semester.

Team Coordinator: Choose a coordinator who will organize meetings, facilitate discussion, and keep me informed of progress and problems in the team. On the first day of class you should determine several times during the week when you are all available outside class.

Exchange Information: Exchange telephone numbers and e-mail addresses among yourselves.

Behavior: Arrive promptly to class and sit with your team. During in-class activities and lab exercises you will work together, so your team members need you there at the beginning to hear the instructions.

FIRST WEEK ASSIGNMENTS

- Read this syllabus carefully! Note especially your responsibilities in the course.
- Read the appropriate parts of the assigned chapters for Week 1 and complete Outlines 1 and 2 for the next class; before 7:00 a.m. on the day of the next class, e-mail me any questions or subjects you would like explained further.
- If you have not activated your university "@maine.edu" e-mail account, contact Computer Services in the library (768-9626) for help.
- If you forgot your password, you can reset your password using the following website: *http://mail.maine.edu.*
- I will communicate via Blackboard using your "@maine.edu" account. If you check a different e-mail account more frequently, use the UMS Mail Server (*http://mail.maine.edu*) to forward your "@maine.edu" e-mail to your preferred account.

READINGS AND OTHER HOMEWORK

Before each class, read appropriate parts of the chapters listed on your Topic Schedule. Determine which parts of the chapter you should read by looking at the outline. Complete any other assignments listed in the left-hand homework column of the Topic Schedule. You are expected to be familiar with this material before the first class for which it is relevant.

WRITTEN ASSIGNMENTS

- One point is deducted for each day that any part of written assignment is late, including the consultation at the Writing Center.
- Both individual writing assignments explained below require a consultation at the Writing Center. You should make an appointment well in advance by going to the Writing Center, located on the first floor of South Hall. Make your appointment *before* your draft is written! Students from many different classes use this service so getting an appointment at the last minute may be impossible.

SCIENTIFIC REPORT OF LABORATORY INVESTIGATION
Each student writes one scientific report about one of the following inquiry-based laboratory exercises: Diffusion and Osmosis (Weeks 3–4); *In Vitro* Gas Suppression: Beano—Enzymes to the Rescue (Week 5); Photosynthesis vs. Respiration/Cellular Respiration in Plants (Week 6); Effects of Experimental Variables on Fermentation Ability in Yeast (Week 6).

On closed reserve in the UMPI library I have placed the book *A Student Handbook for Writing in Biology* by Karin Knisely. Although Chapters 1 through 3 may be useful to you, Chapters 4 and 5 give instructions for preparing and revising a laboratory report. Chapter 6 is a sample student laboratory report. Carefully follow the scientific report of laboratory investigation grading criteria in the front portion of your coursepack, which I derived from this book, and submit this with your completed report.

Due dates:
- **By Wednesday, September 5,** submit a list of students in your learning group and indicate which laboratory report each student will write.
- **By the Monday following completion of the lab exercise,** accomplish your consultation about your scientific report draft with one of the UMPI Writing Center tutors.
- Two copies of the final report are due on the ***Wednesday* following completion of the lab exercise.** On this due date, submit your report with the scientific report of laboratory investigation grading criteria sheet stapled to the front. Behind the final copy, attach the first draft along with notes made during the consultation at the Writing Center. Graph paper in the front portion of your coursepack can be used for the final report.

BOOK REVIEW
Choose and read a book from the Biology 112 book review choices on Blackboard or my website. Each student must read a different book. Write a review of its appropriateness for Biology 112 students by carefully following the book review grading criteria in the front of your coursepack.

Due dates: (See the Homework column on your topic schedule. You do not have to wait until the due date to complete each part!)

- **Wednesday, October 24:** Tell me the author and title of book. Since each student must read a different book, borrow your book from the library early to increase your chances of getting your first choice.
- **By Friday, November 29:** Complete your consultation with one of the Writing Center tutors.
- **Wednesday, December 5:** Submit your final book review with the book review grading criteria sheet stapled to the front. Behind the final copy, attach the first draft along with notes made during the consultation at the Writing Center.

LEARNING TEAM PROJECTS

There will be two projects (both due on **Wednesday, November 7**) that you will organize and complete as a group: (1) Supermarket Botany and (2) Thermoregulation: How Do Plants Deal with the Cold? Detailed instructions will be distributed Weeks 9 and 10.

TESTS AND EXAMS

TEST REVIEW ACTIVITIES. Before each test you will have an opportunity for extra credit points. To be eligible, carefully follow the guidelines for writing test review questions in the front of your coursepack and submit your typewritten question and answer during the class before the test review so that I can edit and organize them. No late submissions accepted! Learning will compete for extra credit points by answering these questions and scratching off answers on an IF-AT Form. If you do not submit appropriate questions on the due date (see Homework column on your topic schedule), you may still participate in the review activity with your team, but you are not eligible for extra credit points.

TYPES OF TEST QUESTIONS. Questions emphasize critical thinking skills acquired during in-class and laboratory activities, as well as laboratory skills. For each test you may bring one 8½- × 11-inch paper on which you have written important facts (on one side only) and your name. This will be stapled to the back of your test when you turn it in.

MAKE-UP. If you know in advance that you will be absent during a test or final examination, you must obtain permission from me at least two school days *before* the day of the test. Unanticipated absences will result in a grade of F (zero points) unless you call me on the day on which the test was scheduled (you may leave a voice mail message and I will call you back) and present medical or legal documentation at the earliest possible date after the class period.

If you have just read this entire syllabus, e-mail me before 7:00 a.m. on the second day of class with a statement of the most important thing you learned from the syllabus, and you will begin the semester with three extra credit points!

GRADING PROCEDURES:

The total possible points for the course is 350 (excluding extra credit) distributed in the following way:

3 topic tests @ 50 points each	= 150
1 final exam	= 100
Scientific report	= 30
Book review	= 30
Supermarket Botany	= 15
Thermoregulation in Plants	= 15
Outline preparation + class participation	= 10
Total course points	**= 350**

To determine the letter grade for a test or exam or for the course:
1. Calculate your percentage based on the total possible points using this ratio: points obtained/total possible points $\times$ 100 = %
2. Convert the percentage to a letter grade using the scale below:

A	= 93–100%	B–	= 80–82.9%	D+	= 67–69.9%
A–	= 90–92.9%	C+	= 77–79.9%	D	= 63–66.9%
B+	= 87–89.9%	C	= 73–76.9%	D–	= 60–62.9%
B	= 83–86.9%	C–	= 70–72.9%	F	= 00–59.9%

Examples of Grading Criteria, Rubrics, and Point Distributions

B-1. THREE EXAMPLES OF COURSE GRADING SYSTEMS DEMONSTRATING HOW EACH ASSESSMENT REFLECTS A CORRESPONDING COURSE LEARNING GOAL

(See box in Chapter 3, Step 2, for the numbered learning goals for these three courses.)

For General Biology I (Biology 112)

List of Graded Assessments	Points Possible for Each Assessment	Chapter 3 Learning Goal Number
3 topic tests @ 50 points each	150	1, 2
Final exam	100	1, 2
Scientific report	30	3
Book review	30	1, 4
Supermarket Botany	15	5
Thermoregulation in Plants	15	5
Outline participation/Class participation	10	1, 4, 5
Total course points	350	

For Human Nutrition (Biology 300)

List of Graded Assessments	Points Possible for Each Assessment	Chapter 3 Learning Goal Number
3 topic tests @ 50 points each	150	1, 4
Complete nutritional assessment of service-learning partner	100	2
Book review	35	4, 5
Homework activities	20	3, 5
Outlines and participation	10	1, 5
Total course points	315	

For Case Studies in Science Seminar (Biology/Environmental Studies 489)

List of Graded Assessments	Points Possible for Each Assessment	Chapter 3 Learning Goal Number
Write 3 topic ideas with outlines for possible case study @ 10 points each	30	1, 2, 3
Write an original dialogue	30	1, 2, 4, 5
Oral presentation of case study from National Center for Case Study Teaching in Science case collection	36	7
University Day oral presentation (with learning team)	10	7
Write original case study and teaching notes, and present orally to class	100	2, 3, 4, 5, 6, 7
Class participation	10	8
Total course points	216	

National Science Teachers Association

B-2. GRADING CRITERIA FOR TOPIC IDEA AND OUTLINE FOR A CASE STUDY IN A SPECIFIC STYLE

Assigned Style/Format of Case Study (Whole Class Discussion, Small Group Method, or Interrupted Case Method): _____

_____

CRITERIA Each criterion worth up to 2 points	POINTS
TOPIC: A specific topic, described in one phrase or sentence that would be appropriate for a single case study.	
STORY: A brief description of your "story with an educational message." The story can be based on an actual event or can be totally fictitious.	
OBJECTIVES: A list of the "blocks of analysis" or issues you want the participants to analyze during the presentation of the case study. The objectives are what you want participants to understand at the conclusion of the activity.	
OUTLINE: A brief description of how you would design an effective presentation in the assigned style or format. This would constitute part of the Teaching Notes in a completed case study.	
WRITING QUALITY: One to two pages, typed, double-spaced. Use of correct spelling, grammar, and sentence structure is expected.	
TOTAL POINTS (out of 10 possible)	
COMMENTS:	

B-3. GRADING CRITERIA FOR AN ORIGINAL DIALOGUE AS A CASE STUDY

(Criteria are adapted from Herreid [2007])

Title of Dialogue as a Case Study: _____

Assign points to each of the eight criteria according to the rating scale defined below:

    0 = Less Than Satisfactory
    1 = Satisfactory
    2 = More Than Satisfactory
    3 = Outstanding

1. The paper is at least five typewritten, double-spaced pages, but not limited to this length. (Points =   )

2. The dialogue concerns a current controversial topic. (Points =   )

3. The issue or issues are explored in depth. (Points =   )

4. The paper is a dialogue between (at least) two people on opposite sides of the question. It is written in the form of a script or play, as demonstrated in Chapter 35: Dialogues as Case Studies—A Discussion on Human Cloning, and Chapter 36: Student Paper on the Atlantic Salmon Controversy in your textbook. (Points =   )

5. At least 20 exchanges occur between people in the dialogue. In other words, if there are two people participating, each one speaks at least 20 times. (Points =   )

6. The exchanges are serious, substantive, and courteous comments made between two intelligent people grappling with an important issue. (Points =   )

7. A short paragraph introduces the paper and indicates where the dialogue is occurring and the circumstances surrounding the discussion. (Points =   )

8. A final paragraph to the paper describes the author's personal opinion and reasons behind it. (Points =   )

9. A list of references at the end of the paper is complete and uses American Psychological Association (APA) bibliographic style. (Points =   )

10. The author uses correct spelling, grammar, and sentence structure throughout and follows the guidelines described in Chapter 52: The Way of Flesch: The Art of Writing Readable Cases in your textbook. (Points =   )

TOTAL POINTS (out of a possible 30): _____

Comments:

REFERENCE

Herreid, C. F. 2007. Dialogues as case studies—a discussion on human cloning. In _Start with a story: The case study method of teaching college science_, ed. C. F. Herreid, 239–245. Arlington, VA: NSTA Press.

B-4. GRADING CRITERIA FOR A ONE-HOUR ORAL PRESENTATION OF A CASE STUDY CHOSEN FROM THE NATIONAL CENTER FOR CASE STUDY TEACHING IN SCIENCE CASE COLLECTION

(Criteria are adapted from Field [2003])

Title and URL of Case Study: _____

Style/Format of Case Study: _____

Assign points to each of the nine criteria below according to the rating scale defined below. Zero points are given if the presentation does not meet a criterion.

   1 = **Strongly Disagree**
   2 = **Disagree**
   3 = **Agree**
   4 = **Strongly Agree**

1. The presenter chose a case study from the National Center for Case Study Teaching in Science Case Collection (Case Studies in Science) that was relevant to the group of students in the Science Seminar. (Points =   )

2. Background information could be easily comprehended by the intended audience within the approximately 25 minutes allotted. (Points =   )

3. The case story was clearly presented in 5 to 10 minutes. (Points =   )

4. The small group discussion of the case study questions was completed within 15 minutes. (Points =   )

5. The whole class discussion of case questions was completed within the remaining time. (Points =   )

6. The presenter involved all class members in the case study activities. (Points =   )

7. The presenter had good clarity of speech and vocal diction. (Points =   )

8. The presenter demonstrated good teaching skills by being well prepared and knowledgeable about the topic and giving clear directions for what individuals and groups should do. (Points =   )

9. The presenter provided appropriate closure to the case in the form of a summary at the end of the hour. (Points =   )

Total Points (out of a possible 36): _____

Comments:
REFERENCES
Case Studies in Science, State University of New York at Buffalo. National Center for Case Study Teaching in Science. *http://ublib.buffalo.edu/libraries/projects/cases/case.html*.

Field, P. R. 2003. Senior seminar: Using case studies to teach the components of a successful seminar. *Journal of College Science Teaching* 32 (5): 298–301.

B-5. GRADING CRITERIA FOR AN ORIGINAL CASE STUDY INCLUDING ORAL PRESENTATION AND TEACHING NOTES

(Criteria are adapted from Field [2003] and Herreid [2007])

Title of Case Study: _____

Style/Format of Case Study: _____

Assign points to each of the 25 criteria on a scale of 1 to 4 according to the rating scale defined below. Zero points are given if the case does not meet a criterion.

    1 = **Strongly Disagree**
    2 = **Disagree**
    3 = **Agree**
    4 = **Strongly Agree**

STORY STRUCTURE

1. The story follows one of the case study style structures described in Chapter 5: Case Studies in Science. (Points =   )

2. The author uses correct spelling, grammar, and sentence structure throughout and follows the guidelines described in Chapter 52: The Way of Flesch: The Art of Writing Readable Cases. (Points =   )

   Criteria 3 to 6 are described in Chapter 7: What Makes a Good Case?

3. The narrative/dialogue is completely developed. (Points =   )

4. Empathy for the main characters is evident. (Points =   )

5. The content is relevant to the intended audience. (Points =   )

6. The educational/teaching function is clearly elucidated. (Points =   )

ORAL PRESENTATION—APPROXIMATELY ONE HOUR

7. Background information could be easily comprehended by the intended audience within the approximately 25 minutes allotted. (Points =   )

8. The case story was clearly presented in 5 to 10 minutes. (Points =   )

9. The small group discussion of the case study questions was completed within 15 minutes. (Points =   )

10. The class discussion of case questions was completed within the remaining time. (Points =   )

11. The author involved all class members of the class in the case study activities. (Points =   )

12. The author had good clarity of speech and vocal diction. (Points =   )

13. The author demonstrated good teaching skills by being well prepared and know-ledgeable about the topic and giving clear directions for what individuals and groups should do. (Points =   )

14. The author provided appropriate closure to the case in the form of a summary at the end of the hour. (Points =   )

TEACHING NOTES
Criteria 15 to 24 are described in Chapter 56: And All That Jazz.

Introduction/Background
15. Courses for which the case is appropriate are described. (Points =   )

16. Student populations (majors/programs/grade level) or other specific audiences that would benefit from this case are described. (Points =   )

Objectives of the Case
17. The purpose of the case is clearly stated. (Points =   )

18. The objectives of the case are described by specific statements and written in the form specified in Chapter 56. (Points =   )

Major Issues
19. Major issues of the case are presented. (Points =   )

20. The teaching notes provide support for the major issues. (Points =   )

Classroom Management
21. The schedule for how to conduct the case during a one-hour class is outlined. (Points =   )

22. One or more of the following types of study questions are used to effectively facili-tate the discussions. (Circle types used.) (Points =   )

Introductory   Challenge   Decision Forcing   Summary

23. Suggestions for board work are described. (Points =   )

24. Suggestions for providing closure to the case are described. (Points =   )

References
25. References are cited correctly using American Psychological Association (APA) style. (Points =   )

TOTAL POINTS (out of a possible 100): _____

Comments:
REFERENCES
Field, P. R. 2003. Senior seminar: Using case studies to teach the components of a successful seminar. *Journal of College Science Teaching* 32 (5): 298–301.
Herreid, C. F., ed. 2007. *Start with a story: The case study method of teaching college science.* Arlington, VA: NSTA Press.

B-6. SCIENCES II BOOK REVIEW GRADING CRITERIA AND POINT DISTRIBUTION

TOPICS TO INCLUDE IN THE BOOK REVIEW	POINTS FOR FINAL REPORT
Complete bibliographical reference (at top) using APA or other standard style; no title page (1 point)	
A total length of approximately two double-spaced pages (1 point)	
Use of correct spelling, grammar, and sentence structure (2 points)	
One or two introductory paragraphs consisting of a brief synopsis of the book (in your own words) (4 points)	
Ways in which the book relates to the upcoming Environmental Action Project (list specific examples) (6 points)	
Major scientific contributions described in the book. How these enhance your understanding of science (4 points)	
How the scientific process was or was not used by the scientists who wrote the book or about whom the book was written (Describe this in terms of the steps of the scientific method, giving examples of observations, hypothesis, experiments, and conclusions.) (3 points)	
The personal characteristics of the scientist(s) who wrote the book or about whom the book was written (2 points)	
Personal, physical, political, or professional obstacles the authors or scientist(s) had to overcome. These obstacles should include things such as race, ethnicity, gender, religion, political events, and scientific thought at the time the book was written. (3 points)	
Your personal feelings about the book, the author(s), or the scientist(s) about whom the book was written. Was this book appropriate for a Sciences II student and for the upcoming Environmental Action Project? Why or why not? (4 points)	
TOTAL POINTS OUT OF 30	
Additional comments:	

National Science Teachers Association

B-7. SCIENTIFIC REPORT OF LABORATORY INVESTIGATION SCORING RUBRIC

(Adapted from Knisely [2005] and Walvoord and Anderson [1998])

First Author's Name: _____

Topic of Laboratory Exercise:_____

Signature of Writing Center Tutor:_____

Date of Writing Center Consultation: _____

TOTAL POINTS OUT OF 30 = _____

TITLE AND AUTHORS

2   Title is written at the top of the report (not on a cover sheet) and is descriptive, concise, and appropriate in tone and structure for a scientific journal. Title allows reader to anticipate the experiment's design. First author is listed first with contributing learning team members listed as second, third, and fourth authors.

1   Title is descriptive but does not allow the reader to anticipate the experiment's design. Names of authors are incomplete or misspelled.

0   Title and authors are on a separate cover sheet; title is the same as the general topic of the laboratory exercise (as given in the coursepack).

GENERAL CONSIDERATIONS

2   All material is placed in the correct sections as described below and organized logically within each section; the organization is parallel among the different sections. The report is neatly typed, single-spaced, with correct spelling and grammar. Pages are numbered in the upper right corners. The entire report is in paragraph form. All measurements are in SI units with proper abbreviations; genus and species are underlined or italicized, with genus capitalized. Underlining in the text is not done for any other purposes (as for emphasis).

1   The materials are placed in the correct sections, all of which are written in paragraph form, but the report does not have a neat appearance, or contains frequent errors of spelling and grammar, or does not use SI units, or incorrectly writes genus and species of organisms.

0   As for 1 but the materials are incorrectly located in the sections or the sections are missing.

ABSTRACT

3   Contains 100 words or less and explains the purpose of the experiment and a brief description of methods, results, and conclusions.

2   Lacks one of the elements listed for 3 and/or is too long or too short.

1   Lacks more than one of the elements listed for 3 and/or is too long or too short.

0   Abstract missing or does not contain the elements listed for 3.

INTRODUCTION

5   Contains background information from the literature (primary references) that directly relates to the experiment. The in-text citation form is correct and citations are paraphrased (quotation marks are not used). Purpose of the experiment and the hypothesis are clearly stated. Information from the coursepack is not copied, but rather the topic is described in the author's own words, using information gained from Biology 112, both in class and from student's own reading.

4   As for 5 but background information from the literature is lacking, along with citations.

3   As for 4, but purpose or the hypothesis is lacking.

2   As for 3, but both purpose and hypothesis are lacking.

1   Information in the Introduction belongs in another section of the report.

0   Introduction is missing or is not written in student's own words.

MATERIALS AND METHODS

5   The materials are described in paragraph form (not listed like ingredients in a recipe). Section is written in past tense and contains all relevant information, in an appropriate chronology, to enable a reader to replicate the experiment. The exact procedure is described, not necessarily what was suggested in the coursepack. Information is complete enough so everything in the rest of the report can be related back to Materials and Methods, but the section avoids unnecessary, wordy descriptions of procedures. Precise measurements are given using SI units.

4   As for 5, but contains unnecessary or wordy descriptions.

3   As for 5, but gives sequential information in a disorganized, confusing way.

2   Describes an experiment that is marginally replicable, so that the reader must infer parts of the basic design. The procedures are not quantitatively described.

1   Describes the experiment so poorly or in such a nonscientific way that it cannot be replicated. Contains information that belongs in a different section.

0   Materials and Methods section is missing or is not written in student's own words.

RESULTS

5   Contains quantifiable experimental data with units clearly defined and labeled in both text and graphics. Drawings, graphs, and tables are included where appropriate. Figure captions are placed below the figure; table captions above the table. Figure and table captions are informative and can be understood independently of the text. Results are described in paragraph form in the text, and the text refers to each table and figure. Actual results are described, rather than extrapolations or what was expected (save this for Discussion). No explanation is given for the results.

4   As for 5, but figure and table captions cannot be understood without reading the text.

3   As for 4, but the data reported in the text, graphs, or tables include information that is irrelevant to the purpose of the experiment or the hypothesis.

2   Quantifiable experimental data are present, but the quantities or intervals are inappropriate, or information is not displayed graphically when appropriate.

1   The section does not contain or communicate quantifiable results. The information belongs in another section of the report.

0   The Results section is missing.

DISCUSSION

5   Both observed and expected results are summarized. Errors and inconsistencies in procedure are pointed out. Possible explanations of unexpected results are given, as are suggestions for further and/or improved experimentation. A statement of whether the hypothesis is accepted or rejected is made by comparing the original hypothesis with the data.

4   As for 5, but accepting or rejecting the hypothesis is lacking.

3   As for 4, but suggestions for further and/or improved experimentation are lacking.

2   As for 3, but unexpected results are ignored.

1   The results are summarized but are not interpreted.

0   The Discussion section is missing.

REFERENCES

3   References are primary journal articles, textbooks, or peer-reviewed internet sources (e.g., from a journal, not from a source such as Wikipedia). References, listed using American Psychological Association (APA) style, are correct, complete, and consistent. All references are cited in the text (author's name and date), and all citations in the text are in the References section. The reference list is arranged in alphabetical order according to the first author's surname. First names are given as initials. (For examples of reference style, see any issue of *The American Biology Teacher*, a journal located in the UMPI library.)

2   As for 3, but consistent APA style is not used.

1   As for 2, but some references are inappropriate (e.g., are not from primary journal articles, textbooks, or peer-reviewed internet sources) or are not cited in the text, or citations in the text are not included in the References section.

0   The References section is missing.

REFERENCES

Knisely, K. 2005. *A student handbook for writing in biology*. Gordonsville, VA: Sinauer Associates.

Walvoord, B. E., and V. J. Anderson. 1998. *Effective grading: A tool for learning and assessment*. San Francisco: Jossey-Bass.

B-8. ENVIRONMENTAL ACTION PROJECT REFLECTION PHASE GRADING CRITERIA AND POINT DISTRIBUTION

TOPICS TO INCLUDE IN REFLECTION FOR ENVIRONMENTAL ACTION PROJECT	INDIVIDUAL POINTS FOR FINAL PROJECT
Use correct grammar, spelling, and sentence structure in all parts of the writing project. (2 points)	
Participation in your learning group. (2 points)	
DESCRIPTION OF ENTIRE PROJECT	
In one or two typewritten pages, describe your involvement in the Environmental Action Project. (2 points)	
Explain why you chose your particular personal environmental action. (2 points)	
Describe your seven days of taking the personal environmental action. (2 points)	
Describe your second environmental action. (2 points)	
Tell whether it was at the University of Maine at Presque Isle campus, the city or town in which you reside, the state or province in which you reside, or the country in which you reside. (2 points)	
Explain why you chose the level and the action, and briefly describe the action. (2 points)	
Tell what you learned from the entire Environmental Action Project. (2 points)	
LETTER TO THE EDITOR OR GOVERNMENT OFFICIAL	
Write a letter to the editor of an appropriate newspaper or a letter to the appropriate governmental official on the topic of your second environmental action. The letter should make realistic suggestions for change. (4 points)	
The writing should be persuasive because of its scientific information rather than emotional rhetoric. (2 points)	
The length of the letter should be long enough to include important information but short enough that it will be read. (2 points)	
Scientific information should be referenced correctly. (2 points)	
The final letter should be READY TO MAIL with correct names and addresses in the letter heading. (2 points)	
Additional comments:	
TOTAL POINTS (minus days late for any part of the project)	

National Science Teachers Association

B-9. NUTRITIONAL ASSESSMENT PROJECT REFLECTION PHASE OUTLINE, GRADING CRITERIA, AND POINT DISTRIBUTION

SERVICE-LEARNING PARTNER # _____

AGE (years):   HIP CIRCUMFERENCE (in.):

SEX (male or female):   RIGHT WRIST CIRCUMFERENCE (cms):

HEIGHT (in. and cm):   RIGHT ELBOW BREADTH (in. w/calipers):

WEIGHT (lbs):   BIACROMIAL DIAMETER (cm):

WAIST CIRCUMFERENCE (in.):   BITROCHANTERIC DIAMETER (cm)

When writing the assessment, personalize the narrative below for your partner. Do not repeat the questions or statements below when reporting the results. Define and explain all components of the assessment; you are writing the assessment for your partner, not for your professor.

A. ASSESSMENT OF HEALTHFUL WEIGHT. (2 points for each part)

1. BODY FAT DISTRIBUTION
   a. What is participant's waist circumference and waist-to-hip ratio?
   b. Does participant have a healthful body fat distribution, or do you recommend that he/she pursue a program of weight loss or weight gain? Explain why.
   c. Is participant at a higher or lower risk for any chronic diseases due to his/her body fat distribution? Explain why.

2. BODY MASS INDEX (BMI)
   a. Define body mass index and explain how it is derived.
   b. What is participant's body mass index (BMI)?
   c. According to the standard BMI table, does he/she have a healthful weight or do you recommend that he/she pursue a program of weight loss or weight gain? Explain why.
   d. Explain the disadvantages of using BMI to determine a healthful weight range.

3. FRAME SIZE ESTIMATE: FOR EACH OF THE THREE METHODS YOU PRACTICED DURING CLASS, EXPLAIN THE MEASUREMENTS, TELL HOW YOU OBTAINED THE RESULTS, AND GIVE THE ESTIMATED FRAME SIZE.
   a. Method 1: Height-to-Wrist Circumference Ratio
   b. Method 2: Elbow Breadth
   c. Method 3: Stature and Two Bone Diameters
   d. Are there differences among the estimates from each of the three methods? Why?

4. **HEIGHT-WEIGHT TABLES: ACCORDING TO EACH OF THE THREE TABLES LISTED BELOW, EXPLAIN:**
    a. Whether participant has a healthful weight
    b. If you recommend that he/she pursue a program of weight loss or weight gain, and why
    c. The advantages and/or disadvantages of using the particular table to determine a healthful weight
    d. 1983 Metropolitan Life Insurance Company Height-Weight Table (NOTE: This is not to determine frame size.)
    e. USDA Height-Weight Table
    f. Report on Dietary Guidelines for Americans

B. **ASSESSMENT OF ENERGY BALANCE (2 points for each part)**
    1. **TOTAL ENERGY USE: CALCULATE PARTICIPANT'S AVERAGE TOTAL ENERGY USE ON ONE DAY DURING THE SEVEN-DAY RECORDING PERIOD BY FOLLOWING THE STEPS. (DEFINE ALL TERMS AND EXPLAIN/ DEMONSTRATE ALL STEPS AND CALCULATIONS.)**
        a. Estimate participant's basal metabolic rate (BMR) in kcal/day.
        b. Estimate participant's physical activity in kcal/day.
            (1) Remember that less active people may overestimate their activity level.
            (2) Multiply participant's BMR by the decimal equivalent of the lower and higher percentage values for his or her activity level to estimate how much energy he or she expends at both ends of this activity level.
            (3) Participant expends between an estimated _____ and _____ kcal/ day in physical activity.
        c. Estimate partcipant's total daily energy use:
            (1) Add together estimated energy use contributions from basal metabolic rate and physical activity.
            (2) Participant's estimated total energy use is between _____ and _____ kcal/day.

    2. **MAKE THE FOLLOWING THREE COMPARISONS BETWEEN YOUR CALCULATIONS ABOVE AND DINE HEALTHY 6 SOFTWARE CALCULATIONS. EXPLAIN WHAT YOU COMPARED, AS WELL AS THE RESULTS AND MEANING OF THE COMPARISONS.**
        a. How does the estimate of participant's total daily energy use that you calculated above compare to his or her DINE Healthy 6 program calculations of average energy output based on activities during the seven-day recording period?
        b. How does the estimate of participant's total daily energy use that you calculated above compare to his or her total energy intake (average kcal/ day of food consumed according to DINE Healthy 6) during the seven-day recording period?
        c. According to the DINE Healthy 6 program calculations, how does participant's average energy intake compare to his or her average energy output?
        d. According to all of these estimates, is participant in energy balance?

3. **ASSESSMENT OF NUTRITIONAL INTAKE: EXPLAIN IN DETAIL THE STRENGTHS AND WEAKNESSES OF PARTICIPANT'S SEVEN-DAY FOOD RECORD WITH RESPECT TO EACH OF THE FOLLOWING NUTRIENTS. DEFINE EACH NUTRITIONAL COMPONENT, AND FOR EACH COMPARE PARTICIPANT'S AVERAGE DAILY VALUE TO RECOMMENDED VALUES. (4 points for each part)**
   a. Kilocalories
   b. Carbohydrates
   c. Proteins
   d. Fat
   e. Saturated Fat/Trans Fat
   f. Fiber
   g. Cholesterol
   h. Vitamin A
   i. Vitamin C
   j. Calcium
   k. Iron
   l. Sodium

4. **HOW CAN PARTICIPANT IMPROVE HIS OR HER DIET? LIST SPECIFIC AND REASONABLE SUBSTITUTIONS TO IMPROVE THE DIET. (6 points)**

5. **PRINTOUTS OF DINE HEALTHY 6 FOOD AND ACTIVITY RECORDS (INCLUDE WITH PARTICIPANT'S COPY ONLY) AND ANY OTHER INFORMATION THAT PARTICIPANT MIGHT FIND USEFUL.**

6. **EVALUATION BY SERVICE-LEARNING PARTNER OF HIS OR HER STUDENT ASSESSOR'S WORK. (6 points)**

NOTE: Your final grade for Biology 300 will not be recorded until you have met with your service-learning partner and he or she has submitted the written evaluation. If these two events do not occur before the end of the semester, you will receive an Incomplete for the course.

B-10. STUDENT-LED TEACHING MODEL GRADING RUBRIC

- Each of the seven traits can be awarded up to 3 points. To earn all 21 points for your teaching model presentation, you must fulfill the criteria described under the "3 Points" column for each trait.
- You are expected to improve on your assigned article's suggestions for presenting the model, as well as on the materials and handouts used by Genetics students from previous years.
- Your presentation should facilitate active participation by all of your classmates and challenge them to use higher-order thinking skills as they learn the factual information.
- Teaching models that are scheduled for multiple dates will be graded after all parts are completed.

Your name:_____

Date(s) of your presentation:_____

Title of journal article on which your model is based:_____

TRAIT	3 POINTS	2 POINTS	1 POINT
ORGANIZATION (Points =)	Presenter is well prepared before scheduled class begins and has all materials ready. He or she presents sections of the teaching model in a logical order, improving on the sequence suggested by the article when necessary to make smooth transitions.	Presenter completes his or her preparation just before the scheduled class begins. Presenter follows the exact order suggested by the article.	Presenter arrives late to class and/or organizes materials at the beginning of the class meeting. Order in which model is presented is confusing and/or lacks coherence.
CONTENT (Points =)	Presenter reviews background material and explains how his or her model applies to the week's content outline topics and textbook chapter(s). Presenter uses model to clarify genetics principles, molecular biology processes, and/or laboratory techniques, with visual and tactile experiences that clarify textbook descriptions.	Presenter uses the model to demonstrate relevant topics from the week's outline and textbook chapter(s).	Presenter does not relate the model to appropriate topics for the week.

National Science Teachers Association

ACCURACY (Points =)	Presenter clearly and correctly defines what each manipulative in the model represents. Presenter accurately explains all factual material; correctly answers questions posed by instructor or classmates; and assumes the role of class expert on this topic.	Presenter uses manipulatives correctly during the presentation, but does not explain to classmates what each represents. Presenter explains factual material accurately, but cannot answer questions that go beyond the factual information in the article.	Presenter incorrectly defines what each manipulative represents and/or makes factual errors during his or her explanation.
MATERIALS (Points =)	Presenter prepares an appropriate quantity of materials so that each individual, each pair of classmates, or each learning team has a "kit" with which to work. The quantity of kits is determined by planning for each classmate to have a role requiring active participation. Presenter uses creativity to improve on materials or substitute materials either suggested by the article or left over from previous years.	Presenter provides minimal amount of materials for the class so that some classmates are passive onlookers rather than active participants.	Presenter demonstrates the model to the class, but does not engage individuals or groups of classmates in manipulating the materials.
PARTICIPATION (Points =)	Presenter uses creativity to ensure that all classmates think and learn during the activity. Presenter poses at least one question that is different from those suggested by the article.	Presenter encourages classmates to think as they participate, but allows some classmates to be passive and simply listen.	Presenter demonstrates the model with cookbook-type instructions that do not compel classmates to think.

TEACHING SKILLS (Points =)	Presenter speaks confidently and clearly so that all classmates can hear. Presenter walks around the room to answer questions and to observe and help individuals and groups correctly manipulate the model. Presenter does not automatically provide answers to questions, but instead facilitates thinking through each challenge.	Presenter provides accurate and clear instructions but then waits passively for classmates to complete each section of the model before proceeding to the next. Presenter observes individuals and groups as they work on the model but does not offer suggestions or challenge them with additional questions.	Presenter reads instructions directly from article. He or she stands in front of the room and makes little eye contact with classmates. Presenter does not engage in spontaneous teaching with individuals or small groups while moving around the room.
CRITIQUE OF MODEL (Points =)	During or near the end of the activity, presenter highlights strengths and weaknesses of the model and explains how it could be improved to be more accurate or useful. Examples of things the presenter may describe are as follows: genetics principles that were portrayed inaccurately, elements that were missing, factual errors made in the article, and how the overall model design could have been enhanced.	At the end of the activity, presenter lists strengths and weaknesses of the model without suggestions for improvement.	Presenter offers no suggestions for improvements or thoughts about the strengths or weaknesses of the model.
TOTAL POINTS =			

Examples of In-Class, Laboratory, and Homework Activities

C-1. INHERITANCE OF ABO BLOOD TYPING IN HUMANS

For years I taught genetics to my General Biology I students in the traditional sequence—the sequence followed by most textbooks. First I lectured by defining terms such as *gene*, *allele*, *locus*, *genotype*, *phenotype*, *heterozygote*, *homozygote*, *dominant*, and *recessive*. Then I demonstrated basic Mendelian principles by drawing Punnett squares on the board, showing the results of monohybrid and dihybrid crosses for traits with clear dominance and recessiveness. In a later class I moved on to "exceptions" to Mendelian inheritance, such as codominance and incomplete dominance. Students were chronically confused about the difference between genes and alleles; they could not get their minds around the concept of an allele being just one of several possible forms of a particular gene. Another almost universal misconception was that all alleles were either dominant or recessive and that each gene had only two possible alleles.

I had always used human ABO blood types as an example of a gene with multiple codominant alleles, but this content came *after* students' misconceptions were firmly entrenched. When I switched the order of teaching by beginning the genetics unit with blood types, an example both familiar and engaging for students, the confusion vanished and students competently used genetic terminology for the rest of the semester. Even if they have not read or fully understood the assigned chapter, most students have heard of ABO blood types and are interested in their own inherited blood type. While participating in the in-class activity below, they apply nearly all of the genetics terms in Content Outline 10, Genetics (Appendix A-7).

In-Class Activity

Using information in your textbook and coursepack, answer the following questions with your learning team:

1. List all possible ABO blood phenotypes in humans.
2. The gene that determines ABO blood group is usually designed as *I*. List the designations for the three common alleles of this gene.
3. Explain what *Gene I* actually does and how the function of each allele you listed above differs from that of the others.
4. Using the designations for each allele that you listed in #2, write *all* of the possible genotypes that produce each phenotype.
5. Place your Paper Chromosome 2*, pink and blue, in a Punnett square formation, and show how parents with different genotypes for ABO blood type could produce various phenotypes in their children.
6. Blood typing is sometimes used as a preliminary test of paternity. The table below gives phenotypes of mothers and their children. Complete the table on your own, and then compare your answers with those of members of your learning team.
7. ABO blood typing cannot be used to prove that a man is definitely the father of child; rather, it can only be used to prove that he is *not* the father. Explain why.
8. What is a far more definitive paternity test?

---

* For this activity, students use paper models of three fictitious chromosomes (Chromosomes 1, 2, and 3), each of which has a sister chromatid. The models are in pink and blue to represent which chromosome comes from the mother and which comes from the father. Students use the paper chromosomes to model mitosis, meiosis, and, in this activity, inheritance of ABO blood types.

The template for these chromosomes comes from Heather R. McKean and Linda S. Gibson, "Hands-On Activities That Relate Mendelian Genetics to Cell Division," *American Biology Teacher* 51 (5): 294–300.

Phenotypes of a Mother and Her Child

For each pair, complete the row with all of the possible genotypes of the mother and of the child and the impossible father phenotypes.

Mother Phenotype	Mother Possible Genotypes	Child Phenotype	Child Possible Genotypes	Impossible Father Phenotypes
A		AB		
A		O		
A		B		
A		A		
B		AB		
B		O		
B		B		
B		A		
AB		AB		
AB		O		
AB		B		
AB		A		
O		AB		
O		O		
O		B		
O		A		

National Science Teachers Association

C-2. BEANO AND LACTAID: ENZYMES AT THE GROCERY STORE

(An inquiry-based laboratory activity adapted from Frame [2002])

Prelaboratory learning team reports on homework activity: Enzyme dietary supplements

1. What do these products have in common?
2. Do concerns about flatus exist in all cultures?
3. What sorts of traditional herbal remedies for flatus exist in families and ethnic groups?

Introduction to the laboratory protocol

1. Two students prepare bean solution for use by the entire class:
   A. Place 100 grams (approx. half a can) cooked canned beans and 200 ml distilled water into a blender and blend for five minutes or until the mixture appears smooth. If it is too viscous, add more water.
   B. Filter mixture through two layers of cheesecloth.
2. Each learning team places two test tubes in test tube racks:
   A. Grind up one Beano tablet in a mortar and pestle and dissolve in 2 ml distilled water.
   B. Label test tubes: #1 (bean solution + Beano) and #2 (control).
   C. Add 4 ml of filtered bean solution to each test tube.
   D. Take a baseline reading of glucose concentration in Tubes 1 and 2 at Time 0 by adding a drop of liquid from each tube to a glucose detection strip. Wait 30 seconds, and then make a reading by comparing the color of the strip to the chart with the glucose detection kit. Record your readings in milligrams per deciliter (mg/dl) and be sure to read at exactly the time specified by the manufacturer.
      i. After 30 seconds take a second measurement.
      ii. Tape your glucose detection strips to your data page and record which test tube and time each represents with the corresponding glucose reading.
   E. Use a clean pipette to add one Beano tablet dissolved in 2 ml water (accomplished in A above) to Tube 1. Pipette the mixture up and down to be sure it is mixed well. Use another clean pipette to add 2 ml of water to Tube 2 and pipette the mixture up and down to ensure that it is mixed.
      i. Take glucose measurements every 5 minutes for another 15 minutes and record your data.
      ii. Explain why you observed your results.

Design an *in vitro* experiment with your learning team.

1. The following supplies are available for your experiment:

- Can of cooked beans
- Half bag of same kind of beans soaked in distilled water overnight
- Milk
- Beano and Lactaid tablets
- Glucose detection sticks
- Safety glasses (wear when using acids and bases)
- Vinegar
- Dropper bottles of hydrochloric acid (HCl)
- Dropper bottles of sodium hydroxide (NaOH)
- Wax pencils
- Test tubes/test tube racks
- Thermometers
- 10 ml graduated cylinders
- Disposable pipettes or washable droppers
- 500 ml beakers
- Water baths
- Hot plates
- Ice
- pH meters/paper, pH buffers
- Mortars and pestles to grind up tablets
- Blender
- Balances

2. Read the instructions on the Beano package and discuss them with your team members in terms of what you know about factors affecting enzyme activity (review your notes on Outline 5, Cellular Energy and Enzymes).

3. You may choose canned, cooked beans or the soaked, uncooked beans, or both.

4. After considering what you know about enzymes, state a hypothesis and design an experiment to test your team's hypothesis.
   A. Your hypothesis must be something quantifiable.
   B. Frame your hypothesis statement using an "if . . . then" format.

5. Have Dr. Wood approve your hypothesis and experimental procedures before you begin.

6. Perform your experiment. (Use safety glasses when working with acids and bases.)

7. Graph your results.

Presentation of experimental designs, results, and conclusions
1. Each learning team presents their hypothesis, experimental design, results, and conclusions to the rest of the class.
2. Students critique the experiments and findings of each team.

Discussion
1. What conclusions can we draw from the results of all team experiments?
2. What part of a plant is a bean?
3. Why does gas form in the human colon when beans are consumed?
4. What would be the effect of leaving all of your test tubes intact and testing again in 24 hours? Why?

Design an *in vivo* experiment.
Include this design in your scientific report.

Design an analogous experiment using Lactaid and milk.
If there is time, perform this experiment.

A Summative Assessment to Follow Beano and Lactaid: Enzymes at the Grocery Store

Materials
1 quart of 2% milk
1 quart of 2% Lactaid milk
Small disposable cups (2 per student)

Test Question
Taste each of the milks.
Describe the taste of the two milks relative to each other.
Explain why they taste different from one another.

REFERENCE
Frame, K. 2002. In vitro gas suppression: Beano—enzymes to the rescue. In *Shoestring biotechnology: Budget-oriented, high-quality biotechnology laboratories for two-year college and high school*, 125–138. Reston, VA: National Association of Biology Teachers.

C-3. EUTROPHICATION

(An inquiry-based laboratory activity adapted from Gill and Markby [1991])

"Eutrophication (the increase in the nutrient status of water with sometimes disastrous consequences to the organisms living in it) is a serious problem associated with the overuse of fertilizer in areas of intensive agriculture. It may also occur as a result of high levels of nutrient-rich effluent (for example from treated domestic sewage) entering water courses which cannot provide adequate dilution (for example, when summer flow rates are low)." (Gill and Markby 1991, p. 7)

Available to you are the following supplies and equipment:

- Pond/river/creek water
- Distilled water
- Glass beakers
- Chemical fertilizers used in gardening (such as Miracle-Gro)
- Wax pencils to mark water levels
- Grow lights
- Thermometers
- Microscopes (light and dissecting)
- pH paper

1. With your learning team, design and conduct an investigation of the effects of chemical fertilizers on the eutrophication of water. (Have Dr. Wood approve your hypothesis and experimental procedures before you begin.)

2. Your scientific report should include data collected, graphs, and drawings of organisms, along with a discussion of the following questions:

   - What is eutrophication, and why does it have a negative effect on the organisms that live in ponds or rivers? (A detailed explanation of this is required.)
   - Why do ponds and lakes in northern Maine experience eutrophication?
   - What chemical elements are most likely to contribute to eutrophication?
   - Should the citizens of northern Maine be concerned about this? Why?

REFERENCE

Gill, J., and J. Markby. 1991. Eutrophication in a beaker. *Journal of Biological Education* 25 (1): 7–8.

C-4. LEARNING TEAM NAMES (IN BOLD) WITH POSSIBLE TERMS (ONE PER STUDENT) IN EACH CATEGORY

GENERAL BIOLOGY I	SCIENCES I	SCIENCES II	HUMAN NUTRITION	GENETICS
Protista	**Mechanical Energy**	**Alkali Metals**	**Carbohydrates**	**Glycine (Gly)**
Amoeba proteus (amoeba)	centripetal force	lithium (Li)	glycogen	guanine-guanine-uracil
Paramecium caudatum (paramecium)	momentum	sodium (Na)	sucrose	guanine-guanine-adenine
Plasmodium falciparum (causes malaria)	work	potassium (K)	fructose	guanine-guanine-cytosine
Trypanosora gambiense (causes sleeping sickness)	acceleration	rubidium (Rb)	lactose	guanine-guanine-guanine
Phytophthora infestans (causes potato late blight)	power	cesium (Cs)	cellulose (fiber)	
Fungi	**Radiant Energy**	**Alkaline Earth Metals**	**Lipids**	**Leucine (Leu)**
Saccharomyces cerevisiae (baker's yeast)	radio waves	magnesium (Mg)	saturated fatty acid	cytosine-uracil-uracil
Penicillium chrysogenum (produces penicillin)	microwaves	calcium (Ca)	omega-3 fatty acid	uracil-uracil-guanine
Amanita muscaria (poisonous mushroom)	infrared light	strontium (Sr)	omega-6 fatty acid	cytosine-uracil-cytosine
Rhizopus stolonifer (black bread mold)	visible light	barium (Ba)	trans-fatty acid	cytosine-uracil-adenine
Ceratocystis ulmis (causes Dutch elm disease)	x-rays	radium (Ra)	triglyceride	cytosine-uracil-guanine
Plantae	**Electrical Energy**	**Halogens**	**Proteins**	**Threonine (Thr)**
Elodea canadensis (elodea)	coulomb	fluorine (F)	histidine	adenine-cytosine-uracil
Allium cepa (onion)	ampere	chloride (Cl)	lysine	adenine-cytosine-cytosine
Medicago sativa (alfalfa)	volt	bromine (Br)	phenylalanine	adenine-cytosine-adenine
Cannibus sativa (marijuana)	joule	iodine (I)	threonine	adenine-cytosine-guanine
Acer saccharum (sugar maple)	watt	astatine (At)	tryptophan	
Animalia	**Nuclear Energy**	**Noble Gases**	**Vitamins**	**Arginine (Arg)**
Homo sapiens (human)	gamma rays	helium (He)	ascorbic acid	cytosine-guanine-uracil
Homarus americanus (lobster)	beta particle	neon (Ne)	tocopherol	cytosine-guanine-cytosine
Latrodectus mactans (black widow spider)	alpha particle	argon (Ar)	riboflavin	cytosine-guanine-adenine
Lumbricus terrestris (night crawler earthworm)	radioactive decay	krypton (Kr)	folic acid	cytosine-guanine-guanine
Musca domestica (housefly)	nuclear fission	radon (Rn)	thiamine	adenine-guanine-adenine

C-5. EXAMPLE OF QUESTIONS APPROPRIATE FOR PEER INSTRUCTION

If a mother is blood type A and her child is blood type O, which phenotype of a father is impossible?

- A. Father could not be phenotype A.
- B. Father could not be phenotype B.
- C. Father could not be phenotype O.
- D. Father could not be phenotype AB.
- E. Father could be any of the above phenotypes (no phenotype impossible).

If a mother is blood type A and her child is blood type AB, which genotype of a father is possible?

- A. $I^A I^A$
- B. $I^A I^O$
- C. $I^O I^O$
- D. $I^A I^B$
- E. All of the genotypes above are possible.

If both a mother and her child are phenotype B, which phenotype of a father is impossible?

- A. Father could not be phenotype A.
- B. Father could not be phenotype B.
- C. Father could not be phenotype O.
- D. Father could not be phenotype AB.
- E. Father could be any of the above phenotypes (no phenotype impossible).

C-6. EXAMPLE OF AN ANONYMOUS PEER EVALUATION FORM

- On the due date of the project each student must submit this anonymous peer evaluation. This ensures equitable distribution of project points and encourages equal participation by all team members.
- You must list every student on your team (including yourself), and the percent contributions of all the students in the group must add up to 100%. If a student did not participate in this project, you should still list the student and assign 0% as the percent contribution.
- Submit this sheet by folding it over and handing it to me during class, slipping it under my office door, or putting my name on the outside and taking it to the campus post office for delivery to my mailbox.

LEARNING TEAM NAME: _____

NAMES OF TEAM MEMBERS (INCLUDING YOURSELF)	PERCENT CONTRIBUTION TO THE PROJECT
1.	
2.	
3.	
4.	
5.	
TOTAL	100%

If you have designated unequal percent contributions to the project, you must briefly explain why below:

C-7. GUIDELINES FOR WRITING TEST REVIEW QUESTIONS

- At the class meeting preceding the scheduled test review activity, each student who wishes to be eligible for extra credit must submit one carefully constructed multiple-choice question with a justification of the correct answer. Questions must be based on content outlines included in the upcoming test (see the Topic Schedule). Questions and answers will be edited and organized by Dr. Wood for use during the test review activity. No late submissions are accepted.

- Divide responsibility for the content outline topics among your team so that each student writes and submits a question and its answer on a different topic. This ensures a variety of questions to use as practice during the test review session. You may work together to create the question, but each student should submit her or his own question and answer.

- Your question and answer must be typewritten and follow the guidelines below. At the top of your submission, write your name and the general topic of your question. Below this, type your multiple-choice question and possible answers (preferably five choices, only one of which is correct) and the fully explained answer. ("Fully explained" means you must justify why you accepted the correct answer instead of the incorrect answers.)

- During the test review activity your learning team will compete for extra credit points by correctly answering questions that require higher-order thinking skills. You may not use your notes or textbook, but your team will work from memory to discuss and answer questions.

- The key to successfully winning extra credit points during the test review activity is for each team member to submit an appropriate question and to study in advance the material for the upcoming test.

- To be eligible for extra credit points during the test review activity, write questions that are appropriate to the depth of knowledge for this course. Do not make your questions too simple or have them require only memorization, and do not ask questions about material not included in the coursepack outlines.

A good multiple-choice question does at least one of the following:

- Tests a student's ability to apply the scientific method: You can describe an experiment and then give a series of possible conclusions or ways to better control the experiment. You can provide a set of data or a graph and ask your classmates to choose from among a set of hypotheses, asking which hypothesis is best supported by the data. You can get ideas for the experiment from your book, from what we have done in class, or from other sources, such as magazine or journal articles.

- Tests a student's understanding of a scientific process: You can describe a scientific process we have studied and ask your classmates to choose from a set of possible outcomes if some aspect of the process is altered.
- Tests a student's ability to solve a scientific problem: You can pose a scientific problem that might confront a real investigator and provide alternate ways to solve it.
- Makes the incorrect choices plausible: Write the multiple-choice question so that your classmates must think carefully about each possible answer. An excellent way to do this is to use common misconceptions that your classmates are likely to hold. Because you have recently learned about various scientific concepts, you are familiar with common misconceptions—ideas that confused you and your fellow students not long ago.

How to write a good multiple-choice question:

1. Think of a scientific statement (something you and your classmates should know and understand).

   a. The statement should include only one idea.
   b. The statement should be written clearly and simply.
   c. The statement should have no clues about the correct answer.

2. Rephrase the statement as a question.

3. Write a clear and concise answer to the question.

4. Develop plausible distracters or incorrect answers (see above).

   a. Include computational or conceptual errors that students regularly make.
   b. Avoid using "all of the above" and "none of the above" as answer choices.
   c. Avoid using paired opposites in the choices (e.g., positive and negative, male and female, or homozygous and heterozygous).
   d. Be cautious about distracters that end up coming together at the right answer.
   e. All choices should be approximately the same length.
   f. Be careful with grammatical cues (e.g., asking for something in the plural but having distracters that are singular).

C-8. INSTRUCTIONS FOR PARTICIPATION PHASE OF HUMAN NUTRITION SERVICE-LEARNING PROJECT

A. CONTACT YOUR SERVICE-LEARNING PARTNER.
1. After midterm select a partner from among the volunteers on the list. To protect the person's privacy, the number next to his or her name is the assigned participant number that you will use in place of a name on any written materials or in any discussions with me.
   i. After learning about the Institutional Review Board (IRB) application and approval process during class, call or e-mail your service-learning partner. Introduce yourself and make an appointment to meet your partner in a private room at the Health Center. The appointment should occur after the class session in which you learn and practice skills for estimating frame size.
   ii. Once you have chosen a mutually agreeable time, call the Health Center to reserve the room for a 60-minute time slot.

B. PREPARE FOR THE FIRST MEETING WITH YOUR PARTNER.
1. Choose the layout of the forms you want your partner to use to record her or his physical activity and food intake.
2. Make seven copies of an activity record form and seven copies of a food consumption form to supply your partner with a week's supply.
3. Write a list of hints for your partner to help him or her accurately estimate food intake and physical activity. Your list can be adapted from the list brainstormed during class.

C. FIRST MEETING WITH YOUR PARTNER.
1. At the Health Center, I have placed a box containing the measuring tape, calipers, and food-serving-size models with which you practiced during class and that you will use during the first meeting. There is also an accurate scale for measuring your partner's weight and height.
2. Explain in detail to your partner the methods you will use to accomplish the nutritional assessment, and answer any questions. If you are unsure of the answer to a question, check with me and get back to your partner at a later time.

3. Have your partner carefully read and sign the Informed Consent to Participate in a Human Nutrition Service-Learning Activity at the University of Maine at Presque Isle.
   i. Write your partner's participant number at the top of the consent form.
   ii. Return the signed consent form to me. I will keep the original in my office files and send a copy to your partner through campus mail.
4. After the consent form is signed, collect and record all of the information about age, sex, height, weight, waist circumference, hip circumference, right wrist circumference, and elbow breadth using the equipment at the Health Center.
5. Explain in detail to your partner how you would like him or her to record daily food intake and physical activity.
   i. Give your partner copies of any hints you have for recording this information accurately.
   ii. Give your partner seven copies of each form you would like him or her to use.
   iii. Emphasize that for this assessment to be accurate, your partner should eat normally and engage in his or her usual level of physical activity. The goal of a nutritional assessment is to evaluate a typical seven-day period.
   iv. Emphasize avoiding changes in either physical activity or diet without the supervision of a health-care provider.
   v. Tell your partner not to write his or her name on any of the information submitted to you. You will instead label the information with the participant number.
6. Look at a calendar and determine a convenient consecutive seven-day period during which your partner will record his or her activities and food intake.
7. Make an appointment to meet briefly with your partner after the first 24 hours of recording to be sure he or she is writing down all of the information you will need to complete the assessment.

D. SECOND MEETING WITH YOUR NUTRITIONAL ASSESSMENT PARTNER.

1. Before your partner continues with the week's data collection, look over what he or she has recorded during the first 24 hours, answer any questions, and make suggestions for more precise terminology or record-keeping. This will ensure that future data input into the DINE Healthy computer program goes more smoothly for you.

E. THIRD MEETING WITH YOUR NUTRITIONAL ASSESSMENT PARTNER.

1. Arrange a time and place no later than the twelfth week of the semester.

2. Collect your partner's seven-day physical activity and food records.
3. Give your partner a written invitation to the healthful luncheon that you and your classmates will prepare.

F. FOURTH MEETING WITH YOUR NUTRITIONAL ASSESSMENT PARTNER.
1. After meeting with me to go over your draft nutritional assessment, make appropriate changes, corrections, and improvements.
2. Meet with your partner at a pre-arranged time in a private location to explain and discuss the results.
3. Give your partner a final copy of the assessment, and submit another final copy to me for grading.

C-9. E-MAIL MESSAGE TO RECRUIT VOLUNTEER FACULTY AND STAFF PARTICIPANTS FOR THE HUMAN NUTRITION SERVICE-LEARNING PROJECT

Subject: FREE NUTRITIONAL ASSESSMENT!

Hurry to volunteer to participate in a service-learning activity with Biology 300 (Human Nutrition) students during the spring semester!

In March you will be paired with a student who will teach you how to keep a seven-day food consumption and physical activity record. Your student partner will use the data from this record, plus other information about you, to complete your nutritional assessment. You will receive a copy of the nutritional assessment, along with a verbal explanation, at the end of the semester.

As a reward for your participation, you will be invited to a healthful luncheon planned and prepared by the Human Nutrition students and their professor.

The Institutional Review Board for the Protection of Human Subjects (IRB) has approved this activity, and your privacy will be protected.

Please e-mail me ASAP if you wish to participate. I will record the date and time on your e-mail and accept participants in the order in which they respond.

If you have any questions, please contact me.

C-10. INFORMED CONSENT FORM

INFORMED CONSENT TO PARTICIPATE IN A HUMAN NUTRITION SERVICE-LEARNING ACTIVITY AT THE UNIVERSITY OF MAINE AT PRESQUE ISLE

- The purpose of the Human Nutrition Service-Learning Activity is for each Biology 300 (Human Nutrition) student at the University of Maine at Presque Isle (UMPI) to complete a nutritional assessment of a volunteer participant who is a member of the UMPI faculty or staff, who is a UMPI student, or who is a minor child of a UMPI faculty or staff member. Objectives are to foster a lifelong interest in nutrition among both the Biology 300 students and the volunteer participants, to teach both the students and the volunteer participants to make effective dietary choices, and to increase wellness among members of the UMPI campus community.

- This activity has been designed for Biology 300, Human Nutrition, at the University of Maine at Presque Isle, and will be supervised by Dr. Bonnie Wood, professor of biology.

- To ensure confidentiality, after signing this informed consent, you will be given a number that will be used in place of your name on all written information pertinent to the activity.

- During approximately the ninth week of the semester, you will meet with your assigned student partner in a campus location where your privacy will be protected. The student will record your age; sex; height; weight; circumferences of your waist, hip, and right wrist; and your elbow breadth. The student also will teach you how to keep a seven-day record of your typical food consumption and physical activity.

- The recording of your typical daily food consumption and physical activity will be over a period of seven consecutive days, during a week convenient for you, between Weeks 9 and 12 of the semester. You will meet with the Biology 300 student with whom you have been paired for about one hour during the week before you begin your record, for approximately 10 minutes one or two days after you begin your record-keeping, and for approximately one hour during Week 13 or 14 of the semester for your student partner to explain your completed nutritional assessment and give you a written copy of the results.

- You will receive a copy of this signed Informed Consent form through campus mail.

Expected benefits of this activity are as follows:
- Biology 300 students will learn the importance of confidentiality and informed consent when working with human subjects.
- Biology 300 students will learn to apply the principles of human nutrition.
- Biology 300 students will learn to teach the principles of human nutrition to another person.
- Both Biology 300 students and UMPI faculty and staff will learn about their own nutritional status and how food consumption and physical activity contribute to their overall energy balance and health.
- Wellness will improve among members of the University of Maine at Presque Isle campus community.
- As an optional "thank you" for volunteering for this activity, participants are invited to a meal of healthful food prepared by Biology 300 students and their professor.

Possible risks or discomfort as a result of your participation are as follows:
- A negative psychological reaction upon learning that the status of your nutrition and energy balance is not healthful. If this occurs, you should contact Student Support Services (768-9615) for counseling.
- A breach of your confidentiality if Biology 300 students and/or instructor do not follow the Institutional Review Board for the Protection of Human Subjects (IRB) guidelines for ensuring privacy of human subjects.
- Undermining of your dignity by having your height, weight, and body measurements, as well as your seven-day food intake and exercise record, scrutinized by a student.

Participation in this activity is entirely voluntary. Voluntary participation also means the following:
- You need not answer any questions you consider inappropriate.
- You may stop participating in this activity at any point.
- If you decline to participate, any information that has been gathered about you will be returned to you or destroyed.

FOR PARTICIPANTS OVER THE AGE OF 18:

- I am at least eighteen (18) years of age.

- I have read and understand the information above concerning the Human Nutrition Service-Learning Activity. I understand that I should not make changes to my food consumption or physical activity without the supervision of my health-care provider.

- I hereby volunteer to be a participant in the Human Nutrition Service-Learning Activity being conducted at the University of Maine at Presque Isle by Dr. Bonnie Wood, professor of biology, and

  _____.

  (Printed name of Biology 300 student partner)

- The nature and purpose of this activity have been provided in writing and completely explained to me as described above. I understand further that I may withdraw at any time.

- In the event that photos or videotapes are made at the optional meal at the end of the activity, I give my consent to be photographed or videotaped. Yes_____No_____

  _____

  (Signature of volunteer participant)   (Date)

FOR PARTICIPANTS UNDER THE AGE OF 18:

- I have read and understand the information above concerning the Human Nutrition Service-Learning Activity. I understand that I should not make changes to my food consumption or physical activity without the supervision of my health-care provider.

- I hereby volunteer to be a participant in the Human Nutrition Service-Learning Activity being conducted at the University of Maine at Presque Isle by Dr. Bonnie Wood, professor of biology, and

_____.

(Printed name of Biology 300 student partner)

- The nature and purpose of this activity have been provided in writing and completely explained to my parent/guardian and me as described above. I understand further that I may withdraw at any time.

- In the event that photos or videotapes are made at the optional meal at the end of the activity, I give my consent to be photographed or videotaped. Yes _____   No _____

_____

(Signature of parent or guardian of volunteer)   (Date)

_____

(Signature of volunteer participant)   (Date)

C-11. E-MAIL QUESTIONNAIRE SENT TO SERVICE-LEARNING PARTNERS

As part of my evaluation of your student partner's final project in Biology 300, I would appreciate your answering the following questions as soon as you have received your written nutritional assessment. You may submit the answers electronically or via hard copy through campus mail. Thank you very much for your participation in this service-learning project!

Bonnie Wood

NAME OF YOUR STUDENT PARTNER: _____

Initial Contact via Phone, E-mail, or in Person
- Did your student partner contact you promptly after midterm to arrange for your first meeting?

First Meeting
- Did your student partner arrive promptly at a mutually convenient time at the UMPI Health Center?
- Did your student partner adequately explain the methods that he or she would use to complete your nutritional assessment?
- Did your student partner adequately answer any questions or concerns you had?
- Did your student partner adequately explain the information on the informed consent form?
- Did your student partner adequately explain how to keep your seven-day food and activity records?

Second Meeting
- Did your student partner meet with you approximately 24 hours after you began your record-keeping to let you know whether you were doing it correctly?

Third Meeting
- Did your student partner meet with you before or during the week of April 19 to collect your records and to invite you to the thank-you lunch on May 4?

Fourth Meeting
- Did your student partner meet with you before the end of the semester to explain your completed nutritional assessment?

- Did you receive a written copy of your completed nutritional assessment?
- Were you satisfied with the quality of the assessment?

General Questions
- Do you feel that your privacy was respected and that information about you was kept confidential?
- Did you find participation in this service-learning activity personally useful?
- What did you like best about participating in this activity?
- What did you like least about participating in this activity?
- What suggestions do you have for improving this activity?
- Other comments?

C-12. COURSES IN WHICH A CASE STUDY IS THE INITIAL COOPERATIVE LEARNING TEAM ACTIVITY

Titles and abstract excerpts of cases are from the National Center for Case Study Teaching in Science Case Collection (*http://ublib.buffalo.edu/libraries/projects/cases*).

- **Sciences I:** Thinking Inside the Box (Bailey 2002). Students working in groups are given sealed boxes containing objects about which they must make indirect observations that they report to the class in a simulated conference setting. An effective lead-in exercise to a discussion of the scientific method, this activity can also be used in a general chemistry course to teach students about atomic structure and how experimental evidence can be used to infer structure.

- **Sciences II:** Love Potion #10 (Holt 2002). Students are asked to consider whether there is evidence to adequately support a series of scientific claims made in an advertisement for pheromones. The case teaches students about the scientific method and the process of science; it was designed for use in high school biology classes as well as in an introductory college biology course.

- **General Biology I:** Cell Phone Use and Cancer: A Case Study to Explore the Scientific Method (Parilla 2006). Students examine a particular piece of scientific research, first by analyzing news articles reporting on the research and then by reading the original research article. In working through the case, students identify the basic elements of a scientific research study, evaluate the study and offer suggestions for improvement, analyze the appropriateness of the headlines of news articles in relation to their content, and compare the accuracy of information offered to the public in a news article with the information presented in a scientific paper. Designed for an introductory course in biological sciences for nonmajors, the case could be used in any course that includes the study of the scientific method, as well as in a scientific journalism course.

- **Genetics:** A Sickeningly Sweet Baby Boy: A Case Study on Recessive Inheritance in Inbred Populations (Washington and Zayaitz 2007). When a newborn develops symptoms eerily similar to those of an older sibling who died shortly after birth, his Mennonite parents are understandably alarmed. They soon discover that their son has Maple Syrup Urine Disease (MSUD), a recessively inherited metabolic disorder. This case explores the genetics of the disease and the ultimate dilemma of treatment options. Developed for an introductory nonmajor's biology course, the case can also be used in other science or health-related courses such as human genetics and biochemistry.

- **Science Seminar:** A Cool Glass of Water: A Mystery (Yang 2007). Does an ice cube melt more quickly in saltwater or in freshwater? The answer surprises the group of student science teachers portrayed in this interrupted case study. To explain the phenomenon, they must figure out the interactions between two clusters of concepts: (1) density and its relationship to floating or sinking, and (2) three modes of heat or energy transfer due to a temperature difference (particularly conduction and convection, with an optional discussion of radiation). The case can be adapted for use in general education science courses or for introductory physics or chemistry courses.

REFERENCES

Bailey, C. T. 2002. Thinking inside the box. National Center for Case Study Teaching in Science Case Collection. *http://ublib.buffalo.edu/libraries/projects/cases/box/box1.html*.

Holt, S. 2002. Love potion #10. National Center for Case Study Teaching in Science Case Collection. *http://ublib.buffalo.edu/libraries/projects/cases/pheromones/pheromones1.html*.

Parilla, W. V. C. 2006. Cell phone use and cancer: A case study to explore the scientific method. National Center for Case Study Teaching in Science Case Collection. *www.sciencecases.org/cell_phone/cell_phone.asp*.

Washington, J., and A. Zayaitz. 2007. A sickeningly sweet baby boy: A case study on recessive inheritance in inbred populations. National Center for Case Study Teaching in Science Case Collection. *www.sciencecases.org/sweet_baby/sweet_baby.asp*.

Yang, L. 2007. A cool glass of water: A mystery. National Center for Case Study Teaching in Science Case Collection. *www.sciencecases.org/melting_ice/melting_ice.asp*.

C-13. SCHEDULE AND CONTENT TOPICS FOR STUDENT-LED TEACHING MODELS IN BIOLOGY 350, GENETICS

Week 1

DNA Structure:
- ❑ Teaching Outside the (Cereal) Box (Byrd 2000). Grade the professor! Demonstration of a teaching model.

Week 2

DNA Replication:
- ❑ Modeling the Classic Meselson and Stahl Experiment (D'Agostino 2001) and Meselson-Stahl Experimental Simulation Using Lego Building Blocks (Templin and Fetters 2002b).
- ❑ Modeling DNA Replication (Bennett 1998).

Week 3

Transcription and RNA:
- ❑ DNA Puzzle Kit: Student Worksheets (Carolina Biological Supply Company, Burlington, NC).

Genetic Code and Translation:
- ❑ Modeling Protein Folding and Applying It to a Relevant Activity (Nelson and Goetze 2004).
- ❑ Demonstrating Translation with a Student-Centered Activity (Poole 2006).
- ❑ A Working Model of Protein Synthesis Using Lego Building Blocks (Templin and Fetters 2002a).

Week 6

Recombinant DNA Technology:
- ❑ Linguini Models of Molecular Genetic Mapping and Fingerprinting (Thompson, Gray, and Hellack 1997).
- ❑ Teaching DNA Fingerprinting Using a Hands-On Simulation (Schug 1998).
- ❑ Recombinant DNA Paper Model Simulation: The Genetic Engineer (Wagner 1998).

Week 8

Genomics:

- ❏ A Demonstration of Automated DNA Sequencing (Latourelle and Seidel-Rogol 1998).
- ❏ Microarrays Made Simple: "DNA Chips" Paper Activity (Barnard 2006).
- ❏ Understanding the Human Genome Project: Using Stations to Provide a Comprehensive Overview (Soto 2005).

Week 9

Eukaryotic Cell Reproduction (Mitosis):

- ❏ Hands-on Activities That Relate Mendelian Genetics to Cell Division (McKean and Gibson 1989).
- ❏ Students as "Human Chromosomes" in Role-Playing Mitosis and Meiosis (Chinnici, Yue, and Torres 2004) and Students as Human Chromosomes, in 3-D (Bednekoff 2004).

Eukaryotic Cell Reproduction (Meiosis):

- ❏ Hands-on Activities That Relate Mendelian Genetics to Cell Division (McKean and Gibson 1989).
- ❏ Students as "Human Chromosomes" in Role-Playing Mitosis and Meiosis (Chinnici, Yue, and Torres 2004) and Students as Human Chromosomes, in 3-D (Bednekoff 2004).

Week 10

Principles of Heredity:

- ❏ Cookie-ases: Interactive Models for Teaching Genotype-Phenotype Relationships (Seipelt 2006).
- ❏ Using Manipulatives to Teach Basic Mendelian Genetics Concepts (Grumbine 2006).

Week 14

Chromosome Variation:

- ❏ Modeling Mitosis/Meiosis: A Problem-Solving Activity (Clark and Mathis 2000).
- ❏ Using Ribbon Models of Chromosome Modifications to Explore the Process of Meiosis (Levy and Benner 1995).

Week 15

Eukaryotic Chromosome Linkage and Mapping:

- ❏ FISH-ing for Genes: Modeling Fluorescence *In Situ* Hybridization (Baker and Jones 2006).

REFERENCES

Baker, W. P., and C. B. Jones. 2006. FISH-ing for genes: Modeling fluorescence *in situ* hybridization. *American Biology Teacher* 68 (4): 227–231.

Barnard, B. 2006. Microarrays made simple: "DNA chips" paper activity. *American Biology Teacher* (online publication) 68 (3): 8–12. *www.nabt. org/sites/S1/File/pdf/068-03-0002.pdf*.

Bednekoff, P. 2004. Students as human chromosomes, in 3-D (letter to the editor). *American Biology Teacher* 66 (5): 328.

Bennett, J. 1998. Modeling DNA replication. *American Biology Teacher* 60 (6): 457–460.

Byrd, J. J. 2000. Teaching outside the (cereal) box. *American Biology Teacher* 62 (7): 508–511.

Carolina Biological Supply Company, Burlington, NC. DNA Puzzle Kit: Student Worksheets. *www.carolina.com/product/life+science/biotechnol ogy+kits+%26+materials/teaching+resources/dna+puzzle+kit.do?sortby =ourPicks*.

Chinnici, J. P., J. W. Yue, and K. M. Torres. 2004. Students as "human chromosomes" in role-playing mitosis and meiosis. *American Biology Teacher* 66 (1): 35–39.

Clark, D. C., and P. M. Mathis. 2000. Modeling mitosis and meiosis: A problem-solving activity. *American Biology Teacher* 62 (3): 204–206.

D'Agostino, J. 2001. Modeling the classic Meselson and Stahl experiment. *American Biology Teacher* 63 (5): 358–361.

Grumbine, R. A. 2006. Using manipulatives to teach basic Mendelian genetics concepts. *American Biology Teacher* (online publication) 68 (8): 117–123. *www.nabt.org/sites/S1/File/pdf/068-08-0021.pdf*.

Latourelle, S., and B. Seidel-Rogol. 1998. A demonstration of automated DNA sequencing. *American Biology Teacher* 60 (3): 206–211.

Levy, F., and D. B. Benner. 1995. Using ribbon models of chromosome modifications to explore the process of meiosis. *American Biology Teacher* 57 (8): 532–535.

McKean, H. R., and L. S. Gibson. 1989. Hands-on activities that relate Mendelian genetics to cell division. *American Biology Teacher* 51 (5): 294–300.

Nelson, A., and J. Goetze. 2004. Modeling protein folding and applying it to a relevant activity. *American Biology Teacher* 66 (4): 287–289.

Poole, T. M. 2006. Demonstrating translation with a student-centered activity. *Journal of College Science Teaching* 35 (5): 14–15.

Schug, T. 1998. Teaching DNA fingerprinting using a hands-on simulation. *American Biology Teacher* 60 (1): 38–41.

Seipelt, R. L. 2006. Cookie-ases: Interactive models for teaching genotype-phenotype relationships. *American Biology Teacher* (online publication) 68 (5): 48–53. *www.nabt.org/sites/S1/File/pdf/068-05-0009.pdf*.

Soto, J. G. 2005. Understanding the Human Genome Project: Using stations to provide a comprehensive overview. *American Biology Teacher* 67 (8): 475–485.

Templin, M. A., and M. K. Fetters. 2002a. A working model of protein synthesis using Lego™ building blocks. *American Biology Teacher* 64 (9): 673–678.

———. 2002b. Meselson-Stahl experimental simulation using Lego™ building blocks. *American Biology Teacher* 64 (8): 613–619.

Thompson, J. N., Jr., S. B. Gray, and J. J. Hellack.1997. Linguini models of molecular genetic mapping and fingerprinting. *American Biology Teacher* 59 (7): 416–418.

Wagner, J. 1998. Recombinant DNA paper model simulation: The genetic engineer. *American Biology Teacher* 60 (7): 531–534.

INDEX

Index

Index

Lecturing, 1, 4, 5
    vs. active learning, 6–7, 162–163
    disadvantages of, 5–6, 162
    in online courses, 156
Length of class meetings, 2, 22–23, 69–70
Light, Richard, 10, 11, 13, 91, 98
Literature research articles, 31

M

Manipulative models, 32, 139
Marbach-Ad, G., 105–106
Mazur, Eric, 7, 54, 99, 146, 155
Michaelsen, L. K., 113
Minute Paper, 63
Misconceptions related to prior knowledge, 8, 26, 29
Murkiest Point, 27, 28, 29, 44, 54, 63–64

N

National Association of Biology Teachers, 161
National Center for Case Study Teaching in Science Case Collection, 30, 31, 88, 128, 130, 134
National Institutes of Health, 159
National Research Council, 128
National Science Education Standards, 138, 144
National Science Foundation (NSF), 159
National Science Resources Center, 159
National Science Teachers Association, 159
New York Times Book Review, 93
Note-taking on content outlines and reading, 25, 29, 55–57
NSF (National Science Foundation), 159
Nutrition Aptitude Test, 114

O

Online course-management system, 35, 62–63

P

PBL (Problem-Based Learning), 102–103, 161
Peer evaluation of group work, 103–105
    anonymous peer evaluation form for, 103–104, 121, 231
Peer Instruction, 8, 9, 54, 58, 99–100, 106, 161
    questions appropriate for, 230
Penalties for late submission of work, 34, 35, 92
PFF (Preparing Future Faculty) program, 160
Physical Science Study Committee (PSSC), 144, 160
Physics First, 161
PKAL (Project Kaleidoscope), 161, 162

Positive interdependence for cooperative learning, 101
Post–9/11 Veterans Educational Assistance Act of 2008, 145
Preparation for Lecture-Free Teaching, 53–59
    by instructors, 58–59
    by students, 53–57
Preparing Future Faculty (PFF) program, 160
Problem-Based Learning (PBL), 102–103, 161
Problem-based service-learning (PBSL), 117
Project Kaleidoscope (PKAL), 161, 162
Project-Based Science, 161
PSSC (Physical Science Study Committee), 144, 160

R

Research experiences for students, 161
Role-playing of case studies, 129

S

Scaffolding, 50
SCALE-UP (Student-Centered Active Learning Environment for Undergraduate Programs), 161
Scholarship of teaching, 156, 164
Science, 7
Science Education for New Civic Engagements and Responsibilities (SENCER), 161
Science education journals, 7, 30, 31–32, 93, 138, 156
Science education reform, 1–2, 14–16, 40, 79, 143–150
    current needs for change, 144–146
    organizational support for, 156
    rationale for, 147–150
    recent initiatives for, 159–162
    resistance to, 153–157
    student opinions about, 156–157
    what educators and administrators can do to effect, 162–168
        advocating for higher value for teaching, 163
        beginning with reforms of secondary and postsecondary education, 165
        establishing reliable instruments to evaluate teaching, 164
        sharing enthusiasm about reform, 166–168
        transforming basic courses, 165–166
    after World War II, 143–144
Science educators, 145
    active learning approach and satisfaction of, 9